The Transformative Powers Of Near Death Experiences

How The Messages Of NDEs Positively Impact The World

Dr Penny Sartori
Kelly Walsh

EasyRead Large

Copyright Page from the Original Book

This edition first published in the UK and USA 2017 by
Watkins, an imprint of Watkins Media Limited
19 Cecil Court
London WC2N 4EZ

enquiries@watkinspublishing.com

Design and typography copyright © Watkins Media Limited 2017

Text copyright © Penny Sartori and Kelly Walsh 2017

Penny Sartori and Kelly Walsh have asserted their right under the Copyright, Designs and Patents Act 1988 to be identified as the authors of this work.

All rights reserved.
No part of this book may be reproduced or utilized in any form
or by any means, electronic or mechanical,
without prior permission in writing from the Publishers.

1 3 5 7 9 10 8 6 4 2

Designed and typeset by JCS Publishing Services Ltd

Printed and bound in the United Kingdom

A CIP record for this book is available from the British Library

ISBN: 978-1-78678-033-1

www.watkinspublishing.com

TABLE OF CONTENTS

ACKNOWLEDGEMENTS	xvi
PREFACE	xviii
FOREWORD: A LOVE LETTER FROM GOD	xxiii
PROLOGUE	xxxvii
INTRODUCTION	lxv
1: THE POWER OF DIVINE LOVE	1
2: TOUCHING THE VOID … AND THE VOYAGE BACK	33
3: BEYOND HEAVEN	60
4: READY WHEN YOU ARE	84
5: TIBOR PUTNOKI AND THE LIGHT OF LOVE FOUNDATION	101
6: PURPOSE, PURPOSE, PURPOSE? WHAT PURPOSE?	113
7: LOVE BROKE THROUGH	135
8: LIFE HAPPENS BUT YOUR JOURNEY NEVER ENDS	159
9: NATURAL TRANSFORMATION THROUGH THE GIFT OF LIFE	176
10: A MID-COURSE CORRECTION	199
11: THE GIFT	227
12: A LOST DOG, A VAST UNIVERSE AND A PRECIOUS GIFT	238
13: THE CONNECTION	260
14: THE VORTEX CHILD	284
15: THE SHARED CROSSING PROJECT	308
16: THEN THERE WERE WORDS	320
17: GOD'S BOOT CAMP	342
18: LITTLE GIRL SOLDIER	363
19: COLLECTIVE CONSCIOUSNESS	387
20: THE GIFT OF BEING	396
POSTSCRIPT CROSSING OCEANS TO LOVE	417

CONCLUSION	431
EPILOGUE	452
AFTERWORD	460
CONTRIBUTORS	464
REFERENCES AND FURTHER READING	467
Index	475

"An enthralling read that encapsulates the positive impact near-death experiences are having on people and the wider world. The work done by Dr Penny Sartori and Kelly Walsh truly reinforces the important message that we are all one, all connected and that love is the most powerful source in the universe capable of healing the world. I highly recommend this well-written and thought-provoking book. Not only are the proceeds earned from the book being used to make a difference in children's lives, it has the power within its pages to open the hearts, minds and souls of every person that reads it."

Anita Moorjani
***New York Times* bestselling author**

"Extraordinary transformation results from near-death experiences in the lives of the experiencers themselves, and this book explores many such life-changing stories in a most revealing fashion. One of its greatest gifts is its comforting portrayal of the infinite healing power of love, and the sense of connectedness with the universe that arises from such profound experiences. Science is on the cusp of a major awakening as NDEs, and similar spiritually transformative experiences demand more complete explanations, all opening the door to a more meaningful understanding of the nature of consciousness, and of all of existence."

**Eben Alexander MD
Neurosurgeon and author of *Proof of Heaven* and *The Map of Heaven***

"I was extremely touched by the personal and very intimate accounts of the transformative power of an NDE. This book helps to break the taboo about NDEs and their after-effects, and it makes clear the impact of such an overwhelming experience on those who have had an NDE. But above all it can also teach us about how to live our own life to the full. Highly recommended."

**Pim van Lommel
Cardiologist, author of
*Consciousness Beyond Life***

"*The Transformative Power of Near-Death Experiences* grabs your heart and won't let go. True, there are a number of books out now about such things, but none of them, I repeat *none of them,* packs the punch this one does."

P M H Atwater LHD, author of 15 books on the near-death phenomenon.
Her latest, *A Manual for Developing Humans, fulfils a promise she made during her third NDE*

"There are few experiences that transform a person's life as profoundly as a neardeath experience. This book helps us to understand what that experience is like and why people change in response to it. It also helps spread the word to people who have had NDEs that their experience is real and they are not alone. Yet for those of us who have never had an NDE, the authors inspire us to make changes in our lives without the need for nearly dying. For one book to accomplish all of this is extraordinary. I highly recommend *The Transformative Power of Near-Death Experiences.*"

Bob Olson

Author of *Answers About The Afterlife* and host of AfterlifeTV.com

"*The Transformative Power of Near-Death Experiences* is itself a powerful and transformational read. The many different accounts converge on some key themes of self-love, acceptance, forgiveness and renewal. Underlying all this is the realization of Oneness and the consequence that we are all deeply connected to each other and that the nature of this connection is Love. Highly recommended."

David Lorimer
Former Vice-President, International Association for Near Death Studies (UK) and Programme Director of the Scientific and Medical Network

"Experiencers from around the globe show how their NDEs led to consistent messages of peace and love, and to an appreciation of the truth that we are all interconnected. Just as NDEs forever change experiencers' lives, so too may this book change yours."

Bruce Greyson MD

Carlson Professor Emeritus of Psychiatry and Neurobehavioral Sciences Division of Perceptual Studies, University of Virginia Health System

"The authors demonstrate that the subject of transformation remains just as relevant today as when Kenneth Ring and Evelyn Elsaesser-Valarino first published their related work *Lessons from the Light* in 1998. The phenomenon deserves much more research into specific processes and possible applications, ranging from medicine to coping with grief and psychotherapy."

Titus Rivas MA MSc
Co-author of *The Self Does Not Die*

"With each turn of the page you will find a treasure trove of insights and inspiration. This exceptional book is expertly written, remarkably easy to read, and enthusiastically recommended."

Jeffrey Long MD
Author of the *New York Times* bestselling *Evidence of the*

Afterlife: The Science of Near-Death Experiences

"Within reading the first chapter of Dr Penny Sartori's and Kelly Walsh's powerful book I had tears of gratitude in my eyes; that is a sign of a powerful book that will touch hearts and souls.

I saw an immediate overlap in the messages Kelly and other featured 'experiencers' obtained from their brush with an altered state of consciousness with my own; we are all intrinsically connected, equal parts of the same whole, and it is the realization of this interconnectedness that will save humanity and the world."

Katie Mottram
Author and Founding Director of the International Spiritual Emergence Network

"This extraordinary book is an inspiring, breathtaking breakthrough in the dynamic field of chronicling near-death experiences. This is a deeply personal book, something others on the subject have somehow intrinsically missed. *The Transformative Power of*

Near-Death Experiences lovingly and fearlessly opens the door for us, a cherished guide to the power of love. With great courage it declares 'we are love', and for this I am most grateful."

Pietro de la Luna
Author of the series *Yeshu'a: The Story of the Hidden Life of Jesus*

"In this much-needed book Dr Penny Sartori and Kelly Walsh have collected together a series of intriguing personal experiences which demand further investigation. Our modern scientific model is based upon something known as empiricism. This means gaining an understanding of the world about us through our experience of that world. If this is to be taken literally then subjective experiences such as the NDE should not simply be dismissed as hallucinations created by the dying brain. Their cultural and historical consistencies suggest that this experience is a universal and, as the accounts in this book describe, involves a powerful transformative effect on those who have perceived it first-hand."

Anthony Peake

Author of *Opening the Doors of Perception*

"Reading this uplifting book is transformative in itself and its power lies in the authentic voices of the contributors. Although their journeys and NDEs were all different, what is remarkable is the transformation that occurred in every one following their NDE and their call to action to share passionately with the world universal messages about unconditional love, oneness and the existence of an extraordinary other world. This book will educate family, friends and healthcare workers about the challenges faced by people who have had this experience, and the subsequent changes that can occur. It highlights the need for understanding, validation and support. A transformative book!"

**Maggie La Tourelle
Psychotherapist and energy healer and author of *The Gift of Alzheimer's***

"*The Transformative Power of Near-Death Experiences* shows us that everyone has an individual spiritual path, and yet all paths have the same purpose – to help us become love, the highest state of consciousness possible. This book is not so much about the beauty and mystery of Heaven as it is about the wisdom of that realm in being able to use any tragedy to facilitate our transformation."

Reverend David Maginley MDiv CSCP Author of *Beyond Surviving: Cancer and Your Spiritual Journey*

"This beautiful book is the light at the end of a tunnel. It should be required reading for anyone who has ever questioned the meaning of this life and wondered whether there is an afterlife. You will cry and smile when you read it – always a sign in my book that something is heaven sent."

Theresa Cheung *Sunday Times* bestselling author of *The Afterlife is Real*

"A wonderfully inspiring collection of stories of transformation, which in themselves become transformational for the reader, pointing to a wider and deeper view of reality in which love and connection are fundamental qualities of the universe."

Steve Taylor PhD
Author of *Waking From Sleep*, *The Calm Center* and *The Leap*

"This remarkable book by Dr Penny Sartori and Kelly Walsh is an extraordinary collection of testimonies of NDEs. It is the focus on the life-changing effects of NDEs, which makes *The Transformative Power of Near-Death Experiences* one of the most fascinating and moving books I have ever read.

NDErs have gained an understanding of the interconnectedness of all life, an awareness of the essential Oneness, which leads them to their most profound message, which is one of Love – of self, of others and for life. This all-encompassing love, which overwhelms them and then is offered by them to others, is at the heart of their transformation. This important book records profound, enriching insights into the meaning of life and death, but above all, it offers Love."

Marianne Rankin, Director of Communications, Alister Hardy Trust, author of *An Introduction to Religious and Spiritual Experience*

Courtesy of Kay Byrne

Dr Penny Sartori PhD, RGN is a world-renowned expert in NDEs. She was an intensive care nurse for 17 years and undertook the UK's first long-term prospective study on NDEs, for which she was awarded a PhD. She wrote the bestseller *The Wisdom of Near-Death Experiences* (2014), which was serialized in the *Daily Mail,* as well as *What is a Near-Death Experience?* She has had her work featured, and been interviewed, across national and international press and radio. She lectures across the world, and currently teaches at Swansea University.

*Courtesy of
Kirstine Doherty photography*

Kelly Walsh is the founder of the Positivity Power Movement and Love Care Share charitable foundation. Her life's work has been inspired by an NDE she had in 2009 following a suicide attempt, and spiritual experiences she has had since. The words she shouted out following her experience – "like-minded souls would collaborate to change the world" – have been the driving force for the creation of this book and the work she now does. She is currently developing a children's character brand, inspired by her NDE, about the adventures of Positivity Princess from Planet Positavia, who is on a mission to rid negativity off the planet and create a more loving, caring, sharing world. The brand will fund the continued work of the charitable foundation she has set up in conjunction with Dr Penny Sartori, aimed at making a positive difference to children's lives globally affected by poverty and suffering.

*Penny: I dedicate this book to my son Sol,
the greatest gift I've ever received.*

*Kelly: I dedicate this book to my late father, David Walsh.
Love you dad to the moon, stars, Planet Positavia and beyond.*

ACKNOWLEDGEMENTS

We would both like to thank so many people who have helped make this book become a reality, which will help raise funds from its sales for children's projects around the world.

First, we would like to thank each other and our respective partners, Kelly's fiancé Neil and Penny's husband Enrico, for supporting us through the highs and lows of completing this book.

Heartfelt thanks also to each contributor: Sue Stone, Dr Mick Collins, Neale Donald Walsch, Gigi Strehler, Krista Gorman, Ainsley Threadgold, Tibor Putnoki, David Bennett, Penny Wilson, Mike Moon, Jeff Olsen, Diane Goble, Barbara Ireland, Deirdre DeWitt Maltby, Erica McKenzie, Katherine Baldwin, William Peters, Robert Tremblay, Paul Ammons, Jessica Harper, Dr Bernie Siegel, Dr Barbara Mango and Shelley Parker. Your love and dedication to the project have never gone unnoticed.

We would also like to thank Peter Furness from Stratagem for his design work, Alex Young from Wish Designs for developing and building our online community and charitable foundation website, Alistair Ruane from Awakening Media/Voices and Video for producing our promotional videos and animated princess, 11-year-old Beth Vizard from the UK for the princess's voice, Joshua Graham from Living in your Truth coaching and mentoring, contributors Penny Wilson/Barbara Mango for assisting with editorial and Susan Dolan from Google Expert UK for managing and growing our social media campaigns. Your combined efforts, together with other volunteers' support, will help to promote this book globally and raise additional funds to make a positive difference to children's lives.

Last, but certainly not least, we would both like personally to thank Michael Mann, Jo Lal and the team at Watkins for believing in us and our vision for this thought-provoking and potentially world-changing book.

PREFACE

By Sue Stone
Founder of The Sue Stone Foundation, Sue is a Happiness, Empowerment and Confidence Coach, and is recognized as one of the UK's happiest and most positive people

In my "former" life, I had no understanding of consciousness and "reality creation", let alone how powerful our thoughts and emotions are and that there were ways to be *intentional* about our experience of life.

When I say my "former" life, I am referring to my life prior to my "annus horribilis" in 1999. It was a time when I lived very much in the drama of life, viewing it as full of problems that I had to overcome; a time of an unhappy marriage, growing debt and worries. I had most certainly forgotten what it felt like to be happy, and longed for that childlike innocence of bouncing through life, free from adult emotions and responsibilities.

Shortly before this, in 1997, my husband and I had separated, and I had a belief at the time that once one thing had gone wrong, numerous other things would go wrong ... what a self-fulfilling prophecy that proved to be!

Things went from bad to worse and I had no idea at the time that I was *unconsciously* creating what I was experiencing. The turning point came one day (I remember it vividly) when I had just £10 left in my purse, was at the borrowing limit on credit cards and overdrafts, facing repossession of my home, with no income and three young children to feed, and feeling very alone.

I was consumed with fear and desperation, but at some level I *knew* I had to do something. To take full responsibility, I started by reading self-help and spiritual books, researched quantum physics and, as a result, began "waking up" to the bigger picture and realized very quickly that I was "doing it all wrong"; I was visualizing and thinking about all the things that I didn't want to happen, which intensified my levels of fear and created more of what I didn't want!

In brief, I made it my mission to "work" on myself and change my thinking and attitude to life. The rest is history and I now dedicate my life to helping others live their greatest lives, to "be" the change we all wish to see in the world. I share a message of peace, love and respect; to "treat others as you would wish to be treated yourself".

I am honoured to be writing the preface to this enlightening book, which totally embodies this message. In addition, I am happy to share that I too had an NDE in 2002. To me it was more an out-of-body experience. My blood pressure is always at a healthy low, but following a routine operation and general anaesthetic, it dropped dangerously low. For my daughter, Natalie, who was 16 at the time, it was a traumatic experience as, bless her, she thought I had indeed died. For me, I remember feeling amazing; that incredible feeling of what I now know to be unconditional love.

People talk about their life flashing before them, and that's exactly what happened to me. I was looking down on all the chaos, and my whole life literally flashed before my eyes. I had no concept of time; it felt like years but in reality it was only a few minutes. Following my out-of-body experience the most noticeable transformation for me was when I started to channel spiritual guidance and ancient wisdom, which I found incredible and truly humbling.

What I particularly love is that science now "backs up" the ancient wisdom that has been spoken by all the masters and sages across the centuries. Science also acknowledges that *everything* in the universe is energy, and mathematically it has proven that every cell, every photon in our universe, is connected to every other one. Now that is hugely powerful! When people say, "We are all connected, we are all ONE", we truly are.

Every thought we have, every word we speak, affects us at the quantum (energetic) level and is projected into the surrounding ether and returned to our reality. When a collective reality is being projected, it becomes a very powerful force for either positive or "negative" purposes.

As Above So Below, As Within So Without.

When situations are presented to us, we are given an immediate choice to respond with either love or fear. Fear creates more fear and love creates more love. Love is vastly more powerful than fear and is our natural essence and the most powerful force in the universe. Remember this, as your heart has the ability to move mountains.

The Transformative Power of Near-Death Experiences is a powerful and enlightening read. Enjoy and embrace!

FOREWORD

A LOVE LETTER FROM GOD

By Dr Mick Collins,
author of *The Unselfish Spirit: Human Evolution in a Time of Global Crisis*

Synchronicities tend to appear with uncanny regularity at significant moments in our lives, bringing meaningful connections, or new opportunities that make us sit up and *take note.* It was through such a synchronous event that the invitation to write the foreword for this wonderful book happened. I had just spent months writing about transformation for a new publication, which also touches on the subject of NDEs. Within an hour of handing the new manuscript to my editor I received an email from Penny Sartori saying that she and Kelly Walsh were co-authoring a book on NDEs and asking whether I would consider writing the foreword. The timing was impeccable and I said yes without hesitation. Synchronicities reveal a subtle realm of interrelations, where we are interwoven in a world of quantum possibilities.

The Transformative Power of Near-Death Experiences is a truly inspirational book, one that is capable of opening our hearts and souls to a sacred reality. This is a book that invites us to live in alignment with our higher purpose. The revelatory knowledge shared in this book is like consulting an ancient oracle, which conveys wisdom and insights gleaned from another dimension. The narratives are not dissimilar to the other-worldly journeys of shamans, who are taken beyond the veil of earthly existence and who then return to daily life with vital information that is spiritually nourishing. Within indigenous cultures such sacred knowledge is shared for the benefit of the collective, and so it is with this book, as we hear about people's travels through their NDEs. We learn about people's immersive experiences of being enmeshed in an interconnected reality, which profoundly alters their understanding of life. Indeed, the stories shared in this book are powerful exemplars that underline the importance of transformation at this time in our specie's spiritual evolution.

We are living in an extraordinary time of global crisis and it is evident that Western ways of living, which are overly invested in individualism, materialism, consumerism and hyper-rationalism, are outmoded in terms of helping humanity navigate the challenges of collective transformation at this time. Mainstream Western attitudes and behaviours have yet to wake up to the sobering reality that our lifestyles are soul destroying for people, and disastrous for planet Earth. Collective transformation cannot happen in a world dominated by self-interest, which continues to fracture our relationships with fellow humans, other species and the natural world. So, the question is, where do we turn for inspiration to augment collective transformation at this time? It is a question we ignore at our peril, particularly as we drift aimlessly into an era dominated by the worsening effects of climate change, escalating rates of species extinction, a burgeoning world population and the threat of dwindling natural resources due to desertification of the land and acidification of the oceans. Let alone the political and social instability that is causing further chaos in the world. At its core, this book is about soulful transformation and action, which has the potential to inspire humanity to work toward the co-creation of an improved future.

There are no easy answers to the collective issues we are facing at this time, but, as I discuss in my book *The Unselfish Spirit: Human Evolution in a Time of Global Crisis,* humanity is more than capable of great cooperation and unstinting collaboration. It is for this reason that *The Transformative Power of Near-Death Experiences* is like a sacred spark that ignites and illuminates new possibilities for inner and outer soul work. This book is a clarion call for the awakening of our psycho-spiritual potential, where each of us is capable of manifesting gratitude, harmony, wholeness and love in our relationship to life. Research has shown us that people's life-changing transpersonal encounters, through NDEs or spiritual emergencies, etc., often act as a catalyst for a renewed sense of meaning and purpose in life. This book reveals how people's transformational potentials were activated by their NDEs, and how they were emboldened to explore new ways of living. Trusting the process of spiritual unfolding takes courage, but this is how transformation is seeded, which grows through the cultivation of our renewed ways of being and doing.

We know that experiences of deep transformation in consciousness are often out of step with mainstream consensus realities. It is for this reason that familial tensions or experiences of social alienation can occur, especially in the early days of a transformational process when people are feeling vulnerable. Yet, the pull to wholeness is like the navigation system of migrating birds that know intrinsically the direction that must be taken. In a similar way, the transformational imperative is strong when people have been opened up at a soul level, such that they intuitively "know" there is no turning back. This book is full of rich examples, where people share their journeys of healing and integration, which in some cases took many years. We read heart-rending stories of transformation in the face of great loss and trauma. One person came through their NDE and shared the experience with a doctor, which led them to be admitted onto a psychiatric unit. However, despite the difficulties they experienced, a common thread that is woven throughout all of the stories in this book is how people were inspired and determined to turn their spiritual revelations into renewed ways of living in gratitude, love and service.

It is evident to me after reading the stories in this book that the journey of transformation following NDEs is about creating a sacred connection to life. For example, one of the strongest themes that emerged in all the NDEs is feeling the power of unconditional love, which inspired people to be more loving when they returned to their earthly existence. Another theme that emerged with regularity was the experience of a life review, where the contributors were shown the fruits of their earthly actions, both good and bad, which were reflected back to them. Interestingly, any judgements they experienced were self-generated. They experienced firsthand the consequences of all the thoughts, intentions and actions that had been directed toward others during the course of their life. This "warts and all" life review exposed people to the reality of how they had lived their lives, and how their thoughts, intentions and actions have impacted on others, for better or worse. It is without reservation that I say, *The Transformative Power of Near-Death Experiences* is an essential spiritual teaching for these troubled times. The life review is a wake-up call for humanity to understand the profound lesson: "what we do in the world to others, we also do to ourselves."

I have been involved in psycho-spiritual transformation work, both personally and professionally, for four decades and I have always considered myself first and foremost a student of life. It is from this perspective that *The Transformative Power of Near-Death Experiences* has become a powerful teaching resource for me. Reading this book has underlined the importance of engaging in processes of deep reflection, which connects to the craft of living in wholeness. Before reading this book, I was already doing regular mini life reviews, and I have often reflected on the good and bad I have done in this life. In this way, the life review is an opportunity to open our hearts and cultivate an attitude of forgiveness toward self and others for the mistakes we have made, as well as cherishing the good we have done. This book has reaffirmed for me the importance of doing regular life reviews, which can act as a spiritual compass in our alignment to sacred ways of living. It is through such honest self-reflection that we can transform our thoughts, intentions and actions into a path of service and love. I frequently ask myself: why should I wait until I die to have a grand life review? If we are open to the wisdom in *The Transformative Power of Near-Death*

Experiences, it could encourage each of us to participate in a *Full-Life Experience,* where our renewed ways of being and doing contribute to the evolutionary spiritual shift that is gaining momentum at this time.

As humanity continues to lurch from crisis to crisis, it is my hope that more and more people will be inspired by the sacred messages revealed in this book. Each of us can be empowered to radically change the way we live our lives, and when we embark on such a transformative journey all manner of providence arrives in mysterious ways. When we summon the courage to live transformative lives in the service of the greater good, as all the contributors in this book have done, powerful reverberations are created in the world. Our active participation in sacramental ways of living brings us into synchronistic connection with kindred spirits, which can evolve into local and non-local networks of transformation, as is happening via this book.

It is impossible to share all the insights that are ricocheting in my heart and soul after reading this book, but I do want to mention a couple of additional themes that stood out for me. I was delighted to read about the energetic life force that was seen around plants following one person's NDE. It reminded me of the wise words from indigenous elders who have been trying to tell us for centuries that the mineral, plant and animal worlds are alive with sacred energy. Other outlier themes in the book make reference to meeting shadow characters that are capable of stealing our precious life energies. These shadow figures reminded me of the disavowed shadow material that lurks in each of our unconscious processes, where our negative projections and counter-projections deplete our life energies, as well as creating more havoc in the world. We should not fear the shadow in our earthly life reviews, for, as we learn from the great psychologist Carl Jung, 80 per cent of the shadow is pure gold. It is simply part of the transformational process.

The Transformative Power of Near-Death Experiences inspires us to live in love, not fear. Therefore, transforming our relationship to the shadow is an essential part of our evolutionary spiritual development at this time. This leads on to another outlier theme in the book, when a person was given a glimpse of the terrors of Hell in their NDE. This interested me as much as the more frequently reported experiences of light and love. I reasoned that these powerful experiences (good and bad) reveal to us the reality of our thoughts, intentions and actions, which are capable of creating Heaven or Hell on Earth. From this perspective, *The Transformative Power of Near-Death Experiences* is a prophetic book, because it gives us intimations of different realities we are capable of creating on Earth with our precious life energies. It underlines how we all have free will and choice, which can be directed toward the co-creation of a better world, if we are inspired to do so. And, for all those people in life situations whose liberties have been eroded, it is incumbent that our soulful activism and collective transformation includes working for a just and fair world for all.

I was inspired to title this foreword, "A Love Letter from God", simply because all the chapters in this book are Divine revelations. When you read this book, I urge you to open yourself to feeling the sacred forces that are working in your soul. Notice how the words or themes in each chapter resonate with the deeper calling and purpose in your life. This is a profound and life-changing book for anyone who takes the time to reflect on the "inner scripts" that are directing their thoughts, intentions and actions in daily life. Making a commitment to live a transformational life is also about composing a "life script" for how we wish to live. We can begin this journey by framing our intentions and returning a "Love Letter to God". This is a simple way of responding to the sacred messages that leap from every page in this inspiring book. It is also a way of declaring our commitment to live in alignment with a Divine connection. If we read *The Transformative Power of Near-Death Experiences* as a "Love Letter from God" it heralds a new dawn for sacramental living in each of us. It means we will be challenged to think, feel and act in soulful ways.

There is much work to do in this time of global crisis, but as this wonderful book informs us, soulful activism is initiated when we embrace the depth of "who we are" in our journeys of spiritual awakening and wholeness. This is the beating heart of collective transformation, where each of us plays a part in bringing forth a world of forgiveness and love, which incubates the flowering and flourishing of our emerging sacred potential. Despite the numerous complexities and challenges that accompany processes of deep change, which are well illustrated in this book, the trajectories of our personal transformations are strengthened when we connect in communities of compassion. It is through the creation of networks and hubs of loving-kindness that a movement of soulful and collective transformation can grow. This book is a shining example of the desire to put transformation into action. All the royalties from this book are being channelled into a charitable foundation that supports children. In this way, the book exemplifies the core values of the foundation it supports, the motto of which is: *Love, Care, Share.* It is the very essence of transformative living and service, which starts with our thoughts, intentions and actions, right here, right now.

PROLOGUE

by Neale Donald Walsch,
international bestselling author of the
Conversations with God series

It can be no coincidence ... no coincidence ... that I received an electronic copy of the manuscript you are now reading when I did. It was forwarded to me by my literary agent in the US, who received a request from Watkins Publishing in London to send it on to me, to see if I might be willing to write an afterword.

Nor was it happenstance that, noticing the topic, I felt the urge to download the manuscript immediately, which I did ... and that I dived into the reading of it at once ... and that I read it in four sittings over two days ... and that by sheer coincidence just as I was finishing this remarkable book by Penny and Kelly, the firm's copy of my own book arrived. I could not miss the connection of it appearing in my hands at the very moment that my reading nine words from Penny and Kelly's book had been vibrating in my centre. What nine words am I talking about?

"...like-minded souls would collaborate to change the world."

Because I wanted the publishers to know that I related on a very personal level to the contents of this book, I sent along the narrative below. I thought I might refer to it briefly in the afterword I had been asked to contribute, but Penny and Kelly suggested that the entire account be added, word-for-word, to the book itself. I was happy for it to be included, because I agree with the authors that more and more of us need to share publicly what we have experienced in our most sacred spiritual encounters. Only by such mounting personal testimony will what once was seen as "paranormal" come to be understood, at last, to be a window into the actual nature of things, and – most importantly – the true nature of God.

I don't know whether an out-of-body experience and an NDE are cousins or twins, but I do feel that in many ways I "died" to who I was, coming "back to life" as a new version of myself following an extraordinary occurrence in my life nearly 30 years ago. Here is my memory of it...

On the evening of 8 January 1980 my wife and I had been arguing. It was one of those silly arguments that many couples often have. I can't even remember what it was about. I'm sure it was absolutely nothing of consequence. What I do remember is what happened next. It's something I will never forget.

Stomping out of the TV room on the lower floor of our split-level house, I left my wife in the middle of our heated discussion, dismissing her with a wave of my hand and disappearing into the master bedroom with a slam of the door.

I threw myself on the bed in utter frustration and then, staring at the ceiling, began to cry. *My God, I thought, why can't we just get along? What does it take for people to just get along? How can the world be expected to live in peace if people can't even do it in their own home?*

I was overwhelmed with deep sadness. It wasn't just the spat with my wife, but the whole of my life that was weighing on me as I was lying there. I remember thinking, *How can people who say they love each other separate themselves emotionally so completely at times like that?*

It was a moment of complete and total surrender to the question – and then to the realization that I had no answer; that I just didn't understand life. I just didn't understand it.

I turned my head into the pillow and whimpered, "Please, God, help me. I don't want life to be like this. And *I* don't want to be like this ... a man who argues over nothing. Help me. Help me..."

I suddenly felt utterly exhausted. As I lay fully clothed on the bed – though it was barely eight at night – I watched myself falling into a deep sleep. Somehow I sensed that it was going to be the deepest sleep of my life. I think I even said that to myself. I remember hearing myself telling myself in my mind: *This is ... going to be ... the ... deepest ... sleep ... of ... your ... life.*

And I was gone.

But not for long. Abruptly, I was awakened by a shocking sensation of being lifted off the bed. I felt like I had been swooped up. The feeling was ... well here's how I've described it since then. Imagine there's a fly on a table. Now imagine that I had a vacuum cleaner hose and that I was able to get it down on top of that fly and then said, "Okay, turn it on!", and someone turned it on. Now imagine how that fly would feel as it was being sucked up by that vacuum cleaner ... going backward, just being sucked up backward. That's exactly how I felt. I felt like I had been sucked up, my whole body, my whole beingness, and I was hovering near the ceiling.

I looked down and saw my body lying on the bed below. It looked weird, inert, as if it was made out of clay. And I remember thinking, *Is that me? My God, have I died?*

And in that moment I had a powerful and unforgettable direct experience. It was not an intellectualization, it was a direct experience of: *Oh, my gosh, I'm not that. "That" is over there, and "I" am over here.*

So I began pondering, anxiously: Who is the "I" that's looking at what I thought I was? And I looked at this form on the bed once more and studied it. How strange, I thought. How strange that I once imagined I was *that.*

I continued to wonder, now even more anxiously: Well, then, who is doing the *looking?* Who am I?

I glanced down to where I expected to find the rest of my body. You know, the way you'd look down at your shoes. I wasn't looking at my body on the bed, I was looking down from my waist to my toes. But ... *there was no "me".* There was ... nothing. I was just ... consciousness. I felt as though I was just a pair of eyes, floating alone near the ceiling.

I don't know how else to describe it. I don't even know what I was looking out of. I wasn't looking out of physical eyes. It felt like just *consciousness* looking outward. I had no body, no nothing. And I remember now really worrying: *Who am I? What's going on?*

With that, I was turned around by some invisible force and I shot out of that room like lightning. Immediately I found myself in a dark place that seemed like – I know this sounds incredibly predictable, but it did seem like – a tunnel, and then I felt myself being pushed or pulled through that passage at insane speed. There was no feeling of fear during any of this, just a sensation of incredible speed.

Soon, up ahead, I spotted a tiny speck of light, and it was this light toward which I now knew I was racing. The speck grew bigger and bigger, until I felt myself sort of pop out of the tunnel and shoot into the light itself.

Now things got really interesting, because I was in the light, and yet I also seemed to be outside of the light, looking at it. I remember (with deep feeling that still comes over me) that it was almost impossible to look at, because it was so beautiful.

I don't know how to explain how a light can be beautiful, because a light is a light, yes? Except that this light was beautiful. Perhaps it had to do with the way it *felt.* I don't know. I just know that its beauty was something I was almost unable to behold. It felt too big, too glorious, too warm and loving, too all-encompassingly *wonderful* for a human consciousness to experience. I felt small ... embarrassed.

I remember wishing that I could just cover myself, hide myself. I felt like saying, *No, no, not me. Don't look at me. I'm not worthy of being in this light. I'm not worthy of seeing this. With all that I have done, with all the black marks on my soul, with all the times I've hurt others and failed myself ... I'm not worthy.* And I shivered with tears. Why had I not done better? Why had I made the lower choice so many times? I was deeply sorry. More regretful than I can ever remember being.

Then, as shame began to overwhelm me, I felt myself being filled with an energy that I can't describe. Whenever I search for words, there don't seem to be any that fit.

As I think about it now, I want to say that it was as if the rays of that light just reached into me – as if it had arms. But it didn't. I mean, there was no physical being there. But the light just enveloped me and reached into me and opened me, gently pulling my arms apart and causing me to feel ... I'm going to say, *embraced,* even though there was no other physical being there.

The emotion I was experiencing was one of what I would later call being *totally forgiven.* Yet in that self-same moment I knew at the depth of my being that what was occurring went *past* simple forgiveness. It was a feeling that does not have words ... but let me try to put words to it anyway. It was a feeling of *knowing* that "forgiveness" *wasn't even necessary.*

It was a knowing that I was in the space of such love that forgiveness or "pardon" didn't even enter the picture; it wasn't part of the reality. There is no "forgiveness" folded into total acceptance and unlimited love, absolute safety and complete protection, utter serenity and resounding tranquillity. The emotion is one that I can only describe as a profound loss of loneliness.

I was being given peace – true peace, total peace, the peace of knowing that *I was not on my own,* that there was *nothing to worry about,* that *all was well* and *everything was perfect.* Then it seemed almost as though some giant finger was ever so gently tilting my head upward with a touch on my chin. And I felt (not "heard", but "felt") these words melt into my heart...

You are perfect.
You are beautiful, beyond description.
I love you without condition.
You are my Divine Creation,
in whom I am well pleased.

I felt totally ... *accepted,* just the way I was. I felt cradled, embraced, the light surrounding me now, floating me softly in its centre. I was *one* with It now, *inside* of It somehow. All sadness left me. Even regret disappeared. I felt healed. Not in the sense of having been "forgiven", but in the sense of having been "made whole". And I remember my soul filling with gratitude and my heart bursting with love.

Suddenly I was consumed with an *intellectual awareness* of exactly what I had been feeling. It was as if my mind had abruptly processed what my entire being had been – how shall I put this? – *absorbing:* that I will never be forgiven for anything that I do. No matter how sad I am about any action or decision, no matter how regretful, I will not be forgiven. *Because forgiveness is not necessary.*

I knew then that I was a child of God, an offspring of the Divine, and that I cannot hurt or damage the Divine in any way, for the Divine is utterly undamageable, unhurtable. I will be accepted, always, in the heart and home of God, allowed to grow through what I will label my errors, allowed to become more and more of Who I Really Am by the process I engage. Like a child working with her multiplication tables, or an adult acquiring a brand new language, my "mistakes" will be seen as steps toward mastery.

The impact of that revelation was enormous, because it was not simply some concept or theory, it was something that I was *experiencing* – I was knowing it *experientially* – right then and there.

Immediately upon embracing this awareness, I found myself in another reality, swiftly surrounded by a million, nay, a hundred million, tiny ... *particles of energy* is the only way I can describe them. They were everywhere. In front of me, to the left of me, behind me, to the right of me. They seemed to me like tiny malleable cells, or soft globules, each with their own distinct shape.

And the colours! Oh, my, the colours were strikingly, astonishingly, breathtakingly beautiful. The bluest blues and the greenest greens and the reddest reds I had ever seen. And that's saying a lot for me, because I have a severe colour deficiency. So for me, this was a spectacular sight.

Now these cells were vibrating in front of me and all around me, forming a shimmering blanket of beauty. I sensed that what I was seeing was the Essence of All Life. It was life in its sub-sub-sub-molecular form. In its smallest particles. At its basis. At its root.

And now here is something fascinating that I witnessed: as I watched these cells of magnificent colour dance and shimmer before me, I noticed that they were changing. They seemed to be swallowed into themselves, and to re-emerge in a different shape and colour. And as they changed shapes and colours, the cells all around them changed shapes and colours, too, in order to accommodate and complement them.

And the cells around those cells did the same, as did the cells around *those* cells, and so on, on and on ... and I realized that the whole thing was one constantly changing, always adapting, ever-interconnected jigsaw puzzle. A pulsating, vibrating mosaic of pure energy.

The more I looked at all of this, the more my being overflowed with a desire to touch these unspeakably beautiful particles, to become one with them. I wanted to merge. I wanted to melt into them. I don't know why. It was an inner desire, felt at the root of me.

I tried to move forward, to get closer, but with each move I made, the mosaic backed away. I thought I would "sneak up" on it, fake a move forward and then, suddenly, dart to one side.

I

It didn't work. I could not fool the matrix. It seemed to anticipate all my moves. I just couldn't get closer, and I began to weep. The sadness of this denial was more than I thought I could bear.

Then the sadness disappeared, abruptly, as a gentle, sweet voice said:
*Do you not see that you
cannot get any closer to this
than you could move your eyes
closer to your nose?
You can see the end of your nose,
but you can't get closer to it.
Consider why.*

And then I realized that I could not get closer to the energy because I *was* the energy! When *I* moved, *it* moved. Of course. I was *already* merged! I realized that I was one with all of it.

And the voice said:
Behold, now, the beauty of you.

I knew in that moment: *Oh my, there's no separation of anything from anything. What was I thinking? How could I not have known this?*

As with the previous revelations, the impact of this was enormous, because it was not simply a concept or theory, it was something that I was *experiencing,* right then and there.

Once again, as soon as I understood it, I was removed from that reality. It seemed that as soon as I came to a complete comprehension of something through the complete experience of it, I was being moved on. It was almost as if I was going through some sort of *curriculum.* Except it didn't feel that I was learning something, so much as *remembering.*

Now I found myself facing an enormous book. It looked as big as the biggest book I had ever seen. No, twice as big. Three times as big. It looked as big as one hundred volumes or directories of some kind, glued together. And on each page – on *each page* – was enough tiny type to fill one thousand encyclopedias.

As I stood before this mountainous volume, the voice I "heard" when I was embraced by the light (a thought that I "felt" would be a more accurate description) came back to me yet again. It said in the gentlest way:

Okay, Neale, okay.
You have searched your whole life for answers.
You've looked and looked, and your search has been real.
It has been pure and sincere.
It has been an honest quest for truth.
So here.
Here are the answers.

With that, the book flew open and its pages flipped past me as if fanned by some gigantic thumb, or blown by some holy and powerful breath. Quickly they flew past, the whole document exposed, page by page, within a nanosecond. And yet, I was able to read and absorb *every word on every page.*

And then I knew. I knew everything there ever was to know, is now to know, and ever will be to know. I understood the cosmology of the universe and the secret of all of life.

The impact of that revelation was enormous, because it was not simply a concept or theory; it was something that I was *experiencing,* right then and there.

That was my fourth awareness.

First, I remembered that I am not my body. Second, that I am totally loved and absolutely perfect just as I am. Third, that I am one with everything. And fourth, that everything is really simple.

And I remember saying, as the book's final page fanned past and the heavy back cover closed...

Of course.

How simple.

How elegantly simple.

And just as I experienced the fullness of that knowing, I found myself back on the bed, having been once again swiftly shifted from the latest awareness.

Now I felt so heavy, so dense. I remember barely being able to move my head a tiny bit to one side. I managed to open my eyes. (It wasn't easy. My eyelids were so heavy. I remember being shocked at the effort it took just to open my eyes.) And I could not lift my hand. I was shocked that it was so heavy, I could not lift it.

For a moment I thought I was paralysed, that I'd suffered a stroke and had lost mobility. I used all the willpower I had to move even one finger – to prove to myself that I was okay.

I figured then that I'd been dreaming. But in the next moment I realized what must be true. I'd been in a different dimension, I'd visited another plane of existence, and I had just returned to physicality. And I realized then how dense and heavy physicality *is*. And I remember marvelling at how different it was where I'd just come from. I was so *free,* so *light,* so utterly – what's the word here? – *unencumbered.*

When I realized that I was back in my human form I let myself just lie there for a while. Then I thought, "Well, surely it must be morning." I glanced at the clock and saw that I had fallen asleep only about two hours earlier. And I remember thinking: *Am I being played with here? Is somebody kidding me?* You could have told me that I was in a coma for a *month* and I would have believed you.

Then I thought, I've got to write this down. I struggled to reach over – you can't imagine the effort it took for me to just reach over for the pen on the nightstand. And as I started to grasp it, my voice came to me again and said:

That is not necessary.
Your truth will never be forgotten.
It can be neither proven nor disproven.
It simply is.

Then the voice said, with soft and quiet finality, two words that I *never* will forget:

Nothing matters.

Now I lay there pondering. *Nothing matters?* How can that be? *Nothing matters?*

And I looked at that message in terms of the little spat I'd indulged myself in with my wife. *What was I thinking?* What was so important that I had to make such an issue over it, that we would have words about it; that it would be so bad, I'd stomp out of the room and slam the door on her? *What?*

I mean, I just felt so ... inelegant. Inept. So emotionally, so spiritually ... evolutionarily ... *awkward.*

But at the same moment I was recriminating against myself, I looked at myself with the wisdom of some Part of Me that was seeing me from afar, and thought: *Given the illusion you've been living, it's totally understandable.*

With that ... with that sense of release ... I fell back to sleep. And this time, I slept through the night.

I remember waking the next morning feeling more refreshed than I had ever felt in my entire life – before or since. And I just floated off into the bathroom to get into the shower.

As I turned on the water I experienced everything in slow motion, as if I was in an altered state of consciousness from taking some kind of drug. I saw the water coming out of the shower head *one drop at a time.*

Then I looked at the tiles in the shower stall, and I saw the wall *in its sub-molecular form.* I saw it as a pattern of energy, and I realized then that everything was 90 per cent space and 10 per cent matter.

I knew then that even *space* was *physical* – made up of elements of energy vibrating and moving so fast that they can't be seen. Even the air is energy. Even "space" is an energy field. It is the "whispiest" energy of the universe. The thinnest, lightest – I don't know how else to describe it – the least solid, the most permeable essence of all. So permeable is this field that heavier, denser energy particles can pass right through it – like rays of sunlight passing through a cloud, to use a simplistic example.

As I looked closely at the shower stall wall, I realized that nothing is what we call "solid", but that energy moves so quickly from here to there that it creates the *appearance* of solidity.

Now I'm in the shower stall watching this effect in the wall. I could see where the heavier matter was located in the field of lighter energy at any particular moment. And I could see the same thing in my hand. I could then see how I could position my hand to place its denser energy particles where the denser energy of the wall was not.

In this way, like the sunlight streaming through a cloud, I put my hand *right through the wall.* I shocked myself with my ability to do this. I said, "Will you look at that." Very simple, I thought. What a simple trick. I've got to tell everybody about this. It's pretty easy. You just go like this. And I did it again! I put my hand right into the wall! Then I pulled it back out, smiled, and went on with my shower, marvelling at it all, pinning it all together in my mind.

While I was thinking, I tried to remember what I had read in that huge book. I had come back into physicality knowing everything, having it all explained in ways that even my limited human mind could understand. And now I wanted to remember what I had come to *know.* But standing in the shower stall, I couldn't remember a single thing. I could remember that I had the experience of *knowing,* but I couldn't remember *what* I knew!

So I started to weep again, and I cried out in my mind: *Why can't I remember? I want to remember! I want to tell everybody! Why can't I remember what I read in that book?! Come on!*

I was mad at my mind for not being able to bring it all back. So I just stood in the shower stall, tears streaming down my face. And I thought bitterly: what good is it to show this to me if I'm unable to retain it? And the voice said to me very softly:

You are not to know.
Simply know that you know.

Then I received a series of impressions that I can only interpret verbally, but they weren't given to me verbally. They were impressions. And the biggest impression was this: if you were to be given all of this now, and have all of it placed in your finite mind, it would be like trying to soak up the ocean with a sponge. You would burn every connector in your brain. Because you can't put the Infinite into a finite container. It's like plugging too many appliances into a single outlet. Sorry. *Overload.* Fuse blown. Circuit breaker tripped.

So, the voice said: "Just know that when you need to know anything in particular, you can access it. You can reach into the Akashic Records, the Eternality, the All of It. You, and everyone else, can access all the wisdom, all the understanding, all the truth, all the awareness, all the insight you need when you need it, by inviting your mind to go to the level of Soul, which will then reach into the Allness of Everything and bring back a particular piece of information as it serves you to have it. And you will know it clearly when you see it. There will be no problem of recognition."

So I finished my shower and stepped out and reached for a towel, when another amazing thing occurred. My awareness was in such a state that I could feel the thread count of that towel.

I dressed myself, combed my hair, and kind of floated to the kitchen on the second level. Then my wife, God bless her, God rest her Soul (she has since celebrated her Continuation Day), looked at me and smiled, as if we hadn't had any fight at all the night before. It was a brand-new day and she saw the look on my face.

"What happened to you?" she said. "You look ten years younger." And I shared with her what I just shared here. People at work that day noticed the same thing, and *said* the same thing. At least one person offered, "Wow, must have gotten a lot of sleep last night. You actually look younger."

When my wife asked, "Well, how do you feel?", I told her that I felt like I had just been dropped off on a street corner somewhere ... on a busy thoroughfare in the universe. I really felt like somebody had just let me out of a car. The car drove on and there I was, left standing there. There goes God's car, I thought. Bye, God. Thanks. Cool ride. But now here I am in this world again, dropped off in the middle of nowhere, with no map, no directions, not a thought about how to get from there to anywhere.

I remembered being told that I would know whatever I needed to know at any given moment – but that wasn't enough to make me feel safe. *I wanted a road map.* If I'm going on this journey, *I want a map.*

How do I negotiate life? How do I go through my day-to-day? How do I even get through this breakfast with my wife, much less get any work done today? How do I do anything meaningful or worthwhile, if nothing matters?

As I thought deeply about this later, I received another impression: "It is precisely *because* nothing matters that you can get through this life. Since nothing matters *intrinsically,* in and of itself, you get to *decide* what matters to *you.* And by the choices and decisions you make do you form and shape Who You Choose To Be. Is this not the greatest gift?"

Very shortly after that I got back into this world. I had been operating with part of me still hanging out in another dimension. Then I pulled out of it completely and got back into the so-called "real" world. I had my attaché case and my snappy blue sport coat with the grey slacks, and I was making decisions and taking phone calls and pushing paper around and doing, doing, *doing.*

I was back in my power place. And that went on until my whole life came crashing down. It was as if God was saying, "Okay, you didn't get it the other way, so how about this? How about you have a car accident and break your neck, but don't die and, instead, lose everything you think you're working for? How about you lose your house, your car, every penny you've got, lose your marriage, lose access to your children? How about you sitting in a homeless park – not for a week or a month, but for a year – and come to your senses?"

So I had everything taken from me. Everything. I had two pairs of jeans, two shirts, a pair of shoes, three pairs of socks and a knapsack. That's it. Not even a dollar to get through the day. Nothing. I was reduced to asking people if they could please help me with some spare change.

It was after I finally healed enough to find a job I could do, and worked my way back into a little cottage behind someone's house, that I had my *Conversations with God* experience. I realize now that this was my road back to some semblance of that place I had visited on 8 January 1980.

I created a way for me to access a level of connection with the Divine, which we can all access. My lasting hope is that God's blessings will be experienced by every living person through being shared with every living person by every living person. That is why I share my out-of-body experience so publicly, and that's why I have shared my conversations with God with the world.

INTRODUCTION

Dr Penny Sartori and Kelly Walsh

NDEs have fascinated me for over 20 years. I worked as a nurse for 21 years and it was while looking after a dying man at the intensive care unit, that I began to question death and what happens when we die. My nursing career exposed me to many situations that I would otherwise have been totally unaware of. Coupled with my growing fascination with NDEs, I was able to pay particular attention to dying patients, and observe their actions and the whole process as they approached death. In 1997 I began my hospital research into NDEs at the intensive therapy unit where I worked. I interviewed patients and gathered data for five years. It took a further three years to analyse and write up the findings I had amassed. In 2005 I was awarded a PhD for my research.

My research left me in no doubt that NDEs occur, and has led me to conclude that our current understanding of consciousness is incomplete and that we have to consider consciousness from a perspective other than it being regarded as a mere by-product of the brain.

Since then I have continued to gather cases of NDEs, out-of-body experiences (OBEs), deathbed visions, empathic/shared death experiences, spiritually transformative experiences (STEs) and any other kind of anomalous experience that cannot be fully explained. I have seen a massive shift in attitude toward NDEs, and it has gone from one extreme to the other. When I began my research in 1995, it was very difficult to find people who were willing to share their NDEs with me; I was always met with hesitation. Often friends would tell me of people they knew who had memories of an NDE, yet when I asked if they would speak to me about it, very few would.

There are many reasons for this. Often people don't realize that other people have had such experiences too. There are some examples in the following chapters of people who, after watching a movie or reading a newspaper article about NDEs, were pleasantly surprised to discover that others had experienced the same as them. After an NDE, some people may question their sanity and be terrified of sharing it in case they are considered to have mental health issues. Sometimes the experience can be so profound that it is deeply sacred to the person, and they simply don't want to share it. Many know that something profound has happened to them, but they have no frame of reference for it, and if they try to discuss it with someone who has no knowledge of NDEs this can cause further confusion when trying to understand it. There are also many misconceptions about NDEs, and people who are ill-informed often dismiss them as hallucinations or a "trick of the mind", having been influenced by popular television programmes that are frequently one-sided and don't present a full picture of an NDE.

Thankfully there has been a renewed comprehension of NDEs and they are now being taken much more seriously. Consequently, people are feeling more comfortable about sharing their experiences publicly. There are huge benefits to this. NDErs no longer have to suffer in silence, meaning it is easier to get information about their profound experiences. The number of emails I have received in recent years has increased phenomenally. Responding to them over the past four years has been a full-time job and I currently have over 14,000 messages awaiting my reply. This highlights that people are more comfortable with sharing their experiences now and emphasizes the importance of finding a greater understanding of these experiences and learning from such people.

Contrary to the beliefs of those who dismiss the NDE as an aberration of a dysfunctional brain, the experience does not end after regaining consciousness. There are many changes associated with NDEs that continue, in numerous cases, for the rest of a person's life. It is literally as if the person they were before the NDE has died and been replaced by someone who looks the same but has very different values. I want to emphasize that these changes are not always pleasant or welcomed by the experiencer, and the renewed perspective on life can be disruptive to their relationships, work life and personal life. Many people have reported devastating consequences of this change in their viewpoint and feel that they no longer "fit in"; they can no longer relate to family and friends, and feel alienated from society.

On the other hand, many experiencers find that the changes are positively transformative, but it may take some time for them to fully integrate and understand the experience and adjust to this new perspective on life. It is the transformative aspect of the NDE that is the focus of this book and that is of great interest to me, because it has the potential to benefit so many people.

In May 2014, I received an email from a lady called Kelly Walsh. I was going through a particularly busy stage in my life, as my book *The Wisdom of Near-Death Experiences* had been published in February 2014 and since then it seemed that everyone wanted to talk to me about my NDE research.

In the months leading up to when I connected with Kelly I had given many talks all around the UK and Northern Ireland, made television appearances, given hundreds of radio interviews and received thousands of emails from all over the world. To top it off, I was pregnant with my son, and by May I was beginning to get exhausted so had decided to take time off from responding to emails in preparation for his imminent birth.

However, when Kelly's email arrived, though it was only short and didn't give much information, for some reason I felt compelled to read it a second time and respond immediately. This is what it said:

Hi Penny

I had an NDE in 2009 and my life's work and the vision I am working towards is connected to my experience. I am based in Manchester in the UK and I am keen to speak to you about my NDE.

Would it be possible to arrange a Skype call?

Love, Care, Share
Kelly x

I sensed that Kelly's experience had greatly impacted upon her and that, although it wasn't immediately apparent, there was an urgency to her request. We arranged a Skype chat and Kelly described her experience in depth, as well as its effect on her life. Technically, Kelly's experience is a spiritually transformative experience (STE), because it occurred when she was recovering in hospital, after an attempted suicide, in the absence (as far as I am aware) of acute life-threatening circumstances, although her biochemistry had been severely affected. NDEs are the most studied form of STEs and occur in acute life-threatening circumstances. Very similar experiences that have almost identical after-effects can also occur, the main difference being that they do so when there are no immediate acute life-threatening circumstances. This is the type of STE that Kelly reported.

During our conversation, what struck me most about Kelly was how her perception of herself and life had changed so drastically from being suicidal, anxious and depressed to being incredibly positive and loving. As a direct result of her experience she appeared to love and accept herself for who she was for the first time in her life. This love also extended to others and she had made it her "mission" to share what she had learned and put it to good use to benefit others.

Kelly explained that she was developing an online community, the Positivity Power Movement, which would fuel the activity of the Love, Care, Share charitable foundation she was setting up to make a difference to the lives of families affected by poverty and suffering. She also told me that she was developing a children's character brand that had been inspired by her experience. One day, she hoped, Positivity Princess from Planet Positavia would become a global brand, empowering many children and helping to share the important message of love and respect for each other. She described to me a whole list of ideas around the character brand, including a children's book, an animated TV series and a feature film. I was impressed by her focus and how she had already taken steps to put her vision for the Positivity Power Movement and charitable foundation into action. She was not procrastinating about what she was going to do; she was already doing it! This was all undertaken in her own time and at her own cost. She had branded a name for her organization, had designed costumes, logos and websites, and was networking with people from all over the world. Obviously Kelly's message is resonating widely, because she currently has thousands of followers on Twitter and her Facebook Positivity Power Movement group is growing daily.

One of the most important questions we can ask is what is it about NDEs and STEs that makes them so powerful that they change the way people perceive and live their lives afterwards? How can such an experience literally transform suicidal thoughts into the complete opposite? How was Kelly able to change her mindset so drastically? I can't think of any kind of therapy or pharmaceutical drug that could have such radical and prolonged effects.

It is very difficult to grasp how experiencing an altered state of consciousness, as occurs in STEs and NDEs, can facilitate such a massive change. It seems so outlandish that it is easier for some people to overlook this key point and attribute the experience as a whole to an abnormality of a dying brain. I feel very strongly that to discount alternative points of view, simply because they do not fit in with the current materialist view of consciousness, is detrimental to developing therapeutic intervention that could benefit millions of people in the long term, which is one of the reasons for writing this book.

When Kelly first approached me about the concept for this book I was unsure if I could commit to the project, due to my ongoing work commitments and all that was going on in my life. However, Kelly's ultimate vision, combined with her pleasant persistence, persuaded me to be involved.

Kelly says:

The vision for this book was inspired by my experience and I am now acting on what I feel is my soul's purpose. However, it hasn't always been that way. Like a lot of people who have had an NDE, I didn't initially feel mentally strong enough to talk openly about what had happened to me for fear of rejection or potential ridicule. I tried desperately to forget what had happened and to focus on rebuilding my life.

A number of years later I realized that trying to suppress what had happened to me was no longer an option. It had happened, it was part of my journey and I had to deal with the emotional rollercoaster connected to my experience in the best way I could. My life was never going to be the same again. My primary focus was to try to integrate the experience into my daily life, while exploring ways of delivering the message I had been given.

During my experience it was demonstrated to me that we are all one, all connected, all one big global family. Regardless of colour, creed, gender, sexuality, religious beliefs or any other perceived differences, we are all loved equally and unconditionally.

Whether you refer to God, the universe, the Source or any other word is irrelevant; the fact is that the light loves us all beyond any love you could possibly put into words, and its simple desire is that one day we will all see each other as our true soul reflection, which is pure Divine Love. On this day we will be released from all manmade fear, rejoice in the reality that Heaven is already here, and will ultimately create Peace on Earth.

What I have found most fascinating since connecting with other experiencers around the world is that, although each person's experience is unique to them, the spiritual understanding, knowledge and wisdom gained from people's time in other dimensions is relatively the same and reinforces the simple fact that we really are all part of the same whole, and are intrinsically linked.

I am delighted Penny agreed to co-author this book with me. Since my NDE, she has been such a blessing in my life, and was the first person to encourage me to stay on my spiritual path and become deaf to the criticisms of others who totally disbelieve in this important phenomenon and dismiss it as a trick of the mind.

Studies into NDEs and other related phenomena have consistently shown that we are part of an interconnected universe, and that consciousness continues beyond our earthly existence. This realization has the power to inspire a shift in our understanding about life's meaning. It raises thought-provoking questions about whether we actually die, or not? My own experience, and those of my fellow contributors in this book, have left me wondering whether we are dealing with the reality of a No-Death Experience. What I mean by this is, our physical bodies certainly die at the end of our lives, but our journey continues as a more subtle form of consciousness, which appears to connect to an eternal soul. This realization could bring about a positive shift in peoples' understanding of the purpose of their earthly lives. In short, the message of No-Death Experiences is that our spiritual lives matter, now and beyond.

Whether you are a believer or not, or somewhere in between, my hope, dream and desire is that the experiences shared in this book will open your heart, mind and soul to the powerfully transformative aspects of NDEs and to how the messages within them can bring about positive change in the world.

We have both connected with numerous people whose lives have been transformed in many different ways as a result of their NDE. This book will feature just a few of those we have connected with, and hopefully it will provide a snapshot of how transformative NDEs can be. I must reiterate that the transformations are not always necessarily on a grand scale.

Transformation can be subtle and personal, yet it gives the individual in question purpose and meaning. This book is a collection of cases where people have been transformed by their experience. Each chapter has been written by individual contributors in their own unique style. The only exceptions are three chapters written by myself, due to a language barrier and time constraints. I have been inspired by all of the contributors. Their stories speak for themselves and each contributor has had complete freedom of expression, so there has been minimal editing to their chapters, but I have added a short commentary to highlight salient points. After her NDE, Kelly undertook training with Sue Stone, so she suggested asking her to write the preface. When Kelly explained what the book was about, Sue synchronistically said, "Oh I had one of those experiences but I tend not to talk about it."

Similarly, last year I read one of the most powerful books I've ever read and it left a lasting impression on me. I remember reading the book and feeling such deep emotion each time I picked it up, because not only was it written from the heart but it was also thoroughly supported from both an academic and experiential perspective. The author had likewise been transformed by a spiritual awakening that he had experienced many years ago. The book, by Dr Mick Collins, is called *The Unselfish Spirit: Human Evolution in a Time of Global Crisis.* When we had completed the manuscript for this book I knew that Mick would be the perfect person to write the foreword. Neither Kelly nor I had met Mick, but when I emailed him to ask if he would support us he replied instantly and said yes. He mentioned how the timing was perfect, as he had literally just submitted the manuscript of his second book to an editor and it would take approximately three weeks to edit, so he had the time to give our book the attention it deserved. He intuitively felt that we were being Divinely guided together for a reason and that our collective work was vitally important at this critical time in our history's evolution. Kelly and I are delighted to have the support of such a heart-centred and loving man, and feel that this is just the beginning of very exciting things for the future.

Kelly also suggested contacting Neale Donald Walsch to see if he would consider supporting our work. His teachings from the *Conversations with God* series have had a profound effect on Kelly. When she first approached me about the book project, she synchronistically received an email from Neale's organization, Humanity's Team, which referenced how the knowledge and wisdom gained from NDEs will change the world. Kelly intuitively felt that Neale would be involved with our project in some capacity. I agreed with Kelly and I recall, shortly after beginning my research, being invited to a wonderful conference in the Catskills Mountains in Upstate New York, organized by the Lifebridge Foundation who funded my university fees while I was undertaking my PhD. During the conference David Lorimer from the Scientific and Medical Network read out excerpts from a book that really resonated with me. The book was *Conversations with God* by Neale Donald Walsch. On my return journey I stopped at the airport bookshop and bought all three books in the *Conversations with God* series and read them carefully. These books opened me up to another perspective on life and I have gone back and re-read them many times, especially during challenging times.

There are no words to express how I felt at the end of the editing process of this book, when Kelly called me to see if I'd opened an email from Jo Lal, at Watkins (our publisher). Kelly was overwhelmed and could barely get her words out. Through perfect synchronistic timing Neale Donald Walsch had received our manuscript, downloaded it immediately and read it in four sittings, and was as excited about it as we were. He agreed to write the afterword but further to this he also sent us the chapter that you have just read, which describes his own experience. We are both honoured and privileged that Neale has shared his own experience here and that he totally understands the whole ethos of this book. It is very interesting that Neale's experience was a precursor to writing *Conversations with God,* as these books have positively impacted the lives of millions of people. It is as if everything has come full circle as the UK edition of Neale's book *Conversations with God, Book 4: Awaken the Species,* originally published by Rainbow Ridge Books in the US, has been issued and distributed by the same publisher as this book, and at a time when the conclusion of my own research is that the message of these experiences is crucial for our evolution as a species. The sharing of such experiences is paramount in spreading this message to awaken the world. Synchronistically, one of the first people to endorse Neale's *Conversations with God* was Dr Bernie Siegel, who also shares his experience in this book.

This book begins with Kelly describing her experience, followed by chapters from various contributors. Gigi Strehler will describe how her NDE motivated her to initiate a UK NDE support group, launched in 2014. During the birth of her daughter, Krista Gorman's NDE led to her modifying the way she interacted with patients through her work as a physician assistant. Ainsley Threadgold's recovered memories resulted in the full integration of his NDE, which he hadn't consciously recalled. Tibor Putnoki's cardiac arrest led to the creation of the Light of Love Foundation. David Bennett's survival of a disaster at sea resulted in a new way of life and overcoming cancer. Penny Wilson's anaphylactic shock led to her being compelled to share the message that we are all connected. Mike Moon describes how a visit to the dentist led to volunteer work in a hospice. Jeff Olsen was able to cope with the tragedy of a fatal car accident. Diane Goble's fun day out in the rapids led to her following a whole new path in life and initiating one of the first stress management centres. Barbara Ireland's NDE prompted her to change her thinking and write a book to help others also change their thinking. Deirdre DeWitt Maltby will describe how her NDE resulted in her living life in a more compassionate and loving way. Erica McKenzie's battle with her weight led to her helping people all over the world and informing healthcare workers about NDEs. Katherine Baldwin's fall into a swimming pool as a child led to her developing healing techniques that have benefited hundreds of people. William Peter's NDE led him to develop the Shared Crossing Project, which is helping people all over the world. Robert Tremblay's NDE has given him the strength to live with a debilitating disease for the past four years, while spreading the message of love and peace that was so deeply etched into his psyche during his NDE. Paul Ammon's undiagnosed blood clot led to conservation work with bees, while Jessica Harper's experiences led to complete acceptance of who she is and she feels passionately about becoming a voice for those who are suffering with transgender and other painful issues. Dr Bernie Siegel's childhood NDE greatly influenced his medical career as a paediatric surgeon; his goal has been to humanize medical education and medical care. The final chapter by Dr Barbara Mango will describe how her experiences from childhood inspired her to undertake a PhD and write her doctoral thesis on the topic of the spiritual and scientific debate concerning the NDE.

As work on this book was drawing to a close, I had two emails on the same day from people who I immediately thought should feature in the book. One was from Barbara Ireland and the other from William Peters. Both of these chapters are shorter than the rest as there was limited time left before the manuscript was to be submitted, so we've slotted them in between the longer chapters.

The contributors are from all over the world and have connected with either Kelly or me over the previous few years, sometimes with notable synchronicities, which will be described in the individual chapters, highlighting the interconnectivity of us all. We thank all the contributors for agreeing to be part of this book and sharing their story with the world. Each of us has the same vision of making a positive difference in the world and we have agreed that all royalties will be donated to the Love, Care, Share charitable foundation, which supports small projects for children globally.

As I've said in previous books and in all of my lectures, NDEs have a wonderful message for the world. It is one of peace, love and respect, and is ultimately The Golden Rule described by all of the wisdom traditions of the world; namely, "Treat others as you would wish to be treated yourself". We can all benefit from this message without nearly having to die first; all we have to do is take notice of what these people are trying to convey. We invite you, the reader, to engage with NDEs and be inspired by the message that they have for us all.

1

THE POWER OF DIVINE LOVE

Kelly Walsh is 42 years of age and lives in Manchester in the UK. Her experience and the message she was given – that like-minded souls would collaborate to change the world – is one of the driving forces behind this book. Kelly has always maintained in discussions with me the importance of working together to demonstrate the collective power of the NDE message, and is purely acting upon the instructions she believes she was given.

I have little to no memory of my early childhood, but what I do know, is that I always felt different. I can't quite put my finger on why, and perhaps I will never know. What I can tell you, is that like a lot of children, I grew up with deep-rooted emotional issues that affected my ability to truly love and accept myself. Outwardly, I appeared happy with a big smile on my face; but that was a mask I often wore to conceal the pain of my breaking heart. Plagued with insecurity and a deep, unfulfilled need to be loved and accepted, I developed an eating disorder at the age of 16, and in my twenties suffered with periods of severe anxiety and depression.

By the age of 33, my mental and physical pain finally became too much for me to cope with, and on Monday 5 October 2009, I decided to end my life by taking a huge overdose.

I did not go into hospital for three days, so, in theory, I should either be dead or have severe organ damage; but God had other plans. To put it in context, the doctor told me my liver enzymes were so high that I might need a liver transplant. My medical discharge letter states that I had in excess of 20,000 milligrams of paracetamol in my body; the maximum recommended dose in 24 hours is 4,000 milligrams.

It was too late to pump my stomach. I was admitted to the isolation ward and put on a saline drip to help flush out the toxins that were slowly destroying my organs. My parents were not allowed to stay with me, and I remember feeling fearful as I was wheeled away from them into the observation ward. Thoughts of burning in Hell started to play over and over in my mind. I had carried out the cardinal sin of attempted suicide, and now I was going to be punished. How wrong can one person be?

I noticed a Gideon's Bible on the bedside cabinet. I pulled it into the bed with me and started to read it at what felt like 100 miles per hour. Suddenly, a lady dressed as a nurse appeared. She had beautiful blonde hair and a soothing smile. Moving near to my bed, she touched my arm and whispered, "When you get out of here, read the book *Conversations with God*" and, with that, she vanished. On reflection, I believe she was an angel.

Her words didn't calm me. Still extremely fearful, I asked to see the onsite minister. He was kind and caring. He sat with me for about an hour and prayed over me. When he left, he gave me a carved wooden cross that I held onto for dear life and protection.

The following evening, I had what I can only describe as a neardeath experience. I was lying in my bed, holding onto my wooden cross while my body was pumping with sweat. It was dark, my eyes were closed and I was feeling extremely anxious. I had an awareness that there were spiritual beings around me trying to keep me calm. I couldn't physically see them, but I could feel their presence in such a powerful and loving way. They had a soothing, peaceful effect, and I believe they were there to help support me with what I was about to experience. Suddenly, I was transported on a journey and could feel myself going through what felt like bumps in the universe, commonly referred to as dimensions. While this was taking place, my whole life flashed before me and I could see and feel the emotions – good, bad and ugly – associated with my life experience up until then.

This was not a particularly pleasant experience; it felt like a test or battle to survive. I was travelling at what seemed like supersonic speed, having to hold on tight while I faced jolts going through various dimensions in the universe. After passing through the seventh dimension, I felt as though the battle was over and a wave of relief surged over me. I was finally at peace and enveloped by unconditional love. It was the most incredible, joyful, loving feeling, and I wanted to stay lost in that moment forever. A love so beyond any I had experienced before, that it is impossible fully to express it in words.

Suddenly, someone or something spoke to me: "You are strong and powerful. It isn't your time." I cannot tell you who or what it was, as I have no recollection. This seemed ironic considering that I'd just tried to kill myself. The voice then said: "You still have a mission to carry out on Earth. Humans have the capacity to heal physically, mentally, emotionally and spiritually ... through love. Self-love is the most important of all." In that instant, I realized that we are all one, all connected and, contrary to common belief, there is no higher Source passing judgement on us. When our souls leave our bodies, the only judgement we endure is that which we pass on ourselves. We evaluate all we've said and done from a place of fear, rather than from a place of love. In a religious context, this would be thought of as our period in Hell; I prefer to call it a period of reflection. The length and pain associated with our period of reflection depends on how we lived our lives. We are simply here to love and learn, and each of us is at a different level in terms of spiritual growth and development. It is worth remembering that not a single person is lost to God's perfect Divine Love. It's only when we go home that we fully realize this. We are all perfect imperfection in God's eyes; trying our best to live in alignment with our soul's real essence, which is love.

The following morning, after what seemed like an eternity as I had no comprehension of time, I came around from this experience. My arms were crossed over my chest and, as I opened them in slow motion, like a rebirth, I remember thinking, "Why am I in a hospital bed after where I have just been?" I felt powerful – like I could do anything, so I tried to escape from the ward ... naked. My ex-mother-in-law, who was there at the time, said I was proclaiming that I had met God and angels. That evening I had a vision of the world changing, and that like-minded souls would collaborate to make this happen. I was so euphoric that I shared my experience with anyone who would listen. I don't think I was taken too seriously, as I was on a psychiatric ward. Miraculously, I left the hospital a week later with a clean bill of health.

My body was healed by Divine Love, but I still had a long way to go emotionally. I had to get back into the real world while trying to integrate what had happened to me. After speaking to a couple of people about my experience, I decided to put it to the back of my mind. Doubting myself, I wondered if I'd imagined the whole thing, but deep down I knew the truth. I fell back into my old patterns, worrying about what others thought, and letting that concern direct my life. There was little support for people who'd had near-death experiences, so I was left to sort through it alone. I guess I didn't feel strong enough emotionally to deal with it, and I worried about other people's opinions of me. I was frightened of negative reactions because, all too often, what people don't understand they fear or ridicule.

    After my experience, life was a mix of joy and periods of dark depression. I understand now, that those dark periods continued to haunt me because of deep-rooted and unresolved traumas from my childhood. Six months later, I met my soulmate on a dating site. The minute I looked into his gorgeous blue eyes I had a feeling in the pit of my stomach that he was the one. I felt like I had known him before and, the truth is, I probably had in previous lifetimes. Three weeks into our courtship, I told him about my suicide attempt. I trembled and wept as I poured my heart out to him. Finishing my story, I waited, expecting him to end the relationship. He just smiled, held me in his arms and said, "It's in your past; let's move forward." I truly believe he was sent to me as a gift from the heavens to aid in my recovery. Little did we know, the toughest part of our journey was yet to come, and it would require a period of deep soul-searching and healing for us both.

Being in love was wonderful, but the rest of my life, well that wasn't coming together as easily. I found my work to be unfulfilling. No matter what job I took, I was left feeling like I wasn't living according to my soul's purpose ... whatever that was. How was I supposed to have a heart and soul filled with joy, when I didn't even know what I was supposed to be doing with my life? I was on an emotional rollercoaster, questioning everything and going over and over in my mind the experience I'd had in hospital. Why would God tell me I had a mission to fulfil on Earth and not tell me how I was supposed to accomplish it?

It took what you might call "Divine intervention" for me to start acting upon the mission I'd been given. I was brought up as a Methodist, but had stopped going to church in my late teens. Out of the blue, I was invited to meet a new friend at a local Pentecostal church. We were greeted at the entrance by a group of young women who asked if I believed in God. I replied that I had a strong belief in the love of the Divine, but did not fully accept certain aspects of what was still being taught in various religious organizations, e.g. God is to be feared and homosexuality is a sin. The service was lovely and at the end I felt as if lightning had struck me and began to shake and cry.

I decided to explore Christianity further. For the next three months, I spent a lot of time with a group of devout Christians who had very strong beliefs about who was going to Heaven and who wasn't. This didn't feel right to me. How could God love unconditionally and yet punish people? During this time, I attended some prayer sessions and ended up speaking in what they call tongues. It sounded like Arabic. I had no control over it.

On reflection, I realized that God was communicating with me, reaffirming my true path and the message that needed to be delivered to the wider world. Church was the wake-up call I needed. Sermons were preached about love and forgiveness, while at the same time telling me anyone who was not a practising Christian would perish in Hell. This was in direct conflict with the God I'd experienced.

We need to understand that some of the greatest spiritual teachers of all time – Jesus, Moses, Muhammad and Buddha – taught love for humanity, regardless of colour, creed, gender, sexuality, religious beliefs or any other differences. I believe it is the power of this Divine Love that will bring peace and harmony to our beautiful planet and, ultimately, heal the world.

Walking away from the restraints of church life and returning to my spiritual journey proved to be an important step in my recovery: helping me come to full acceptance of what had happened to me in hospital. Emotionally I wasn't healed, and didn't yet have the strength to share the message that I had ultimately been sent back to deliver. It would take another four years, lots of Divine synchronicities (too many to mention in one chapter), and the biggest tragedy of my life, before I was finally strong enough to act on my soul's purpose.

A year later, I was invited to attend a spiritual weekend in Glasgow, which happened to fall on the third anniversary of my overdose. One of the speakers was Neale Donald Walsch, so you can imagine how super-excited I was. His words spoke to the depths of my soul, leaving me in tears. A male friend of mine, who had travelled up with me, looked at me and said, "Kelly, he is saying the same stuff you were saying on the way up here." I replied, "Yes, I know, but how do I know this stuff?"

Later that day, Doreen Virtue was speaking. She asked if anyone had anything they wanted to share. Tentatively, I put my hand up, and for the first time spoke about my experience. The reaction from the audience was incredible. At that moment, I knew in my heart and soul that one day I would be speaking about my experience and what I learned from it, to the world. This was later confirmed when I got a little nudge from the universe. A lady with a bag full of angel cards approached me. She asked me to pick one out. I reached into the sack and pulled out a purple card that said, "life's purpose/master teacher". My friend looked at me and said, "See Kelly, this is your purpose." Five minutes later, as God is my witness, a second angel card fell off the back of the purple card. It was gold, and had the words "grace and Holy Spirit" printed on it. I had no idea how significant the colours purple and gold would become in my journey.

In early 2014, struggling with feelings of isolation and doubting my path, I decided to search the internet for others who'd had an experience like mine. I stumbled upon – or should I say I was Divinely guided to – Dr Penny Sartori. I sent her a two-line email, to which she replied immediately, and we arranged to Skype next day. Penny was heavily pregnant at the time and wasn't responding to emails, but she intuitively felt that we needed to speak. I shared my experience and my heart and soul's desire to create a movement based on uniting humanity in global friendship. Its ideology is love, care, share. I also made Penny aware of a children's brand concept I was working on, which I hoped would one day fund the continued work of my charitable foundation. The intention of the foundation is to make a positive difference globally to children affected by poverty and suffering. It was so cathartic to finally speak to someone who believed my truth, without thinking I'd gone mad. Penny loved and believed in my vision, and since then magic has begun to unfold.

Several months after our connection, I made an appointment with a past-life regression therapist. Prior to the session, the therapist told me she often got channelled messages during and after sessions. I went into a meditative state, but rather than regress, I saw the colour purple and then what appeared to be a golden heart rising up in my consciousness. I cried tears of joy. The therapist brought me out of my meditative state, and told me what had happened to me was very unusual. The reason I had not regressed, she felt, was because this incarnation was so important.

She had drawn a crown on a piece of paper and asked me if the colours purple and gold were significant to me. I replied that prior to my experience, they hadn't, but since then, yes. The crown she had drawn was the exact image of the logo I'd had designed earlier for the movement: purple and gold, complete with a love heart. She suggested connecting me to my spirit guide and told me to shout out the first name I heard, which was Peter. To be totally honest, I was a little disappointed with the session and didn't fully trust what had just taken place. I wasn't convinced Peter was my guide; maybe my conscious brain had randomly picked out that name.

That evening, the therapist texted, telling me to look up Peter, the Rock, one of Jesus' disciples. I laughed and texted that I wasn't well versed in the Bible, but I would check him out. The following day, I met with a lady who had recently become my mentor. She asked what I had been up to. I told her about the regression and the reference to Peter. The woman looked at me in shock and said, "I knew there was a reason I chose this book to read on the train. It was meant for you."

She handed me the book, *The Christ Blueprint: 13 Keys to Christ Consciousness* by Padma Aon Prakasha, which had a chapter inside titled "The Anchor, Peter the Rock".

A passage in the chapter talks about a Christ-orientated civilization built on a simple heart that recognizes love, does its best and lives a good life, yet struggles and has flaws. I smiled as I read those words; they reminded me of myself, and I now understood why Peter was the perfect guide, not only for me, but no doubt, for many others. He had his weaknesses, like we all do, but God can see beyond any of our flaws to what truly lies inside all hearts and souls.

The words from that passage would be of enormous help to me, as I was soon to face the most upsetting and challenging time in my life. Since my NDE, I had come a long way on my healing journey. However, there were still deep-rooted, suppressed issues from my childhood that needed healing.

In June 2015, I sat talking with a friend about her upbringing, and how she and her sister had both been negatively affected by things that had happened to them in their childhood. Tears welled up in my eyes as I listened to her story. Her pain felt as though it were my own. I realized I wasn't just crying for my friend and her sister, I was crying for myself and my inner child too. It was the strangest experience; as if I knew I'd been deeply affected by something, but had no clear memories to anchor the feelings to. I went to my friend's bathroom and prayed aloud to my late grandparents. "I don't know what it is I need to know, but I need to know. Please help me understand why I'm feeling this way."

The following day, I was talking to a gifted spiritual lady. It was the first time we had spoken, and without knowing more than my first name she said, "Your intuition regarding your childhood is correct. This is coming to the surface now because you are finally strong enough to deal with it. It's time to heal." Little did we know, the next day I would have a severe flashback and be admitted to hospital. I had never felt such fear; it resulted in a total meltdown and full-on psychosis. Paranoia overtook me, leaving me distrustful of everyone. My partner and parents stayed with me until they were asked to leave. My partner leant over the bed to kiss me goodnight, and I grabbed the Jesus crucifix from around his neck and snapped it off. I was terrified, and the crucifix seemed my only form of protection. Later that evening, I gave the onsite nursing staff the shock of their lives when I leapt from my bed and started singing and preaching about Jesus and various archangels, who were going to rid the darkness from our planet. I sang and preached for hours. The nurses later told me I had a beautiful singing voice. But, because I'd gone on for hours on end, they eventually sectioned me and gave me an injection to stop my singing and calm me down. When my partner came to the hospital, the nurses took him aside, "Is Kelly religious? Does she sing in a choir?" He replied, "No, she's normally tone deaf". Thankfully, within a couple of days, the mental health team assessed me, revoked my section, and allowed me to go home. It's difficult to understand all that transpired in hospital and we still struggle to comprehend why it happened. However, one thing is for sure; I was in a heightened state of awareness brought on by deeply suppressed trauma. It seemed I was finally ready to face, process, heal and release those pains. I'm also certain that it was an important part of my on-going spiritual awakening, which continues in the writing of this book and the charity work that is connected to it.

I was blessed to be supported by kind and compassionate medical staff. They saw beyond my seemingly odd behaviour, and recognized what I needed was support to get through potential post-traumatic stress symptoms.

Sadly, this isn't always the case for patients who display signs of spiritual connection. Many end up sectioned under the Mental Health Act, forced to take a concoction of mind-altering drugs that suppress their true feelings and identity.

I believe far more should be done within the healthcare system to understand symptoms of spiritual-awakening. Focus and attention should be directed to identifying the potentially deep-rooted cause and effect of people's perceived mental health issues. My personal experience taught me that a person-centred, holistic approach should be considered within the healthcare system, focusing on the collective healing of mind, body and soul.

Out of love and respect for my family, I have chosen to leave out more personal details surrounding my hospital admission and our on-going relationship issues. However, what I will share is that in September 2015, my father sadly transitioned to the other side. Tragically, he ended his physical life through suicide. When we received the telephone call telling us he'd hanged himself, the feelings of shock and loss were unbearable. The repercussions of his passing have been heart-breaking. My mum's side of the family held me accountable for my father's suicide, shunning me and calling into question my character; and ridiculing my experiences and beliefs.

I can't say it hasn't hurt, it has. However, the knowledge and wisdom gained during my near-death experience, and the spiritual and healing path I've been on since, have helped me cope with this tragedy in a more peaceful and dignified manner than possible before. Don't get me wrong, I still have periodic struggles dealing with the enormity and pain of it all and I've sought alternative therapy to help me process and heal the trauma. However, I am blessed to know life continues, and that one day I will be reunited with my dad. I recognize that, since childhood, I have been seeking love and acceptance outside myself, when the person I really needed to seek that from was me. My life experiences have made me who I am, and I wouldn't change a thing. I believe I chose this path coming into this world so that, one day, I'd be in a position to help others with their healing journey to self-love and acceptance. Ultimately, we are spiritual beings having an earthly experience. At times, our lives can be very painful, but I truly believe that all our experiences, including pain and suffering, are perfectly orchestrated to help us to learn, grow and develop. It's only when we go home that everything finally makes full sense. It is worth always remembering that no matter what challenges you face, you are love – and are loved unconditionally; we all are.

I'm passionate about raising awareness of suicide, and speaking openly and honestly about my experience at both ends of the spectrum. I believe more suicides could be prevented if people understood that it is impossible to end life. Our souls and spirits continue after physical death to face the same issues we had difficulty with on the Earth plane. At some point, everything must be dealt with; either through continued healing in the various dimensions, or during our next incarnation. Surely it is better to stay in the physical body with your loved ones around you, and work through your perceived problems so you can heal what needs to be healed, rather than end your physical life. Perhaps if I had spoken to my dad about this in more detail he would still be with us today. Who knows for sure, but I am 100 per cent certain of God's unconditional love and that my dad is continuing to grow and heal in spirit. It's been confirmed to me by Hazel Angeni, a gifted spiritual medium, that my dad is okay. He has had his life review and now understands all the stuff I talk about. This made me smile!

I hope my words help ease the pain and suffering of those who have lost someone to suicide; enabling them to understand their loved ones are not banished to a life in purgatory, and that one day they will see them again. The time has come to end the stigma associated with mental health issues and suicide. We need to encourage people to speak openly and honestly about their feelings rather than hide them, as so many do, as a dark guilty secret.

I believe most people's issues stem from an element of low self-esteem that generally derives from childhood experiences. Broken adults often create broken children, and the cycle continues. More needs to be done to help all children realize how truly special, beautiful and amazing they are. We have a duty of care to help children develop healthy, happy minds and positive outlooks. Education should not be solely focused on academia. It should be more holistic, addressing life skills, creativity and how to be true to our authentic selves.

Since my experience in 2009, I have been studying the power of positivity and have been privileged to train with the Sue Stone Foundation. During the course, we discussed the proliferance of negativity in the world and the impact it will have on the futures of our precious children. In a split second, what I was shown during my near-death experience came flooding back, and my alter ego character, Positivity Princess from Planet Positavia, was born. Positavia is essentially where I went during my NDE and, through the character, I want to empower children to awaken their Positivity Powers and be the positive change we want to see in the world.

My ultimate dream is to create a children's character brand that helps to fund the continued work of the charitable Love, Care, Share Foundation that I have set up. I visualize families going to the cinema to watch an animated movie about the adventures of Positivity Princess from Planet Positavia. At the end of the movie a trailer is played that shows the work of the foundation and the audience's faces light up as they see the impact the profits from the movie and subsequent merchandise sales are having in helping less privileged children around the world. What better way to make Positivity Power – kindness, compassion and an acceptance of all – become cool! Whether you're aged 1 or 101, it's never too late to become a Positivity Prince or Princess who truly loves, cares and shares.

My NDE, and subsequent spiritual experiences, have impacted my life in ways I could have never imagined. They have filled it with so much love and beauty, and led me on a path that has connected me to some truly incredible people. However, there have been fleeting moments when I've wished they had never happened, so that I could live a relatively normal life ... whatever normal is. At times, it's difficult readjusting to an earthly existence after having touched the other side. I'm learning to surrender myself fully, and let God, the universe and the angels lead the way. I know the vision in my heart and soul is being Divinely guided, and my prayers are being answered.

One of the synchronicities almost too poignant to mention, relates to a professional video I needed for the Positivity Power Movement website. I had no budget to cover this. What I had, and continue to have, is trust and faith that the ultimate vision will eventually manifest itself. I was sitting chatting to God and angels, as I often do, asking them for help and guidance. An hour or two later I was browsing on Facebook and discovered a competition to win a professional video shoot and edit. I quickly entered the competition, and a few days later learned that I had won. When I looked into the company doing the video shoot, I was astonished to see their name was Awakening Media, based at Angel Wings in Leeds. I had to smile. When I finally met the lovely man, Alistair Ruane, who was going to shoot my video, he informed me that he was also an animator and voice artist. I shared my global vision to create the first children's brand of its kind aimed at helping less fortunate young people; what happened next sent shivers down my spine. Alistair kindly offered to produce more than one video. In addition, he helped create an animated Positivity Princess; thus, I would have a product to show potential media partners interested in production. He told me he was prepared to help me, because a year earlier, on 9 October, which happens to be the anniversary of my NDE, he had nearly died, and it changed his attitude toward life. He now wanted to be of service to others. I knew in that instant that Alistair would be one of many like-minded souls who I would continue to work with in the future.

While writing my chapter, I was compelled to reach out and connect to a young woman from Wigan, called Caz Simms. She was a patient at the same time as me, in the same ward where I had my NDE. I sent her a message on Facebook asking if she had any memory of anything I said in hospital. I was half expecting her to say, "I don't know what you're talking about", but she replied, "Yes, I do, and it's amazing to see that you are achieving what you set out to accomplish. You said you wanted to change the negativity in the world and prevent it in younger people. You were telling everyone that we are all one, all connected, all equal. You were so full of love, as if you had a message from God to share." This completely blew my mind and I knew in that instant, that I had been guided to reconnect with Caz to reaffirm what I had experienced, and to remind me of the importance of the work I was now doing.

What spurs me on to work for a transformational shift in the world, is that future generations of children will grow up loving themselves and each other. I use my personal story as an example of the deep change that is possible. Learning to love myself has taken over 41 years, and although I still have emotional wobbles from time to time when unhealed issues and insecurities rise to the surface, I am actually very proud of how far I have come. For years I've seen the love and beauty in others, but struggled to see it in myself. This lack of love for myself has, at times, led me down a self-destructive path, and I have said and done things that I now regret. However, I realized holding onto past perceived mistakes serves no purpose. The past is past, and whatever I had done in my former life was part of my awakening. I have learnt that we all do things that do not serve our higher purpose, and these become the lessons for our growth. Judging ourselves and others is counterproductive, because the reality of God's love is Divine and unconditional.

Imagine what the world would be like if we supported each other. Letting go of the guilt and shame of our past, and learning to love ourselves and one another in the same way God loves all creation. Each moment is an opportunity to re-frame and re-set how we live our lives. For example, I use a simple method to do this, which involves standing in front of a mirror. While looking at my reflection I say, "Because

I truly love and forgive myself, I am able to truly love and forgive others." This simple exercise can help us begin the journey of setting our hearts, minds and souls free. When we live in love and forgiveness, the positive ripples resonate powerfully in the world. In this way, the journey of deep healing begins when our hearts and souls are redeemed in the service of love, for self, others, and the world.

Who knows where the next part of my journey will take me, but one thing's for sure: it will be a journey based on love, not fear. I know I am meant to share my truth and work in collaboration with others, to make beautiful and lasting change on our planet. I will never forget the channelled words I read from a real-life princess, the late Her Royal Highness Princess Diana. She said, "It isn't just about loving each other and changing the world; it is loving everything to change the world." Not always easy, I know, but something we can all work toward. She was, and still is, an inspiration to so many people, including me. Her bright shining light lives on and continues to touch the world in such a positive and life-affirming way. Through the work of our charitable foundation, we plan to bring love, joy, happiness and positivity into children's lives the world over, and to leave a beautiful legacy, just as she did.

Since my research began, many people have contacted me after their STE/NDE. They have described the many synchronicities that began to unfold in their life. Often, these synchronicities seem unbelievable, but they have great significance for the individual. Kelly is no exception and this chapter has only touched on some of the many synchronicities in her life. Kelly has been totally transformed by her experience and is completely committed to acting on what she learned during it. She really has been a driving force in this book coming to fruition and her ideas expand way beyond just co-authoring it. She has created the children's character Positivity Princess, set up the Positivity Power Movement (which is fuelling the activity of the Love, Care, Share charitable foundation) and continues to network with people from all over the world in order to spread the message of interconnectivity, peace, love, caring and being of service to others.

2

TOUCHING THE VOID ... AND THE VOYAGE BACK

I first connected with 37-year-old actress Gigi Strehler when she contacted me via my website in 2011, asking for help in understanding her NDE. She was in the early stages of making sense of her experience. We exchanged a few emails but it was a couple of years before she got in touch again. This isn't unusual; it can take many years before someone is able to fully disclose their experience to me. We arranged to have a quick Skype chat which lasted about three hours. I was fascinated to hear what Gigi had to say and how she interpreted her experience. It is conversations with NDErs that deepen my understanding of this multifaceted phenomenon. In our initial conversation, it was very apparent to me that Gigi's life-changes after her NDE were difficult to reconcile with her life prior to her NDE, as Gigi experienced one of the less frequently reported NDEs: a void experience. I later connected Gigi with Kelly, who then connected her with other people who feature in this book.

The process of coming into this world takes significantly longer than it takes to leave it. In some cases, life ends in the blink of an eye; for others, it is an enduring drawn-out exit. I was of the former; my brush with death was so sudden and unanticipated. I find it fascinating that people are often more curious about the details leading up to death than the actual event of dying. I had a friend who committed suicide and I was struck by how many people questioned precisely how he'd taken his own life, rather than immediately acknowledging the absence of that life. We do indeed have a morbid fascination with death and dying. I'll keep my account brief.

It was a usual exam day at the theatre school where I taught. I made it through the exhaustive procedure of rehearsing students and sending them into their individual examinations.

Feeling unusually weak and tired – little did I know I was suffering from internal bleeding – I went to the bathroom before leaving for the evening and collapsed. I was to learn later that the condition I was suffering from was called Meckel's diverticulum, and that I had a perforated ulcer, one with its own blood supply – but at the time, all I knew was that blood was pouring out of every orifice possible. I managed to cling onto the sink and unlock the door – and to my great good fortune the headmistress was walking along the corridor. I managed to get her attention. Knowing that something was very wrong, I instructed her to call an ambulance. Then I passed out. I came to in the ambulance, then arrived at Accident and Emergency (A&E). I had the utmost faith (assumption, really) in the medics, the hospital and the pending diagnosis – and that whatever was wrong would soon be rectified. Somehow I managed to rationalize the fact that blood was pouring out of me, and that I was having emergency blood transfusions to replace my rapidly depleting vital life force. The doctors did their best to investigate, but despite tubes being stuck down me, up me and in me, they couldn't find anything. The blood flow was so intense that it obstructed the camera's images. But I still had faith. And I still rather naïvely believed in luck.

The twists and turns on fate's path can turn on a dime, as they say. Rather unfortunately, and in the end catastrophically, all this took place during the time that nurses and medics were due to strike against government changes to their pay and pensions. Under normal circumstances, I would've been out there on the picket line with them. Their very act of striking was to be my demise. I still have very neutral sentiments about it. However, as the years pass I constantly readjust my relationship with words such as chaos, chance, luck, fate, destiny, coincidence, serendipity, accident and mishap ... The nurses serving on my ward were bank cover nurses – filling in for those protesting outside. I was approaching my fifth day in hospital, and the bleeding was showing no signs of ceasing. I remember my mother holding my convulsing body upright while a river of red poured forth. Something obviously then went awry in the handover or my medical notes, because I was not given a blood transfusion that evening. The following morning I was due for a scan to try to ascertain the source of the blood – it was to be a lengthy procedure, so I was wheeled to the bathroom so that I had a last chance to relieve myself before it started. Once in the bathroom I promptly passed out, hitting my head against the tiled wall, and started slipping away. This was it. Death was coming.

It's true what they say: your last sense to go is your hearing; all the other senses slowly cease to function as death encroaches from the feet up, but the last to disappear is your hearing. This is an age-old phenomenon. You may have heard accounts of Socrates being forced to ingest the highly poisonous plant hemlock as a method of execution; one that involved ascending muscular paralysis resulting in death. Or perhaps you've seen footage recorded using a thermal-imaging camera of someone passing away: the whole body glows red at first as the camera detects heat (life), then starts to transform through various interim colours to blue (death), spreading from the feet upwards. You essentially leave your physical form through the crown of your head and therefore your hearing remains intact longest.

And I heard a lot during my experience. I heard the medics call for the crash team. I heard them admit fault at having somehow omitted the last blood transfusion. I heard the chaos as they realized the crash unit was on the other side of the hospital. I heard the shouts as quick-fire decisions were being made. I heard fear, panic, confusion, determination and adrenalin. Then everything went to black.

Death is a very beautiful and lulling process. It is a delicious feeling – certainly one that no longer perturbs me. There's no other experience more blissful, no matter how many drugs or mind-altering substances you take. And there is such *grace* and *mercy* in the process. Now, faced with any situation,

I always remind myself that *all things pass* – even pain – and that's the wonderful salvation that death brings.

What is it like to die? Well, for me it was like sinking back into a hammock. It is as if "death" is a backward trajectory and "life" is a forward will/intent/focus. Years later, I still had moments in therapy when I couldn't forgive myself for succumbing so easily to death. We all have an idealized notion that we will fight to the bitter end for that forward motion toward life and existence, at any cost. Not so for me. I separated from my body as easily as a leaf falls from a tree. I knew that my physical form had given up. Though I knew that my only hope was to focus all my mental strength/consciousness/intent into fighting forward back into "life", I chose instead to sink deeper into that wonderful hammock of mercy and grace. I chose death.

Limbo-land. That's the phrase I coined in therapy to describe the space/place I went to. Many people see a tunnel of light, or meet passed loved ones, or even an energy/source/light entity/deity. I did not have an experience that confirmed another consciousness realm. This is a wonderfully and positively affirming feature of a commonplace NDE. Even a "negative" NDE, such as sensing or encountering a demonic presence or destructive forces, can have its positive outcomes. Both experiences leave people returning to this physical realm with a secure and rooted sense of another space – time continuum or existence of the self. Those who have a positive NDE are brought back and bask in their Heavenly experience. Those who have a negative one often return and reform. Either way, they have an unshakable concept of the continued awareness of the self. I was to have an unshakable concept of something quite different. Something only reported in roughly 5 per cent of NDEs. I went to "the void". Total darkness, total silence, total nothingness. Zero. Zip. Zilch. And this was nothingness as an experience, not just as a concept we toy with while alive. *I'll let that sink in for a moment, and then maybe what I'm trying to articulate will really land ...* I experienced true timelessness. Time is not linear; in fact it is a manmade concept. It is bendy, curly; it spirals. In one simultaneous moment you experience all that was, is and will be; everything that you are a part of and at one with. In later months, my analytical mind, once returned to the physical realm, would suffer a severe breakdown, struggling to compute the *concept,* let alone the experience. Grappling to understand what *that place* was – Limbo-land – I started to think that if I hadn't had a Heavenly or Hellish experience, then I had somehow gone to some interim space/place. A doorway between life and death (or rather, a continued, yet altered, existence and state of being) – a sort of purgatory if you will. This idea was to spawn what has since, perhaps, become a lifelong obsession with investigating mankind's concepts of the hereafter. I took my questions to the Rabbi, the Priest, the Imam, the Monk – none had any concrete answers, and by concrete I mean a philosophy, ideology or concept that aligned *100 per cent* with my experience/reality/truth. In my desperation, my psyche began to break apart. Who am I really, I asked myself, given that my self-awareness has effectively velcroed away from my physical form? What *is* that Limbo-land place? *Where* did I go?

Therapy allowed me slowly to let go of the need to define that place in any other words or by any other terms. Instead, when I wish to return to that space, I recall the feeling and wholeness of the experience. The feeling of total *love,* total *mercy* and total *absence of judgement* will cradle my consciousness forever. It is not important for me to describe or articulate that place – what is vital, however, is to absorb the three stark revelations I had there.

Revelations by nature are instantaneous. They are not processes or journeys to a certain awakening – they are immediate and complete and profound. The only way I can articulate this is thus: it was as if three revelations/realizations were instantly downloaded into my brain – though whether the brain still functions as a "brain" during a cardiac arrest is debatable. Whatever term you wish to attach to them, I essentially connected with three pertinent truths that would eventually influence every single breathing moment of my return to life...

Revelation One – *the material world is not reality.* Dead easy to say (no pun intended) as a given statement. But when it happens, it shakes your entire world and existence. It is deeply shocking. It suddenly distorts our notion of ourselves. We take nothing with us. Nothing. Not even our physical form. I am not my body nor my mind. I am not my organs. I am not even my breath. What am I then? *I. Just. Simply. Am.* It's a big notion and a bigger and shocking reality when it happens. Because of this, I found it very difficult upon my return to the physical world to create attachments to things or money or possessions. I became hugely intense in my communication with people – I would gaze deep into their eyes, looking to connect with their deepest and truest self as opposed to their physical manifestation. I could no longer register faces and bodies on any sliding scale.

Nor could I differentiate anymore between beauty and ugliness. I lost all objectivity. I could only subjectively decipher the light and dark energy that people carry within themselves, and the whole spectrum in between. With all our advancements as a species, we have stifled a certain animal instinct/sixth sense. And my animal instinct had been magnified. I would just sense someone's vibrational energy and acknowledge my own individual response to it. I could "sniff" people in an instant, almost read their inner thoughts; regardless of what I was supposed to think of their outward form. Beautiful or not. It became very intrusive, both to the other person and to my own energy. I could "sniff" their innermost thoughts, their deepest fears, their deepest loves. The truth is what it is. There's no escaping that, no matter how it is dressed up and presented to you. In the first few years, then, after my experience, I would call a spade a spade. I'd tell people what they were really thinking and feeling. It scared them or angered them or overwhelmed them. Eventually I just stopped saying things. But the ability to see straight through the physical form still remains an oxymoronic blessing and curse.

Revelation Two – *judgement is an internal process.* Many world religions, philosophies and ideologies speak of a day of judgement or of a balancing of the scales or karmic retribution or day of reckoning: an assessment of a person's actions, words and sentiments. But it is *nothing* like you imagine it to be. Many people who have had an NDE speak of a "life review" in which they are shown their life (by a neutral, non-judging entity) or re-experience parts of it. Often from the greater higher-self perspective or through the "eyes" of the person whom your behaviour or actions or words affected. For me, as well, judgement was not an external process. There was no separate entity determining that good people take the lift up to Heaven and bad people the escalator down to Hell. That is far too simplistic a viewpoint. Judgement is a wholly internal process. It does not take place from the outside in, but rather from the inside out. For me, being in Limbo-land, without physical form, was like being completely transparent. Everything could "see" into me, and I was part of everything. This is maybe where the ideas of "God is everywhere" and "God is all-seeing" come from. You cannot run from yourself on your deathbed. You know the truth behind every *action,* every *word,* every single *thought.* That's right. Every single intention you've ever had is known by you and by *all that is.* And because "time" in the physical realm is finite, once you pass into the eternal realm, you cannot go back and change the ripples and vibrations created in your physical lifetime. You cannot undo any action, any word, any thought or sentiment. It is just *what is,* and now in Limbo-land, forever will be. *That* is for me what created my own personal Hell. Every encounter, every event, every word, every action, every energetic transaction with every other person, animal or natural entity is accounted for because *it happened* – it came into being and you cannot unstitch what is woven into the fabric of life. That smarts. When I came back I had a debilitating need to rectify and resolve every past event that gave me or others any discomfort or emotional pain.

Revelation Three – *it is our deeds, not our creed that matters.* It is the action we take and the things we do that determine our vibrational state in the realm to come. Religion or traditional belief systems or ideologies are not important. It is not *how* you get there, but that you *get* there: to a more elevated state of being/consciousness than when you started. I came to realize that your professed belief (or disbelief for that matter) has no bearing whatsoever on the outcome. What you think, say and do has infinitely more bearing than what you "believe"! As a result, I simultaneously have all the time in the world for religion and yet absolutely none at all! It led me to want to study each major world faith deeply in order to learn how different sacred texts, prophets and wise men, cultures and spiritual processes aid us in our journey and quest to move incrementally away from darkness toward the light. I have a vivid memory of looking at a large book in Religious Education (RE) at primary school at the age of eight or nine ... and remembering only one thing: "Religion is but a multi-coloured lantern; we all look through the different colours, but the candle is always there." It encapsulates exactly my sentiments surrounding this final revelation. I had a sense that it's almost as if God/the Source/the Light/Om/Yahweh/the Universe/the All That Is (delete as appropriate) is much bigger than such trivial complications of needing to define spiritual expression. The energy of All That Is doesn't really have the time or, I imagine, the inclination to be dealing with the nitty-gritty of mankind's quest to find enlightenment through set doctrines, manmade and man-implemented rules, regulation of rituals or perfection of practices. You evolve and elevate or you do not. Simple.

Re-entry into my physical form was rather like a very hard crash landing. I suspect it was due to aggressive medical intervention, but I suddenly felt the shock of my senses being reawakened. I could smell the overpowering disinfectant of the sterile environment. I was blinded by the artificial luminous lights. I could taste the arid dryness of my mouth. I heard the trainee doctor expel a huge sigh of relief while wiping sweat from his panicked and furrowed brow. The pain of needles being jabbed into my veins shot through my entire body. It was indeed a crash landing, but I was here. I was now. I was back.

The first words I said to my mother when she was rushed into the room were: *"J'étais près de Dieu"* – "I was close to God." I should point out that my mother tongue is 100 per cent English. Although my mother speaks four languages, French being the third, and although I took French as a language subject at school, to this day it still strikes me as a rather odd and out-of-place thing to say. Anyhow, however it came out, in whatever language, I do acknowledge that I had somehow comprehended on a very deep level the reality of what had happened. I had touched the void – and come back. I knew I wasn't departing again anytime soon. So as the doctors rushed me into the operating theatre for emergency surgery (they decided that they would just have to go in and see what they could find) and the ceiling lights flashed past me as I was hastily wheeled down corridors, my mother ran alongside me and simply said "Ask for forgiveness", which I admire from her as being a very hopeful and practical piece of advice amid the hysteria and chaos.

Forgiveness best describes the overwhelming sentiment I felt in Limbo-land. A seamless fusion of *mercy, compassion* and *love*. However, I do remember thinking: "forgiveness for what?" in response to my mother's well-intended prayer/hope. Had I really lived a life that was so bad? Yes and no. But at the time, I was perhaps already comforted by the complete serenity I had felt in the other space and which clung to me like a sparkling dewy residue. I was not afraid. And I was forgiven.

When I came round from the anaesthetic and operation, the nurses called for my mother, although family members weren't normally allowed in the recovery room. This time my first words were, "I came back for you Mummy...", and I later learned that they had cut into my stomach, and discovered and removed the Meckel's diverticulum, the perforated ulcer and some of my intestine. I also later learned that they had told my mother they didn't really fancy my chances of survival. Which explains her comment of "ask for forgiveness" as her final parting advice and as an indication of the potential end. But it was in fact to be the beginning of a slow and arduous recovery period: physical, mental and emotional. One that started with my mother literally feeding and bathing me, while I slowly rehabilitated my core muscles and started to walk again. It was as if I were speeding through life's experiences from infancy. As if a reset button had been activated on my life. I marvelled at how bright and colourful the flowers and trees were when I finally left the hospital some days later. Sounds were completely overwhelming. I was learning to sit comfortably in and be housed by my body for the first time all over again.

The most extraordinary things were happening to me. Something must have changed in my electromagnetic make-up because I could tell I was in a slightly different physical form this time. Lights seemed to buzz or flicker when I drew near to them – and I've blown a few fuses! I also became highly photosensitive and had to drive with sunglasses on at night for a long while afterwards. I still struggle in our technologically advanced age with televisions, computers, phones – the artificial light sears into my retina and I seem to cause more interference than the next person on devices. I also knew that something had shifted in my energy. Having grown up without pets, I had no affinity with animals (I loved and respected them, but maintained a neutral stance regarding them), but now they would constantly approach me as the sentient individual beings that they are. I live in a small ground-floor flat in the heart of London. Squirrels would happily come into my living room and foxes would grace my porch. Their "purest instinct" could sniff out that dewy residue of the other space I suppose. It was similar with young children; they would gravitate toward me with all their purity, innocence and love – and I knew that something within me had changed. Not by choice. I never asked for it. Just simply as a side-effect of my NDE.

It is the aftermath of an NDE that really has an impact on your life rather than the NDE itself. For me, all sorts of things happened. My sleep was altered: I had to sleep with my mother because my heart would shudder me awake just as I was drifting off to sleep – as if it remembered the time it stopped and was trying to drag me from the peaceful state I was drifting into, lest I was dying again. My dream life went off the Richter scale – "significant" dreams peaked in intensity and frequency. I can always tell the difference now between a dream where the mind is just sorting all its junk out and one where a connection to the Source has brought a message, such as being introduced to my two guardian angels (I woke up crying, not quite believing I was worthy of one let alone two of these incredible entities) or dreams of prophecy (I began to dream of events before they played out in real life) or of guidance, signs or omens. As a result, I am absolutely fascinated by our sleep state and our relationship to it and what happens during it. It's a large proportion of our daily life (a third) that we spend in this altered, almost coma-like, existence – with differing brain patterns, awareness and altered consciousness. Some channel or connection is made to something, somewhere. I'm convinced of it – and we're only investigating the tip of the iceberg.

Somewhere between the spiritual and the physical lies the mental and emotional. I can say with certainty that there was a time when I completely lost my mind and heart. I think partly my experience of "the void" led me to have a complete existential breakdown, and my experience of "the peace that passeth all understanding" left every emotional encounter in this world paling in comparison. I almost became suicidal, wanting only to return to that blissful euphoric state that was Limbo-land. The way I felt and thought about everything completely changed. As if I'd had a brain and heart transplant; a personality and identity transformation. It was overwhelming. I had a different take on myself, my place in the cosmos, my family, my friends, my environment, my choices, my attitudes, my morals, my values, my ideas of love, children, animals and nature – in the broadest scope of things – right down to politics, career, money, assets, relationships, marriage, religion, faith, sex, prayer, meditation – straight back up to enormous concepts to do with time, energy and consciousness ... As you can imagine, it's a lot to mull over, and a lot to muddle through if, like me, you're whacked on medication to dampen the *effects* of the NDE side-effects and Post-Traumatic Stress Disorder (PTSD).

It was during this time that Near Death Experience UK was born. I had done a couple of years of extensive reading on the subject matter and found huge comfort in the fact that although NDEs greatly differ in their manifestation, there are a few traits that hold true and transcend the age, sex, language, culture, creed and colour of the experiencer. I came to realize that these universal truths linked us all. I supposed that if I was suffering terribly in trying to adjust to life on planet Earth, there must be thousands of others who are experiencing the same pain, confusion, challenges and obstacles. I created Near Death Experience UK as the UK's first support group for experiencers. I had no idea how I was going to help anyone else other than say: "I know. I get it." But I knew it would be a great way to bring the NDE community together to offer *support, love* and *encouragement.* Due to incredible medical advancements, more and more people are being brought back from the brink of death having had the most extraordinary experiences, and the more we share them, the more we can learn from them. My NDE has shaped and changed me in ways I would never have been able to conceive. I am so thankful. I would never take it back. And I hope light fills your "Take Two" – wherever and whoever you are...

During our first Skype conversation, I remember Gigi describing how hard it was to find anyone who could understand her experience. She felt as though she was being a burden on her family and friends because she was talking about her experience so much. This highlighted to Gigi the need for a safe place for NDErs to go to seek understanding from others who had also been through the same or similar experiences. There had previously been an NDE group set up in the 1980s as IANDS (International Association of Near-Death Studies) UK, which was chaired by David Lorimer and Dr Peter Fenwick, but there was no active support group operating at the time that Gigi first contacted me.

As a direct result of her NDE, Gigi spent a great deal of time researching support groups with the aim of setting up the Near Death Experience UK support group. Although Gigi has only briefly alluded to it in her chapter, I feel she has accomplished a great deal. She set up a website, searched for a venue and spent a lot of time, as well as her own money, in setting the group up. Anyone who has ever been involved in setting up an organization will appreciate how difficult this job can be. Her determination paid off and she successfully led the first meeting in June 2014, after which several meetings followed, with what started off as a small group of members.

I feel this is the beginning of something that is much needed and I am confident that this group will grow, for no doubt many people reading this book will find themselves in a similar situation to that which Gigi was in. The group affords NDErs the opportunity to discuss how their NDE has affected them and find comfort in the support of those who have also experienced such changes.

Gigi has great vision for the group and hopes that, with time, it will spread to venues throughout the UK so that there will be local groups in which people can meet without having to travel to London. She also envisages that therapists who specialize in helping NDErs will be contactable through the group so that people are supported as much as possible. If you're interested in being a part of this group and in helping Gigi to develop it further, then please visit the website www.neardeathexperienceuk.com *where there are details of how to contact her.*

3

BEYOND HEAVEN

Krista Gorman is a 46-year-old lady, who lives in Florida. I had an email from Krista shortly after my book came out in 2014. I watched a short film on YouTube of Krista giving a presentation, about her NDE, at an International Association of Near-Death Studies (IANDS) conference. I noticed a slight synchronicity when she mentioned that, while she was pregnant, an ultrasound scan showed that her daughter had a hydronephrosis. When I was pregnant with my son, he too was diagnosed, during an ultrasound scan, as having a hydronephrosis, a kidney condition. I was really inspired by Krista's presentation because here was another healthcare worker who understood the importance of NDEs. Krista has written a book about her experience and has featured on Morgan Freeman's show The Story of God *on the National Geographic Channel. I connected Krista to Kelly and they quickly became firm friends. She also became an active member of the Positivity Power Facebook group, where she met the love of her life through video interaction.*

It was the summer of 2000 and I was at the end of my pregnancy. I'd spent the previous two years working very hard, studying and training to be a physician assistant, and had graduated just three weeks prior to the scheduled delivery of my daughter. I was a new PA and was also going to be a mother. It was such an exciting time!

I'd been scheduled for an induction at 39 weeks due to a congenital abnormality of my daughter's kidney, and on a hot July evening I settled into my hospital room. A medication called Pitocin was delivered through an IV to start labour. Just before the Pitocin, I was also given an antibiotic to prevent infection. Not long after the antibiotic started running through the IV, my chest began to feel funny, like my heart was beating abnormally. I notified the nurse, who immediately stopped the medication, and shortly afterwards the palpitations also stopped. I was at a loss to explain why I'd had the reaction other than I may have developed an allergy to the medication during my pregnancy.

Through the night my labour proceeded uneventfully and by the next morning I'd dilated only three centimetres. Contractions are much stronger with Pitocin, and as much as I wanted to go through my labour without one, I asked for an epidural. Shortly after the catheter was placed into my spinal canal I lay there watching the monitor next to me. Watching the tracing, I could see my baby's heart rate drop dangerously low while I was contracting. Knowing that bradycardia (a slow heart rate) during labour was an immediate indication for a caesarean section, my heart sank as I waited for my midwife to give me the news.

Seconds later she appeared and told me she would need to put an internal monitor into the top of my daughter's scalp in order to watch her vital signs closely before undergoing delivery via a caesarean section. Though I knew the section was absolutely necessary, I was crushed. I wanted to deliver my baby, to watch her come into the world and hold her as she took her first breaths.

However, I recognized the urgency of the situation, so I immediately pushed the thoughts away. I was having my baby! No matter how she came into the world, I would be holding her soon. Excited at the thought of seeing her face for the first time, I laid there as the monitor was placed. Would she look like me? My husband? Both? What colour hair would she have? *I just want her to be healthy.* In the middle of that thought I felt the same fluttering in my chest that had been there the evening before, only this time it was much more severe.

My breath started coming in short bursts and no matter how hard I tried, I couldn't get enough air. As I turned to my mother next to me, I was barely able to get the words out: "I'm having trouble breathing!" That's when all hell broke loose. Immediately, I was yanked onto my left side and an oxygen mask was placed over my face as I was simultaneously being wheeled out of the room and across the hallway to the operating room. I remember the sound

I made as I struggled to get air into my lungs; a tight, frantic gasping. Then, just before everything went dark, a soft, gentle, serenely Divine peace came over me. My heart stopped at 9.18a.m.

My next moment of awareness was of being high above my body, looking down and seeing it lying there on the bed with people all around it. I could see, and I was still "Krista". I was awake, conscious, yet unencumbered by my physical self. I watched as tiny black particles rushed up from my body to where my vision was high above, until I was a floating loose static cloud. There was no pain. No sound. No worry or fear. It felt as if I'd been completely removed from any reality I'd known and the memory erased. I was simply pure, unadulterated consciousness. I didn't know where I was or why, nor did I feel like there was a reason to know. I simply was. I could feel, however, and in that moment I felt a strong sense of curiosity about what was happening down below. What was that thing down there? What were all the other things doing around it? At that point, I had no understanding that what I saw was *my* body lying on the bed below and the things around me were doctors and nurses trying to save my life and the life of my baby.

I had no emotional attachment to the physical forms I saw. The whole scene was almost like watching a movie, and as I watched I became more and more curious about what was happening. I saw my doctor pull my daughter out of my belly and hand her in a blue towel to someone at my right shoulder. They took her and quickly turned around so I couldn't see what they were doing – and I so wanted to see! I watched as someone dressed in blue stepped into the doorway below and stood for a moment as if to assess the situation, then walked up to the bedside to stand across from my doctor, who was already busy working on me again.

As I floated to the other side of the room, I felt myself becoming more and more attached to the scene unfolding below. It felt more familiar, like I almost knew what was going on but couldn't quite grasp it yet. Just as that feeling began to dawn on me, I had the sensation of a tugging from my left side. It was a gentle pull as if to say, "Come on". I resisted, as I wanted to stay and find out what was going on. In response, it pulled harder and I knew intuitively what I was required to do. So, I let go. Once my resistance faded, I found myself shooting to the left like a bullet through the room, through a fluid-like wall, through a flash of bright white space, then out into a place where I was immersed, reabsorbed within the same particulate matter that I was. It was thick and dense and penetrated every bit of me.

What a rush! It was incredible! I zipped along imperceptibly in that space and found myself noticing how the "wall" next to me was fluid in some areas, then densely particulate again. It was beautiful, like a moving piece of art. I felt amazing! Then, in an instant, I was permeated with the feeling of sublimely intense, Divinely pure love. It felt as though every single particle that I was, was also that same love. I was absolutely complete and whole and perfect. I was home.

In the next instant I had what I can only describe as a "download" of information – information I'd subconsciously and often consciously wished to have my entire life. I was given the answers to all the questions I'd ever asked. They came to me in a sort of funnel, where instantaneously they all boiled down to one point, which was love. It was the same love I felt myself to be at that moment. That very love was the answer to everything! I finally knew!

The bliss I felt encompassed me as I continued to speed imperceptibly forward. Then a speck of whitish light caught my attention and I was again curious and wanted to move toward it and, as I did so, it grew, becoming larger and larger until I could see dark grey, shadow-type adult human figures in its smoky, white, round opening. In front of them was the figure of a little boy, about seven years old. He reminded me of what I had imagined a little Tom Sawyer would look like, with a greyish-black, wide-brimmed hat and overalls. The rest of the figures were more indistinct and I knew they'd put the little boy in the front to lure me in, to take advantage of the compassion I felt toward him.

Regardless of that, I could feel how the boy and the others needed me, and my immediate response was a desire to help. As I moved through the opening, the shadow figures drew aside to allow me in. I floated deeper into the room, moving along the line of them, then stopped. As I hovered there I saw how they gathered at a bit of a distance, encircling me in the whitish-grey mist, and I felt their strong desire for my help. I wasn't afraid, nor was I unafraid. I had no idea why they needed help, only that I had an equal desire to give it to them. As soon as I felt that desire to give of myself, they started coming at me very quickly from all directions. One at a time they'd "strike" me and retreat, darting almost instantaneously toward, then away from me. I didn't feel anything, just that I was beginning to get smaller. They were stealing my energy, my essence, and I was rapidly "dying" again, fading away, much like what I'd experienced in the hallway of the hospital as I took my last breath.

Suddenly, I had the very quick realization that these beings would literally destroy me if I stayed. Though I wanted to relieve them of their suffering, I wanted to leave even more. I'd no sooner felt the desire to leave when I was again pulled to my left and found myself racing past the shadow spirits out of that place and back into the static, re-joined with my essence and once again immersed in pure, blissful love.

I quickly came to another opening and went through it, intuitively knowing it would lead to something different than what had come before. Not only was it different, it was the polar opposite! I emerged into the most glorious of scenes, one of utterly breathtaking beauty! For as far as I could see ahead of me, a field of gorgeous yellow flowers blanketed the ground, spanning the distance until they met bright green rolling hills dotted with trees arched by a bright blue sky above. To my left was a tranquil waterfall with moss-covered rocks. To my right was a dense evergreen forest. It was my Eden and I was completely overtaken with gratitude and love for it all. I was it and it was me! The landscape and I literally became one as love moved through and all around me, from flower to flower and tree to tree. We were all connected, one seamless flow of love energy.

    I next found myself flanked on both sides by what I refer to as my angels. They were tan in colour, very tall and thin, and communicated to me through feeling, in the same way as the shadow beings. I was told I could stay in my Eden, I could move beyond it to what came next, or I could return to my life here. I didn't remember anything about my life on Earth, and didn't have any knowledge about what might come next, but after looking around once more I knew what I wanted to do.

    Instantaneously I was moving backwards at a terrific speed and watched as my angels turned toward me and communicated that, having made the choice to return, I needed to share what I'd learned there. I "felt" to them that I would, though I was unaware of exactly what that meant because I still didn't know what I was coming back to or why I'd chosen it. My next memory was of a terrible deep pain in my chest. I'd returned to my body. My pulse returned at 9.26a.m.

The grim reality my family and friends had to face during the first hours after my cardiac arrest was the complete opposite of the incredible, beyond-human-words, glorious experience I'd had in the afterlife. They were beside themselves with fear and grief after being told by my doctors I had a fifty-fifty chance of surviving the first 24 hours after my cardiac arrest and, if I did survive, there was the strong possibility of brain damage that would render me in a vegetative state for the rest of my life. Not only had I spent eight minutes without a heartbeat but I'd also gone into DIC, or disseminated intravascular coagulation, after suffering an amniotic fluid embolism. It was a day where, as my doctor said, "something miraculous happened" – one that also changed his own life in powerful ways.

After about a 24-hour medically induced coma, I opened my eyes. My doctors were amazed at the speed with which I regained my faculties and from there my recovery was, according to my hospital report, "rapid and impressive", alleviating many of my family's and loved one's fears. After eight days in the hospital, I was able to return home.

Afterwards, however, I definitely wasn't myself. I wasn't the "old Krista" everyone wanted back. Although I seemed to function fairly normally, my personality had completely changed and my family wasn't sure what to make of it. There was no explanation for my peaceful, relaxed demeanour. Whereas I had been very much a Type A personality before – somewhat anxious, obsessive, driven and focused, always worried about the future or dwelling somewhere in the past – I was now laid-back and completely relaxed. What I felt was completely accepting of everything, without resistance to anything. I didn't question what "was". I just moved through my day with ease and did it quite well for having gone through what I'd gone through.

I could simply "be". I was able to be present in each moment with no concerns, no anxieties. I did the next thing that needed to be done, with a deep sense of love and appreciation for everything, and it felt so normal to be that way. Every diaper I changed, every dish I washed, every cuddle with my newborn daughter was filled with the sense of love and feeling of awe; a childlike wonder that felt so amazing and effortless. Nothing felt "wrong". Long-held beliefs were replaced by a deep sense of understanding and egoless acceptance of all beliefs. Everything, absolutely everything, was as it was intended to be and for a much higher purpose than most of us can comprehend here in this physical form. This understanding brought me infinite peace, and love was at the core of it.

I never questioned anything about how I was feeling; in fact, I thought everyone felt like I did until that constant, blissful state I'd existed in gradually began to fade. It was then I recognized the changes in me and could see myself from both sides, though I was still not fully in touch with the Krista I'd been before my NDE, and still had no direct memory of my experience. Then, one morning I awoke after having an incredibly vivid dream. It was hyper-real, unlike any earthly reality I'd ever experienced. All the details of my NDE were there, the feelings and what I'd seen – they were now readily available to me in my waking state. I suddenly understood why I'd felt the way I did during the previous weeks and in that moment, I was deeply, completely and utterly transformed. It was as if I'd woken up to my new self, although I'd been there all along.

Elated and beside myself with joy, I yelled for my husband. I wanted to tell him how amazing the afterlife is and how loved we all are. I wanted to shout it from every rooftop! Overwhelmed with emotion as I recounted what I'd been through, Tom held my hand and listened intently. Though he was incredibly supportive and kind, after sharing I felt immediately let down. I could feel he wasn't really able to understand. He couldn't relate to what happened to me, and I knew I couldn't expect him to. I felt I wouldn't be able to expect anyone else to either, except for those who'd experienced the same thing.

With my NDE came a huge transformation of consciousness, yet processing the experience and acceptance of it in the weeks and months that followed was an almost minute-by-minute emotional struggle. My inner scientist made me out to be crazy and argued that my experience was the creation of a brain low on oxygen, yet my true self, my higher self, knew that to be a lie. The reality was, I'd been transformed at the very level of my DNA and there would be no going back, but at the same time it meant fulfilling the promise I'd made to my angels, and I wasn't yet ready.

Because of the cardiac arrest and subsequent lack of oxygen, I suffered from short- and long-term memory loss. Often just getting through the day was a struggle. I wanted to focus on my new baby and that, along with all the other demands of everyday life, drained my energy, leaving me none left over even to begin processing all I'd gone through.

At a point of needing to understand it better, some online research led me to Dr Jeffery Long, an NDE researcher who is also a physician. Being in medicine as well, I felt more comfortable reaching out to him but, because I struggled with my story being judged by others, I held back. Rather than coming out and saying I'd been to the afterlife, I decided to test the waters and told him I thought something might have happened while I was in cardiac arrest, but I really wasn't sure. His reply stopped me in my tracks. "Pay attention to your dreams." Dr Long had written words I couldn't ignore. Relieved and a bit frightened, I understood. My experience was real and I'd have to accept it. Maybe then I could stop torturing myself. It also meant I'd need to fulfil my promise – the promise I remembered and now understood – to share the love I had experienced in the afterlife. But how? How was I going to live as that Divine Love in this world?

The profound shift in consciousness from one way of viewing who and what I was to another shook my foundation and I hadn't yet acquired the tools necessary to rebuild myself in this 3D world on my new foundation of love. My calling was to share the love I was, that incredibly blissful and transcendent, Divine, everlasting love, yet I had to do it in this body, this skin suit I had come back to, and had to figure out a way.

The thing was, I hadn't a clue as to how to go about it. I loved others and myself, but only to a point, always holding myself back from full expression. I allowed fear of being the full expression of my essence, that pure particulate love energy I was in the afterlife, to keep me from it and didn't realize for many years afterwards how much that fear grew and restricted my self-expression as I integrated back into my life here. I felt as though I had to do everything I could to fit back into the old mould just to survive. I had to function within the heavy demands of being a new mother, starting a new career, being a wife. At the same time, I was also healing my body and getting my memory and cognitive functioning back, all the while moving further and further away from who I knew was my true self.

Integrating back into this 3D experience, I again fell into my old mindset of viewing myself as essentially separate from everyone and everything. I'd lost my conscious connection to the Divine Love I was and had to get it back, going through many trials and struggles over the years in my attempts to do so. I needed a new template on which to rebuild myself as the love I was. Eventually, I formulated Twelve Principles in my attempt to summarize my NDE and what it encompassed. They are simple, but not easy. What they did for me was help transform how I exist in this three-dimensional world. They opened a doorway to an existence where I was most able to remain in alignment with who I felt and knew myself to be in the afterlife. They quite literally brought Heaven to Earth for me and, when I began to heal, those

around me began to heal. The Twelve Principles are:
- Live in Awareness
- Live Willingly
- Live Lovingly
- Live Fearlessly
- Live Compassionately
- Live Patiently
- Live Presently
- Live Spiritually
- Live Faithfully
- Live Purposefully
- Live Creatively
- Live Miraculously.

As we move through each moment, we exist within a multitude of relationships, each one unique and purposeful and present for a reason. It's through our relationships with others that we learn about who we are. The key to developing and maintaining loving relationships is to develop and maintain a loving relationship with ourselves. When we're able to treat ourselves as the amazing, brilliant, Divine beings we are, we are then able to treat others in the same way. We are each a mirror reflecting all those around us. In my life up until the point of my death, I hadn't cared for myself in the way I always knew I needed and wanted to; now I had no choice but to figure out how to do it.

Love was the key to everything. Just like the universe, of which I was an integral part, I had to love myself first, without condition. It would require the healing of very deep wounds; all the scars my ego had left on my heart had to be loved better. The shadow beings had taught me the importance of self-love, of putting my own well-being first before anyone else's. Although that may sound selfish, it's absolutely necessary in order for us to be the best version of ourselves so that we may better serve others. Not by bowing down to them, but through sharing our love, whether that be through our role as mother, father, spouse, co-worker or stranger on the street.

In order to honour and love myself better, there had to be a major change in my life, namely the decision my husband and I made to end our marriage. It was not an abrupt end, but rather a mutual decision made after many years of working really hard to stay together. Eventually, we were able to come to the understanding that we were not the same people we'd been when we first met and fell in love, and that we could not maintain the type of relationship our marriage required. The silver lining is we continue to love and respect one another as individuals on our separate paths, and that is a direct reflection of the love and respect we have for ourselves.

My NDE and subsequent practising of the Twelve Principles changed how I viewed myself, not only as a soul in this body, and with all the ways I relate to and interact within the greater world, but specifically in my professional role as a physician assistant. There is an eternal connection we all share with one another, a connection some of us are consciously aware of and others aren't. For those who aren't and who are met face to face by another who has this conscious awareness, there lies the potential for awakening in them. We are mirrors; like Indra's Net, we are jewels in the great net of the universe, reflecting one another's Divinity.

I see that Divinity in my patients, when I look in their eyes. There is a recognition there. They know I truly care; they can feel it. It's love they're recognizing in that instant, and within those Divine moments a connection is made that transcends earthly bounds. They are miracle moments where true healing begins. I try to use the Twelve Principles in all my interactions with my patients. To be loving, compassionate, patient and present. I try to be willing to listen and see the Divine, powerfully creative beings they are. I try to recognize the little miracles that occur all the time, the synchronous happenings which fill me with awe.

I have so much appreciation for being given the opportunity to re-experience myself as the Divine being I am in this body, and that grows every day. My purpose for returning is simply to love, to the best of my ability, without conditions or judgement in all aspects of my life. Choosing to love more is how we can heal and create a more loving world. It is my life's practice, the *art* of living. Much love to you.

Krista's experience was very deep and extensive and has instigated many life changes. The question is, how could Krista describe such a deep, lucid, heightened state of awareness when she was in cardiac arrest? This was an intricate experience that required the ability to make decisions, but it is not clear how Krista's brain could possibly have had any cognitive ability at such a time.

I was particularly interested by the conflict she described arising from what she experienced and what her "inner scientist" thought. That must have been a very confusing dilemma, yet it appears that the experience itself was able to override those externally learned traits of her "inner scientist".

It is apparent that Krista has done a lot of soul searching since her experience, which has left her with deep insights shaping the way in which she now lives her life. She was able to devise a 12-step approach to her healing and the integration of her NDE, and she continues to use that approach many years later.

4

READY WHEN YOU ARE

Ainsley Threadgold, aged 37, had an NDE at the age of 13. Ainsley's experience is of particular interest to me because, initially, he had no recollection of his NDE. Remarkably, however, uncovered memories appear to have remained in his subconscious mind for over 20 years. Once these memories were recovered, he struggled to understand his experience and reached out to Gigi at the NDE support group website. Gigi connected him with Kelly and he engaged with the Positivity Power Facebook group, where he became friendly with Krista who wrote the previous chapter.

Before I begin telling my story I want to say thank you to you the reader: thank you for drawing this book and my words into your life. I want this to find you where you are. I want you to know that you are loved, loved as I know I am loved. I have lived a life of feeling completely unworthy of love, yet I have been provided with more love than I could possibly describe.

I spent many troubled years wishing to be living a different life, to be able to go back and undo life events that had caused me deep pain. I have felt the agony of losing people close to me, I have felt the sadness of having been, at times, unloved or unwanted, and I have also felt the shame of acting in a manner that has caused others to feel the same. Yet now I abound with gratitude for all of these events because they have brought me through the cosmic ocean; they have forged me and guided me to the most sublime of synchronicities, events that have found me my purpose and also found me true love.

I wake up every day with a smile in my heart, knowing that I have chosen this life, that my every step has been Divined. I am the creator and the co-creator and I have someone to share this with, someone who, like me, had an NDE, someone else who desired nothing more than to feel her purpose and to share and feel the love we all have innately inside.

In 1993, when I was 13 years old, two very distinct elements marked my life. Following years of struggling with dyslexia, dyspraxia, being bullied and subsequent weight problems, I was moved from an all-boys school to a mixed school where I finally found myself a good set of friends and a chance to be happy. During that period of my life, I also developed an unhealthy fascination with broken bones. I was obsessed with what it would be like to have them. I now realize that I had pre-cognitive awareness of events that followed and simultaneously helped to create them.

One evening my younger brother and I were out with my father helping to deliver leaflets around the village. I remember wanting to get it over with because my mum was going to cook a Chinese meal. The last memory I have was of my father driving onto a country lane where we were to deliver the last of the leaflets.

Six hours later I opened my eyes. I was greeted by a vague orange glow from lights outside a room that wasn't my own. I looked around, and my parents and brother were sitting on some plastic chairs near to the bed. Dazed, I turned to them for answers. "What happened?" I asked. "You were run over," they told me, "and you have a badly broken leg." I should have been scared, I should have had a sense of fear but I felt strangely calm. I looked down and could see a temporary cast on my left leg coming up to my hip. What had happened? Why couldn't I remember? Looking back now, I can't help but ask myself: why wasn't I scared or in agony?

Those were my only memories of the incident. I had no concept of how serious it was or how badly I'd been hurt. I later discovered that I had been hit by a car at around 40 miles an hour: an impact that should have been fatal! So why was I here? Why wasn't I more injured? I shouldn't be typing these words, I should actually be dead.

That wasn't the only strange thing. After I left the hospital, I noticed that I couldn't wear a watch without it stopping or breaking. My presence also seemed to affect radio signals and electrical equipment. On top of this, I had a gnawing need to know why I was here. Had I a purpose? If so, what was it?

Twenty-one years after my accident, a series of events finally led to me recovering my lost memories. At the age of 34 I developed acute sciatica. This affected the same leg I'd broken when I was run over and also the same parts of it. Being a police officer, I needed and still need to be physically fit for duty, so I sought the help of an osteopath. The subject of my accident came up in conversation with him; I was fascinated by the relationship between where my leg was affected and why it had appeared in exactly the same area that I had broken it. I also talked to the osteopath about my blank memory and the other strange after-effects. He handed me a book. It was a study of NDEs by Dr Penny Sartori. He told me that he'd had an NDE and suggested that I may have had one too, just without the recall.

The book was a revelation! For the first time, I could see a light at the end of the tunnel. I saw and could feel why I had for so long felt different. After finishing the book, I contacted the NDE UK site, which Dr Penny Sartori was associated with, for advice. I also looked into regression hypnotherapy. I felt that this would be my best chance of recovering memories that had been lost for all those years.

I found a therapist shortly afterwards. On speaking to her I knew that I had been gifted with the right person. We spoke on the phone for over an hour, her genuine enthusiasm shining through, so I booked an appointment for the following week. On the day of the appointment I went in with an open mind. I was now ready to face reliving the accident and the after-effects that had caused me so much pain. I knew that, whatever I discovered, it would lead to a great healing.

Karen, the therapist, spoke to me about the process and ensured that I understood what was going to happen. I felt safe, with an inner knowing, that she would prove to be the perfect guide. As the process started, Karen got me to visualize relaxing, then took me further into myself. In my mind's eye, I was led to a path with a series of doors to my right-hand side. I was asked to choose a door then, when I was ready, I could step through. Once I was through, she got me to describe who I felt I was, what I was wearing and where I was in time.

As I stepped through the doorway, I found myself on the floor, half buried in a ditch at the roadside. I was 13 again and I had just been run over. I was back at the scene of my accident. I remember becoming my 13-year-old self again. Dazed and confused, I became increasingly upset. I just wanted my mum, but couldn't get up. Why couldn't I get up? Next, I felt the sensation of being carried into an ambulance. While inside, I felt a presence next to me; it was my mum's dad Tom. He had died three months before I was born, but was now with me.

He held my hand and comforted me, telling me how brave I was; he also wanted me to tell my mum that he was so proud of her. Then he told me to close my eyes. As I did so, I felt myself being drawn into an ocean of clouds. Floating through these, I felt myself being pulled toward a place of pure beauty, where a man was standing dressed in a white robe. He came to greet me. Kneeling, he placed one hand on my chest and the other on my cheek. He told me that he was the carpenter and that he knew and loved me as he knew and loved everyone. He told me I had a job to do and that he would speak through me as I spoke for him. Then he sent me back, telling me that I would not remember this part or any other part until the "right time".

I then became the scared 13-year-old boy again, screaming for his mum. Karen gently guided me away at that point and placed me in a state of calm acceptance. I had finally recovered some of my memories and knew why I was here. I knew that I had a purpose, that I actually mattered and that I was here to help. Since then I have recovered more and more of this sublime experience. This was to come in the form of unique experiences during deep meditation.

While in a meditative state, I am brought to a higher place of awareness; one that can be likened to Karen's hypnosis sessions.

I am now aware that originally when I was run over, I was killed outright. The carpenter told me that I would be "put back in circumstances far better than those in which I left", so that I could live the life I needed to, to come to a place where I was ready to do the work I was destined for.

He then handed me a ball of energy. This energy was everything that I had ever been, a culmination of all my past-life karma, and the life between my accident and the 21 years it would take me to remember the NDE. I saw and felt everything, all the pain I would have to release, all the tears I wouldn't be able to cry, but that I would force others to cry for me. It was too much; I didn't want to do it. No! How could I go through it? Then something happened that would change my mind, that would change everything. Suddenly the carpenter's form was replaced by that of a woman. I knew her, but had never seen her before.

She knelt down in front of me and spoke very softly, and her words shook me to my foundation. "Hello my love, you don't know me yet, but you will. If you choose to come back I want you to promise me something ... I want you to come and find me." I know now who spoke these words. This woman was later to become my one true love, my twin flame. She was the reason in spirit I decided to come back; the reason I agreed to live again. To know that one day I would finally meet this woman, fall madly in love and be reminded of her part in my experience every time she spoke, by the vibrational quality of her voice, melts my heart and gives me that sense of peace I felt when I was in that Heavenly space. However, I now realize that before this could become a reality I had a responsibility to myself to heal, to start the path with new steps, conscious steps.

After a few days I heard back from the NDE UK site. This led me to the first time I shared part of my experience, and it felt right, as though my sharing would help not just me, but others too. Divine synchronicity would shine a light on me and I felt a renewed sense of wanting to serve; I offered whatever assistance I could to the group. In response, I was asked if I wanted to help run a support group near to where I lived. I said that I would love to help out wherever I could. I was then given the email address of Kelly, who was also interested in setting up a satellite group.

Connecting with Kelly was like reconnecting. I had a strong sense that we had been siblings in a past life; it felt like I'd found a long-lost sister. When we spoke, we shared our experiences and I discovered that she was linked with Dr Penny Sartori, who was the author of the book I was given by my osteopath. It struck me that the universe was already lining me up with and connecting me to the right people. As we shared our stories, Kelly told me about her vision and about Positivity Power. Her NDE had shown her that like-minded souls would come together to collaborate and effect global change. From that point on, I was sold; this was shared with me for a reason. I felt a strong connection with Kelly and we both knew that we would collaborate, that we were being guided to something greater.

Part of this guidance came in the form of being invited to re-join Facebook. Kelly convinced me to sign up again. I created a new account that would be dedicated to my spiritual growth, so I kept any Facebook friends to just those who would help me grow. I joined a number of wonderful NDE groups and shared my story. I quickly found that my words were an inspiration to those who needed them. I also discovered a passion for writing. I started to write what I Divinely felt. I let the universe write through me. Having dyslexia has made me a unique filter; my writing and my poetry are emoted from a very special place, and I place myself within the energy of the words as they flow.

One of the things I helped Kelly to do was set up a Facebook group. Thus, the Positivity Power Movement was born, a place where like-minded souls could connect and collaborate.

One of the people that Kelly invited to the group was Krista, who lived in the United States; Kelly had been introduced to Krista through Penny. Shortly afterwards, we all started to post video blogs, detailing who we were and the love we wanted to share. My second video post was born from a deep passion I felt relating to a picture I'd seen of a child with her arms held aloft in terror because she thought she was going to get shot. This was a Facebook post of a famous image a photographer had taken in a war-torn country. I felt the frailties of our race and the need to share my passion for this to change, for us all to look inside who we were; to lift our vibrational hearts to a place where love finds peace.

Krista had seen my video post while she was at work and, in her words: "Your energy and passion hit me like a freight train." It was as if her very soul was drawn to the energy of mine. A few days later, on 1 April 2015 at 11.14p.m. GMT, Krista and I shared our first messages. We had found each other. We had crossed the cosmic ocean on a predestined, pre-chosen path.

This was to mark the beginning of a wholly beautiful but at times painful series of changes for me. It was the start of the most profound healing journey, one I am so thankful I have not had to undertake alone. In saying this, I have had to be willing to change, to shed my old skins like peeling those of an onion, to submerge in order to emerge and re-emerge. I am now at the cusp of something amazing; my path is laid before me. It is connected and interconnected with Divine gifts; I call these gifts friends and loved ones.

As is apparent from Ainsley's experience, NDEs are the beginning of deep self-discovery and in many cases continue to be a work in progress. The underlying message of this NDE is one of love: love for ourselves, love for others and love for life. It appears that discovering his NDE, which had been suppressed for all those years, sent Ainsley on an accelerated journey of healing. His transformation has been a very personal one and has enhanced his ability to love – himself and others.

Ainsley's is an important account of an NDE for another reason: the fact that he had no recollection of it until he underwent hypnotic regression therapy. My first reaction to this was one of concern, as I had read some research many years earlier that warned that this type of therapy could re-induce the symptoms associated with neardeath circumstances. In the specific case I read about, the person concerned had undergone hypnotic regression to the time of his NDE. During the regression, he developed symptoms of pulmonary oedema and other associated breathing problems that had occurred at the time of his hospitalization (and subsequent cardiac arrest). These symptoms eventually resolved themselves after the hypnotic regression session was terminated but there is the possibility that his condition could have further deteriorated. I have always warned against such therapy for this reason. However, in Ainsley's case he did not develop any symptoms associated with his NDE.

The fact that Ainsley had no conscious recollection of his NDE raises the question: does everyone who loses consciousness during life-threatening circumstances have an NDE, but not all are able to recall it? Hospital research undertaken in the last decade or so shows that between 11 and 23 per cent of people who survive cardiac arrest report an NDE. Is it possible that the other 77 to 89 per cent are simply unable consciously to recall such an experience? This can only be verified or otherwise by further research.

Another point of interest relating to Ainsley and this book is the way that various synchronicities led to us all becoming connected. When Ainsley read my book The Wisdom of Near-Death Experiences, *everything suddenly made sense to him. Like so many people I've spoken to, he describes developing electrical sensitivity after his NDE, so after reading the book he was able to "join the dots" and make further sense of his experience.*

Through seeking further support and understanding, Ainsley connected with Gigi, who directed him to Kelly, both of whom I knew through my NDE work. I had already connected with Krista, who

I'd also connected with Kelly. On reflection, this aspect appears to reinforce one of the messages of the NDE: that we are all interconnected.

5

TIBOR PUTNOKI AND THE LIGHT OF LOVE FOUNDATION

In March 2015, due to a series of synchronicities, I was able to meet NDEr Tibor Putnoki from Hungary via a lady called Helen Williams. She had recently completed a healing course that had been taught by Tibor Putnoki's Light of Love Foundation based in Hungary. While in Swansea volunteering with another organization, Helen felt overwhelmingly compelled to go into a café near her workplace. She had walked past it on several occasions and each time felt drawn to it. There was no reason for this as she wasn't hungry or in need of a hot drink. Then, one day, for reasons unknown to Helen, she went into the café and uncharacteristically began talking to the owner (whom she'd never met) about her work with the Light of Love

Foundation, and she mentioned Tibor's NDE. Immediately, the owner, who happens to be my mother-in-law, phoned me and handed the phone to Helen so that we could chat. I arranged to meet up with Helen to find out more. In the meantime, Helen told me where I could purchase Tibor's book 9 Minutes: My Path to the Light.

I read Tibor's book with fascination and was ecstatic to hear he would be visiting Lampeter (the university town where I studied for my PhD) a few weeks later. I hoped he would agree to meet me so that I could learn more about his NDE.

It transpired that another talk Tibor was due to give was cancelled at short notice, so I was approached concerning the possibility of him speaking instead at Swansea (where I live). I quickly arranged a venue for this talk and advertised it as best I could. The event was so well received that a second was arranged for the following day and, in between sessions, Tibor granted me an interview, which he allowed us to film and post on YouTube.

This chapter is based on Tibor's talk given in Swansea and on my interview with him. It will summarize Tibor's NDE and discuss the powerful life changes that ensued. This is probably one of the most extensive NDEs that I have come across since my research began over 20 years ago, and my brief summary does it little justice. Since his experience, Tibor has dedicated his life to being of service to others and he travels the world giving talks. Further details about his life, his NDE and the Light of Love Foundation can be found in his book. This is what Tibor described via his interpreter.

Tibor was an orphan who, from an early age, was determined to succeed in life. He studied hard and learned how to fly aeroplanes. However, he faced many challenges throughout his life, including multiple sclerosis and partial paralysis due to a spinal injury. Then his general health began to deteriorate even further.

In 1994 Tibor developed high blood pressure and was intermittently hospitalized several times over a period of months until, one day, his condition deteriorated notably. By the time he arrived at the hospital by ambulance, it was apparent that his condition was serious and he was admitted to the intensive care unit, but his prognosis was not good. He was monitored for a few days, when one morning he awoke with terrible pain in his chest and head.

The pain suddenly intensified and Tibor heard a loud "snap", followed by silence and darkness. The pain disappeared and he slowly left his body. He observed the doctors and nurses doing their best to revive a patient (which was him) and was surrounded by light. He was able to observe a nurse preparing medication in another room and even noted the marks on the packaging of the injection needle.

While still out of his body, he became aware of a patient's call button being activated and observed the patient requesting the help of a nurse in a different part of the ward that he had not previously seen. He followed the nurse to a room where a colleague was talking on the telephone to her husband. He was panicking because their child was ill and the paediatrician's number was nowhere to be found. Tibor then found himself in the midst of some fog, and then in a different location: the apartment of the nurse and her husband. In both his interview and book, he described the actions of the man, what he was wearing, the furniture and rug in the apartment, and even the books on the shelf. Tibor was particularly attracted to the man's socks. They were white but covered with animal motifs, which appeared to be a little eccentric for a grown man.

Tibor returned to his bedside, where his attempts to communicate with the nurse and doctor were futile. He looked at the patient's face and was shocked to see himself; he couldn't understand how he could be lying in the bed and looking at himself at the same time. He realized he was weightless and it suddenly dawned on him that he was dead. The nurse picked up his arm, which was dangling off the end of the bed, and as she touched him Tibor found himself half in and half out of the wall by his bed. He felt panic over his state of affairs, but the fear was soon replaced by a bright light and an overwhelming feeling of love and happiness. Enveloped in light, whilst still out of his body, he found himself looking down on the surgical intensive care unit. This was situated on the floor above Tibor's ward. He acquired knowledge about all of the patients there, even knowing how long they had left to live.

He floated higher and saw the whole city from above, somehow from a perspective that enabled him to see far more than when he had flown over it as an aircraft pilot. He rose higher and was able to view the whole planet. He became a part of the light rising above the Earth and heard what he described as the "music of the spheres".

He experienced an extensive life review in which he saw his good and bad deeds along with the effects of his actions. During this process, he gained insight into how his behaviour had prevented him from experiencing many good things, and he realized just how many people loved him. Although he was accompanied by a Being of Light throughout the life review, Tibor alone judged his earthly deeds; the being acted as a source of comfort, reassuring him that he could make amends for his actions.

Tibor was lifted higher, and in the distance saw gates opening to a city of lights. He was surrounded by beings who communicated to him that they had been waiting for him. As the gates opened wider, Tibor was aware of a threshold, at which appeared the palm of a hand with a triangle in its centre holding within it an all-seeing eye, but a loud voice prevented him from entering. Eventually, beyond the threshold, he saw something indescribable and incomprehensible. Surrounded by other beings, he was engulfed by the incredible light and filled with a sense of overwhelming and unconditional love. The beings in the light surrounded Tibor and opened their hands to display their palms, imparting great knowledge to him, conveying that this knowledge is within each one of us. Tibor became aware of the knowledge of the "collective unconscious" and was amazed that he hadn't been consciously aware of this when he was alive. Throughout this whole process time had no meaning, but he was eventually sent back to life.

Once again he became aware of the body lying on the bed below and realized he was looking at his own body. He became aware of the doctor announcing that he was alive and, once again, he was fully in his body. A few hours later the doctor spoke with Tibor, asked what he recalled and took notes. He was so interested that he set out to prove Tibor's experience by verifying the details given to him.

This is a fascinating case because it appears that Tibor was very much aware of events taking place in other parts of the hospital that were neither within earshot nor in his line of vision. It is intriguing that he even described the nurse's husband's socks, yet this man was at home several miles away from the hospital where Tibor was situated. Tibor did not know the man and certainly had no knowledge of what kind of socks he wore, so how could he describe with such accuracy the conversation, the inside of his home, including a description of the furniture, the rug, books on the shelf and what he was wearing?

It could be argued that he was able to hear the phone conversation, but his hospital bed was in a different room to where the nurse was talking and, at the time, there was a great deal of noise and commotion around Tibor's bed as the staff tried to resuscitate him. From my nursing experience I can assure you that these are not conditions conducive to eavesdropping on conversations going on in the immediate vicinity, let alone in another room. What explanation is there for Tibor's description of the man's home and the kind of socks he was wearing? Could he have previously overheard the nurse discussing the appearance of her home and what kind of socks her husband wore? Even if this were so, what are the chances of her husband wearing those socks at the precise time that Tibor saw them?

Tibor was also able to deduce from the books on the man's shelves that he was an electrical engineer. How could his brain be capable of such cognitive processing while he was in a state of cardiac arrest?

Tibor described being in the surgical intensive care unit, upstairs from where he was situated, so it would have been impossible for him to overhear conversations discussing the patients' details. He was aware of the names and diagnoses of these patients, yet his physical location was nowhere near them. According to Tibor, the doctor who resuscitated him checked Tibor's claims with a doctor in the surgical intensive care unit and the details were verified. How was it possible for Tibor to acquire this information?

The investigating doctor also spoke to the nurse whose apartment Tibor had visited during his NDE. The nurse verified she did not know Tibor and that he had never been to her apartment. How could it be possible, then, for him to describe it in such detail? According to Tibor the doctor even drove with the nurse to her apartment so that he could check things for himself. He returned to the hospital with the unusual socks in his hand.

What I found particularly poignant during his talk was when Tibor spoke

about three questions he'd been asked during his NDE:
1. *Did you have a life before your death?*
2. *Did you live a life worthy of a human being?*
3. *Could you look into other people's eyes with a pure heart and your head held high?*

When I thought about these in depth, they had a profound impact on me, and made me reconsider and reflect once again on the way in which I live my life. To experience them first-hand obviously influenced how Tibor adjusted to life after his NDE. He founded the Light of Love Foundation – a non-profit organization that teaches people self-help techniques, life skills and empowerment. The community has thousands of volunteers and is estimated to have helped over 100,000 people to date. As a result of his NDE, Tibor developed a healing technique similar to Reiki and he teaches this to his community so that it can be used to benefit others. He has also developed a massage treatment that he has passed on to the community. This massage helps greatly with relieving stress and providing relaxation. Each year there is the Pot ceremony in Hungary, and people from all over the world visit and participate in the celebrations of life.

Tibor works tirelessly, lecturing all over the world spreading the message of what he learned during his NDE. He has given over 500 talks and reinforced the philosophy of the Light of Love Foundation whose message is about living in love and helping others. He teaches his healing and massage techniques all over the world. The realizations that Tibor arrived at as a result of his experience have been the driving force for him to help others.

6

PURPOSE, PURPOSE, PURPOSE? WHAT PURPOSE?

Kelly connected with 61-year-old David Bennett via Facebook in January 2015. She sent him a private message and they arranged to Skype. David recalls they shared their thoughts on how to raise the collective consciousness of the planet and discussed the loneliness they had both felt at times following their NDEs. Kelly was in the process of setting up the Positivity Power Movement group and David encouraged her to do what her soul was calling her to do. She mentioned the book and working with me, and although David had never met me he was aware of my research through IANDS (International Association for Near-Death Studies). David has appeared in The Story of God with Morgan Freeman, Doctor Oz, Angels

Among Us, NBC National News, and PBS Documentaries: "Back From The Light: After-effects of Surviving a Near Death Experience". David's NDE occurred while he was at sea, during which time he nearly drowned. David has authored two books on his experience.

One night in March 1983, I was working as the chief engineer on the research vessel *Aloha.* The harbour master radioed to tell us the harbour was closed to incoming vessels of our size due to rough seas. The captain decided to send in some of the crew on a Zodiac (a vulcanized rubber boat that we used to retrieve submersibles). The weather was so rough that the captain directed me to accompany the group, because I knew the harbour.

On our way in, we were in the trough of a swell and we couldn't see the shoreline. It was only when we were on the crest of a swell that we could glimpse the faint harbour lights. I stood on the bow, hanging on to the bowline to steady myself and trying to locate the harbour buoy. The more we moved toward shore the deeper the troughs became. We could suddenly hear roaring waves; then a wave broke beneath us and we were falling. Everyone hung on and, luckily, we were able to stay in the boat as we slid down a wave for 25 to 30 feet. Looking up, all I could see was a ridge of white foam above our heads, as the next wave crashed down on us. It packed an incredible amount of force, folding the boat in half like a peanut butter sandwich. I was catapulted from the bow into the ocean; it was the most raging violent force that I've ever felt. While wave after wave crashed over me I lost all sense of direction as the ocean tossed me around like a rag doll. When I opened my eyes, it was so black I couldn't see which way was up. My years of experience as a diver had taught me not to panic. My lungs burned. The furious sea kept pounding me, and I longed to take a breath of air. I was getting very cold. I hoped the life vest I was wearing would carry me to the surface, but the surface did not come. I couldn't hold my breath any longer. Euphoria from lack of oxygen took over and I finally tried to breathe the salt water. The agony quickly melted away into darkness.

I wasn't afraid. I was surprised by the total darkness and the shocking absence of noise. The sea had dissolved from violent roaring to a complete absence of sound. It was as though the booming percussion of the waves didn't exist where I now found myself. I was in absolute blackness without my physical body. My last experience in life was a violent drowning, so this felt calm, quiet and peaceful. I was warm, as if my consciousness was wrapped in a thick blanket. It gave me a sensation of total tranquillity. I was curious, thinking, *Where am I?* I had not yet come to the realization that I had died because my consciousness was intact. Instead, I wondered if this was yet another stage in the euphoria, or something more, as I had not experienced it in my training.

The darkness was emptiness, not good or bad. It lacked emotion. But I was comfortable and no longer in pain. I began to sense a connectedness to this fertile blackness that seemed infinite. Yet there was something supportive, and I had a knowing that the state I was in was the most natural thing in the world. I started to feel comforting joy and happiness. Although I could not quite grasp the meaning of this perception, I sensed there was more going on around me; something bigger, larger than myself, *more* than myself. I felt as if I should be communicating with this darkness. There was an omnipresent intelligence at hand, and I knew I should move on. Slowly, ever so slowly, light started to appear within the darkness. I could see a brighter light off in the distance. Everything was growing brighter. At the same time, I felt as if I were moving closer to the bright light in the distance. As the light got closer, my feelings intensified. I was being lifted up emotionally, as if it were enveloping me, taking me into what I could only call Love. I was becoming part of its Love.

    I found myself moving at the fringes of this now-brilliant light, continually drawn toward a denser area. It seemed the most natural thing to do and yet it also felt especially familiar. I was happy and filled with joy. I felt so comfortable and loved. I began to realize I didn't have a body. I was a single fragment of this light. My physical body was gone; I was formless, a sliver of light, like that around me. As the intensity of the glow increased, the intensity of my fragment of light increased. I didn't judge this transformation. I just accepted it. I was in admiration of the change I was undergoing. The love was incredibly empowering – it was a part of everything. The light seemed to be composed of billions upon billions of many-coloured light fragments that pulsed and flowed. The light was constantly in motion; even though I remained stationary it moved in unity with a connected mindfulness. I was in awe of the teeming life coming from the light; it was alive with consciousness, as if the souls of all living things past, present and future were interconnected, sharing and shining their Love. They danced and pulsed with their lights to combine into one spectacular illumination of Divine Love and Knowledge.

Three light fragments were becoming brighter, breaking away and moving toward me. I recognized these shapes as other beings. As they grew closer, I could sense them projecting thoughts of *Welcome Home,* as if we were family and there was immense joy in our reunion. I immediately knew who these beings were. I recognized their energy and could sense their individuality through what appeared to be their warm, deep and expressive eyes. This felt stronger and more binding than anything I had ever experienced in my life. They were so excited to be there with me and to see me home again. I just knew unequivocally that I was home, and it felt so extraordinarily magnificent. They were supporting me and helping me by projecting waves of love and compassion. I was overcome with the joy of belonging somewhere: my life from childhood up to then had been devoid of any deep sense of family. More light beings came and joined us. Their way of communicating involved projecting a knowing and comforting energy, which contained more information in a millisecond than our mortal thoughts could assemble in a day. A dozen members in all joined our circle.

We travelled into another area of the light that was a translucent globe. Once this sphere was completely around us, I started to experience my life. It was as if I was living my life through other people's perspectives and simultaneously reliving it through my own. This view was astonishing and wonderful, and the depth of this life review was more than all-encompassing. It was ... ineffable. I could see the effects and consequences of my actions and/or reactions spread beyond the area of the sphere, like ripples in a multidimensional pond. Not only were there images to see, but I also experienced feelings of others and how my actions in life had touched them. I could feel their joy, happiness, heartaches, disappointments and love – all their emotions in regard to my actions. I was aware also of my soul family's excitement and exhilaration to be here experiencing this along with me.

Some parts had a larger significance, and there were certain aspects of my life review that I'd have preferred my soul family not to see. I didn't want to admit things I had done. I was ashamed that my newfound family had to experience those times in my life. Amazingly, they didn't judge me by my experiences, not even the events I was not proud of. They were merely observers, experiencing my life with me. They didn't express any judgement, pro or con. They seemed to relish my experiences. Beyond my soul family's support, I was also aware of the Consciousness of the Light. When I think of God today, I think of it as a Consciousness of the Light, with billions of souls attached. The light seemed to be observing, acting as a supportive and an incredibly loving constant during my death.

God knew me better than I knew myself. I experienced my true nature. I felt as though this review of my life was meant to help me grow and evolve. Surprisingly, some of the smaller incidents in my life took on a greater importance during the life review. At the time, these incidents were forgettable, hardly noteworthy. But once I saw the after-effects, especially how my actions affected others, I became aware of the bigger picture. We are always thinking about leaving a mark and trying to make our lives matter. The accomplishments we think are important, like building something that will exist beyond us, or getting a job promotion, aren't necessarily the things that are going to be the most important in the life review. I learned that it is more important to live our life day by day and do the best we can. Cherishing our experiences, good and bad, big and small. Trying to be as helpful, compassionate and loving as we can. Living life in a loving manner generates the most powerful impact in the life review. Those actions create the largest waves of positive after-effects.

The experiences and feelings then changed. I was shown images that were not from my life. I had no references to them. I was having direct interactions with people I didn't recognize. I was in locations I had never been. My soul family continued supporting me, buoying me up during this, not with words but with thoughts of immeasurable love and compassion. Then I heard a clear, distinct voice that didn't emanate from just my group. I sensed it came from the light itself. I listened carefully to this deep, loving resonant voice, which told me, **"This Is Not Your Time; You Have To Return."** My first response was *No! I want to stay right here! I like it here. I've found love and a family I never knew existed, I do not want to go back and continue living a physically painful life.* I resisted, pleading and arguing against the request. Then I heard the voice again. This time the light said, **"You Have To Return; You Have a PURPOSE."** The word *purpose* kept echoing in my essence, resonating through me. When I heard the second instruction, I couldn't argue because I understood the truth within it. When you are a part of the Consciousness of the Light, you are a part of the all-knowing. I understood that I had to return to my body and continue living my life.

I became aware of my body, lifeless and suspended in the water, it was still being tumbled and blasted by the sea. I watched it without emotion, already longing to return to the light. My being was feeling so much larger than my body, freer and complete. Returning meant losing my sense of connectedness. Separating from the light and re-joining my body was the hardest thing I had ever been asked to do. It was more painful than drowning.

The lines from the Zodiac boat were flailing around the wreckage. Somehow my arm, in all that violence, had become tangled up in the bowline. A wave hit and the rope cinched around my arm and hand; it dislocated my shoulder and thumb as it pulled my body to the surface. I watched as another set of waves slammed my body. They hit me against the pontoon with such force that some of the water was pushed out of my lungs. Simultaneously, my Light Family gave me a shove. I experienced a rushing, buzzing vibration, and then I was back in my body. As I was entering it, my soul family projected within me the knowledge that they would always be around me. Instinctively, I inhaled my first breath of air in a long time. My first conscious thought after returning to life was, *Why do I have to live this life?* At the same time, an understanding nagged at me that I needed to survive. Resonating within me was the question: Purpose, Purpose, Purpose? What Purpose? I only knew I needed to survive because of those words. I knew there was some *purpose* to my being alive and living a life.

Once I recovered from my death and returned to life, I could see the life energy in my surroundings. There was an aura of light around all the plants and rocks in the ornamental flower gardens. I could feel and touch them without physically doing so with my hands. My engineer brain kept trying to figure it out. How is this possible? Not knowing about auras, I didn't have words for it. The palm trees were the most majestic experience. They were all so alive. This new way of sensing life forces made me examine all of what was going on around me. As an engineer, I needed to figure this out. *Why suddenly had life changed? How come I can now see this? How is it possible that I can see and hear what I could never sense before?* I went down to the ocean. I could also sense a larger picture of Earth energies – the rhythmic patterns of the waves with the tides and the moon. I could see Earth as a living, breathing planet. During my youth in Arizona, some of the Native American grandmothers had shared stories with me about Mother Earth. I didn't really take their lessons seriously about how the Earth grows, expands and contracts. They'd say, "She is breathing." Now, after my time in the Consciousness of the Light, I could understand their meaning.

Instinctively, I knew that what I had experienced was something difficult for anyone to understand. Let alone me. I was an old salt, and up until now I'd kept my feet firmly on the ground or on the deck of a ship. I was an engineer who only saw things in black and white. I was afraid to talk about what I had experienced; I was afraid my co-workers would think I was totally nuts. This new way of living, of being able to sense life energy, had left me dazed. I don't believe anyone knew of the extent of my inner turmoil. I didn't want to say anything because no one else seemed to notice my new perspective. If I talked about it, they would think maybe I'd received a severe crack on the head in the storm that had made me a bit crazed. Heck, I honestly thought I was going crazy. I had to find a way to deal with this. I wanted my old life back, but that was not going to happen.

Being back from death was incredibly complicated. I was moving at less than half-speed compared to when I was in the light. My new appreciation for life was so much bigger than I was. Part of me was still connected to the light, and that was freaking me out as well. So I did what I thought was best, which was to focus on the moment. Doing that, I was able to get through the first three days of living in a new reality and processing this radical shift in my life. I had always been a guy who cut a swathe through life in order to survive. Having an experience in the light was a gift all by itself, but exposure to the Light of Consciousness leaves one with clear, new perceptions.

After my experience, I was given three gifts: *acceptance, tolerance* and *truth*. They seem like very simple concepts, but they can take lifetimes to really understand, let alone master.

The first gift I dealt with was acceptance. I suddenly learned how my life could touch others without my knowing it. I know, now, that I am in the perfect place at all times and should be experiencing the present moment. By experiencing my life review with love and non-judgement, I knew who I was. I could accept that I had faults and strengths. I was able to start work on myself to make myself a better human. I no longer needed to beat myself up over my failures. Instead I could learn from a mistake, accept it and move on.

Tolerance allows us to see that others have their own goals and their own paths. Suddenly, I had a way of recognizing and respecting the beliefs and practices of others. From watching my own life review, I recognized that everyone is in their perfect place as well; experiencing what their life's path navigates for their growth. That allowed me to avoid discounting the opinions of other souls. I could be accepting and tolerant of someone's path without feeling I was condoning it. Even conflicting views didn't threaten me anymore, and I found myself able to distance myself when necessary. Unconditional love for all beings brings a reverence for all life and removes the want for others to be something they are not.

Truth. Even as a small child, I had a sense of when I was going against my true nature, or if I behaved in a way that I thought would be more acceptable to the people around me. I knew that was not who I truly was. This self-created fiction would slowly become me, even though it was false. Over time I became lost in the false self I had constructed. The love from the light and the Consciousness of the Light showed me my true self, without the fiction. The light knew me better than I knew myself. It is difficult to shed a false persona overnight. I kept trying to wear the old me after the NDE, but it didn't fit anymore. It took me a few years to accept my authentic self, as I had experienced it in the light.

Now, when I am working with my true self, I call it my truth.

After my NDE, my truth and my philosophy kept changing as I kept growing. I was becoming a more accepting and tolerant individual, but I also tried to hang on to what I had known as my personal truth. Then I would realize that what was real to me had changed because I had changed my philosophy, even if just a fraction. Your truth fluctuates with the growth and direction of your life path. It won't be a straight road, and will take many twists and turns along the way. We need to experience every moment. I spent a great amount of time working on a quiet ministry. What I mean by "quiet ministry" is trying to be a living example to others. I know my existence is going to cause ripples – I saw that in my life review, so I decided to go forward, knowing and accepting universal guidance. My experience shifted my direction; it came at the perfect time, showing me the bearing in which I needed to go. Most importantly, I now understand that we do not die at the time of physical death. We live on with a higher level of consciousness. So with this understanding, I no longer fear death.

No longer having the fear of death offers incredible freedom, a freedom to live life unbridled and to its fullest, filled with joy and gratitude at each encounter and experience. Not fearing death also gives us a sense of calm, which enables us to unwind, no longer caught up in the rat race. When I accomplish something positive, a sense of completion follows, often accompanied by a sign that tells me the direction of a new path ahead. If I have learned anything from my experiences, it is to follow those synchronistic events in life. Even though I may not be able to see the bigger picture when it is happening, I know it will reveal itself at the right time and place. My life has been transformed through this voyage. I receive insights that allow me to view my potential paths. I believe these insights alert me to my soul's purpose, acting like guideposts. I can make the proper choices on my path, which often helps me be in the correct place to help others. In this way, I can be more of service, which is my life's purpose.

In November 2000 I was diagnosed with cancer, which had started in my right lung and metastasized outward, eating away three bones in my spine. Finally, my spine had collapsed because the T2 thoracic bone in my spine was no longer there and the tumour could not support the weight. After many tests, the doctors also found lesions in my hip, kidneys and brain. They felt that the most compassionate solution would be to make me comfortable and allow me to pass away peacefully. In my NDE I'd seen I was going to have cancer and I also saw I would survive it. So, I used the guidance of spirit to find holistic and traditional treatments. My doctors agreed with my treatment wishes and within six months I was cancer free. It took another year to convince them I was going to survive, before they finally agreed to perform three corrective spinal surgeries. I recognize that healing from cancer was also part of my greater purpose, so that I can now help end-stage cancer patients and fellow experiencers with integration.

I always stay mindful of the power inherent in our interconnectedness, especially when passions are at their peak. I just remember my life review and how my passions created some of the greatest ripples, positive and negative. Experiences are what make us grow. They make our spirit grow. How we deal with responsibilities, experiences and opportunities is of great consequence. Because we are all from the light, we don't have to go searching for spirit. Spirit is within us all, and all we have to do is be mindful and listen. When we are able to do that, we gain clarity and understanding of where we need to be, so that each of us may live our lives just a little bit better.

David had a very intense experience, and his life review in particular appears to have profoundly transformed his self-perception, which has also translated into the wider picture of being of service to others. He now lives his life in accordance with what he learned during his NDE. What a refreshing perspective! What if we all made our life choices based on what we will have to face in our life review rather than being concerned about what will impress others? What if we all became more concerned about living our lives for ourselves, doing the things that make us happy, rather than making choices based on what others will think?

It is an important point that David was later diagnosed with a cancer that metastasized to his spine as well as other parts of his body. There are many examples of people having had physical illnesses that later resolved or went into remission after they had an NDE. Being a former nurse, I am fascinated by the mind – body connection and more research is confirming how important the mind and our thoughts are with regards to our health. Those who have had an NDE undergo a radical metamorphosis in the way they think and perceive things. This is another area of focus for potential research that could greatly empower everyone who is diagnosed with a debilitating illness.

7

LOVE BROKE THROUGH

Penny Wilson is a 47-year-old retired nurse from Kentucky, USA. Robert Tremblay (who also features in this book) suggested that Penny connect with Kelly on Facebook to discuss sharing her story. During their initial conversation, Kelly mentioned Dr Barbara Mango, another person featured in this book, and Penny said, "Ask her if she remembers me from the conference in California. We met there and both spoke at length." This once again affirms the interconnectivity of each and every one of us and how we have all been guided together. Penny's NDE occurred during anaphylactic shock.

I'm the mother of three terrific kids, grandmother of two wonderful grandchildren, and engaged to my sweet fiancé, Don. Retired from my work as a nurse, I live in Kentucky. Three years ago, I developed an autoimmune disorder called idiopathic anaphylaxis, which is a fancy way of saying that I go into anaphylaxis and anaphylactic shock without being seriously allergic to anything. It's a sort of glitch in my immune system. This condition caused me to be critically ill on numerous occasions. During three episodes of anaphylactic shock in 2014, I felt my spirit leave my body and subsequently had three NDEs: each a continuation of the one before. My story begins as I stop breathing, am placed in a medically induced coma, and on a ventilator. I wake in a deep, dark place.

    My mind begins to wake, pushing me up from darkness into full consciousness. When I open my eyes, there is total blackness. I perceive that what lies before, behind, above and beneath me is a deep and endless void, through which I seem unable to navigate. A crushing sensation pushes around and against me, though when I move my arms nothing physical is touching me. Where is this terrible pressure coming from? I wonder. The oppressive environment wrings my existence like a wet rag, making each breath a tremendous effort; every muscle in my body drags air into my lungs, then squeezes it back out.

All alone in this place, it's as though no one else has ever existed. Have I been in this soul-oppressing purgatory all along? Maybe it was all a dream, my life and family ... the world. Could that have been a place and time I'd created in my mind to provide some relief from this darkness? It was too terrible to consider. Exhausted, I felt deep sleep encroaching. I begged it to swallow me into its gut and keep me there, so I would never know this awful place again. Hearing my pleas, the deep sleep quiets my conscious mind into blackness, mercifully rendering me completely unaware.

The reprieve from the void seems short as I wake again to the dreaded place. It's not Hell, of that I'm certain, but knowing that doesn't diminish my hopelessness. How long have I tarried in this unending abyss? Every moment here is a second and an eternity all at once. If the life I remember was real, and if I ever get to go back to it, I will live differently. I'll embrace my days with passion and joy; not just let them slip by, as though each one wasn't a gift.

Every time I emerge from the sleeping quicksand, I ask the same questions. Where am I and why am I here? Where has everyone and everything gone? I puzzle, searching my mind, trying to make sense of my state. Maybe I should try to move ... but how and where? Struggling to make some forward motion, each attempt is a tremendous effort, as though trying to move through thickening concrete. The work is draining and so taxing that the deep sleep, in its compassion, takes me in its arms and gives me rest.

Finally, after what seems an eternity, something changes. I've moved through the void, and now find myself on one side of what seems like a glass wall. Floating, I approach the barrier and peer through. On the other side, I can see my physical body lying in a hospital bed. How can I be here and there at the same time? The wall doesn't yield to me, but, as I approach, the scene on the other side becomes clearer. My body is hooked to wires and tubes.

Ah, I must be very ill! The realization brings hope ... It wasn't a fantasy; I hadn't been dreaming it all! I am just sick, and terribly so from the look of it. Squinting my eyes, I make out my daughter standing beside the bed. To the right, a ventilator pumps and churns behind her. I must be in serious trouble to need a ventilator. What brought me to such a state?

My daughter stands at her post in front of the life-sustaining machine, and a longing so deep and profound fills me. I need to touch her – to take her in my arms and make all this go away. Instinctively, I reach forward ... but my hand is stopped by the cruel wall that divides the void from the hospital. I pound it with my fists but it refuses to yield. Then it occurs to me; I know what to do! My mind whirls with hope for the first time ... I must try to wake my body. Of course! Why didn't I think of it sooner?

Focusing all my energy on the me in the bed, I try to wake her, to will her eyes open ... nothing, she lays there motionless, ignoring my efforts. Come on! Why isn't it working? Perhaps I need to start smaller ... get her to move her finger. Determined, I redirect my focus to her hand ... Come on Penny, just a little twitch, you can do it! I let out an exasperated breath. Damn! Still nothing. Why is this so difficult? I try over and over, each desperate attempt landing flat against the stubborn wall. I feel myself being sucked backward with great force; as though all the winds of the earth are pushing me away from the me in the hospital bed, away from my earthly body that lay like a stone, only inches from my daughter. Thrashing and fighting to stay close to the membrane proves useless; my struggle against the invisible vacuum is but wasted effort. I'm sucked back ... back ... back into the heartless, dispassionate void.

Time passes unmarked. How long have I been here? A day? A week? The cruel void holds me in its merciless grip. I shut my eyes tight, then open them slowly, and find myself again near the membrane between the void and the hospital room. Being close to the physical world is a profound relief. This time it's different; the membrane is pulsing, almost like it's breathing. I pop through the now flimsy barrier and find my spirit-self floating over my physical body. I see myself lying there ... motionless, attached to monitors and the ventilator, my body showing no more life than the blankets that cover it.

After only a few seconds, the scene in the hospital room grows dim as I'm forcefully sucked back into the darkness. The void feels heavier; the pressure on my chest makes it difficult to get air into my lungs. I remember I don't need to breathe; the ventilator is doing that. Still, something pushes me to inhale and exhale, to reconnect with the me that lies in the hospital. The effort is exhausting, like trying to swim with cement blocks tied to my limbs. I press forward, struggling, trying to find the membrane. I don't want to be in this dark, hopeless place. Nor do I want to be in the hospital room, watching helplessly from my station in the upper corner. Please let me wake up in my body, or keep me in the deep sleep forever, so I never know the void again. How long must this cycle continue?

Lamenting my situation, it dawns on me, the void isn't a real place! It's symbolic! It represents my apathy; a symbol of the wall I'd spent a lifetime building, the bricks I'd stacked to keep people out and my feelings in. A barrier I constructed with each hurt I suffered. My efforts at self-protection had made me less ... less real, less vulnerable, less joyful, and as impenetrable as the coma I lay in. My physical self in the ICU had no idea how close she was to losing it all.

The realization that I'd built this prison around myself caused the void to shatter with a thunderous boom! A bright light shone before me, and pushed the darkness back, until it was behind and beneath me. I felt myself being pulled, as if by a magnet, into the arms of a glorious spirit. Am I finally being rescued from this terrible place? Oh, let it be so!

The spirit is bold and adorned in light. She holds me tightly to her breast and her energy swirls around me, like a great funnel cloud, holding me effortlessly in the middle. Pulling me in closer with one arm, she thrusts out her other arm. Her fist whooshes past me toward the darkness, landing a blow on the soulless place. The void explodes and the fragments fly all around us, trying to enter her funnel of energy, but unable to penetrate it. Her light shines brighter as the shards collide with it; the radiant glow repels and sends them to a place I'm glad I know nothing of. The void's sickening pressure trickles off me like dew from a blade of grass; each droplet making me lighter as it's consumed by the glorious rescuing spirit. Looking up, I see the face of my champion; her features, soft and feminine, her eyes a brilliant green, returning my gaze and knowing me completely. Our spirits merge, like two rivers meeting and converging to the sea.

She's familiar to me, but when I try to recall how I know her, it falls away like a dream that hides in the curves of your brain, playfully evading discovery. I press further, consumed with a deep need to remember how this spirit is known to me. My eyes draw upward, to her hair ... her brilliant red hair, like nothing I've seen before. To call it red is to describe it with a pitifully inept word, akin to calling the sun a flicker of light. Her hair is like fire on her head. It has an energy that defines her, powerful and bold and ... in an instant I remember her. Lovetta Patrias, my maternal grandmother! Tears spring to my eyes and my heart leaps in my chest.

She was an amazing woman in life and, clearly, that spirit had followed her to the place where she found me. Laughing and crying, my tears came in torrents, purging me of the grief from her loss that I wasn't aware I still harboured. She hadn't died! No, she's more alive in this place than she was in her body. The realization took my breath.

Her gaze, soft and sweet, relaxes me completely and I melt into her arms. For the first time in a long time I feel safe. Ahh, safe! When had I last felt untouchable by harm? It feels as a balm to my soul. Resting in her embrace, I allow my resonance to merge with hers, our energies entwining and encircling us; yet somehow, each spirit is still identifiable as its own. How is it possible to feel such unity and still feel the uniqueness of all that is me? Her energy doesn't consume or diminish mine. In fact, as our forces dance around us, I can feel my energy, my wholeness growing into something so powerful and profound, it escapes earthly definition.

Finally, she speaks to me, but not how we speak here, on the earthly plane. There's no sound, yet it's audible, there are words, but they don't move from her lips to my ears ... she speaks them with her spirit, directly into mine. "Calm yourself, dear one." My spirit envelopes her instruction and breaks it down into molecules.

The energy in her words is digested; each syllable carrying the intended effect. I feel calm and fluid. The words "dear one" diffuse to their smallest components, yet aren't fractured or destroyed. They retain their full meaning in each tiny piece, and course through me like blood through my veins. I feel her words, physically, emotionally and spiritually. In that moment, I know her and feel her loving me, showing me I truly am dear to her. It infuses me and makes me ... more. Finally, I see who I really am and it's clear that I'm so much more than I ever believed I could be.

My understanding manifests in a deep way that's new to me. On a cellular level I feel and know what it means to be dear to someone. Knowing this, in such completeness, overtakes me and I weep in her arms. I weep for pain, and sorrow, and joy. I weep for all the suffering I'd known in life, and all the suffering I'd seen and felt unable to change. I weep for the wall I built, the isolation I'd willingly imposed on myself while in my body. I weep for those in the earthly realm, who are without hope and believe there is nothing but what they call "the here and now". My heart dissolves at the thought. What if they'd been right, and the void had been my eternal existence? Lying forever in a state of ... nothingness? I cry out, trembling at the thought of being consumed by the sleep that I'd once considered a reprieve. "Shhhh, dear one, all is well." Her words pull me back from the awful memory of the deserted place that had, until recently, been my self-constructed prison.

Resting in her arms, a question comes to my mind and I move to ask her, to speak the words, but as soon as the thought forms, the answer appears, from her consciousness to mine. "You are not dead, there is no death except that the body becomes useless and is cast away. You are either alive in the body ... in the earthly realm, or super-alive here ... or a mixture of the two as you are now, part of you there and part of you here, on the Side of the Spirits. Your body lies near death back in that place, and your spirit has left it, but not completely. A sort of ... cord, binds you to it still. If it did not, you would be fully here."

Another question springs to mind and, as before, it is answered without my having to speak. "Your consciousness exists outside your body. It's not contained or housed in the brain. It's eternal and cannot be held inside anything. It exists whether your physical body does or not. You can access it with your brain, but it isn't kept there like some sort of component. Consciousness endures despite the body. You've heard it said, dear one, that energy isn't created or destroyed, it simply changes forms. It is true on the earth plane and it's true here. It is law."

My consciousness is eternal? Not dictated by whether my body is alive or dead? I'd never imagined such a thing. I thought that when I died, I would still have some sort of physical structure that defined me. It's difficult to comprehend that my body isn't me. The information courses through me, billowing into fullness, and I realize that this ... the way I am here ... this is more real, more true, more accurately me, than the person being kept alive in a hospital on the other side. I finally understand who I am meant to be. I ponder the complexity and simplicity of it so deeply that I don't realize my grandmother has moved on, leaving me to float in the bright white light.

All at once, a powerful energy shook me from my thoughts, and everything stopped. When I say "stopped", I need you to understand exactly what I mean, so brace yourself, here come the variations: ceased, departed, evaporated, left town, hopped on a plane, got out of Dodge, took off like a cat with its tail on fire ... do you get it? It was strikingly foreign to have my mental voice stilled and all musings sent away. My brain quit thinking, and ceased its usual busywork. As it silenced, I knew who I was with. Two words formed in my mind – I AM.

I was with the Spirit of God, and I knew Him. I knew Him in a sense that was physical, spiritual and mental. He was indescribable. He held no form, there was no embodiment, for what could hold Him? What could contain the eternal? The white light of His penetrating energy was unstoppable. It couldn't be dimmed. It touched me and went deeper still; beneath my physical self, of whom only a perception remained. His vast white presence soaked into every part of me, diving deep into my core and stealing my breath, of which I had no need, as I was filled with His light. I lay myself bare to this energy, letting it fill every void, every hurt and longing. It took up all those spaces without diminishing me in any way, for the white energy of God does not take from us, only gives ... filling us to overflowing. The radiant light moved with powerful intent toward all parts of me; surrounding and infusing every cell, filling my body with intense warmth and vibration that was an indescribable joy to my ears, my skin and my spirit. I remained intact, retaining what was of benefit to me; while that which wasn't of benefit seemed to never have been. I was unable to recall those parts and had no desire to bring them forth to my understanding.

Floating, I felt the white light filling and permeating me to my tiniest cells. I relaxed my head back, not wanting to feel burdened by the weight of it, and at that moment the white light moved into my neck. It was so warm and caused me to curl my physicality inward, so I could experience it even more. From my neck, it moved up through my jaw and into my mouth, lighting my tongue with the most pleasing of melodies. I wanted to keep my eyes closed, to try to contain the light so it couldn't escape, but that was in folly. My eyelids couldn't contain the power of the Creator. It shined straight through them to the outside, reflecting off the light that surrounded me and raced back in.

The white brilliance warmed my face and poured into my head, buzzing around my brain, lighting it with tingling sensations and creating a sense of floating and weightlessness. Then, the light proceeded to enter each curve of my brain, flowing through as though travelling an expansive winding river; sparking to life previously unused parts of my intellect, and creating within me a "knowing", which made all things clear.

Situations that had tormented me in the earthly realm, were brought to my memory. The dread and sadness that held me captive to the pain of those transgressions was vanquished. Each truth became peaceful and clear in my mind. No words were spoken, no explanations given to erase the hurts and disappointments. Just this deep internal knowing that the reality of those matters had not been what I had believed it to be.

I'd tried for so long to fit my trials into some sort of framework, to understand them. I didn't know my understanding wouldn't come through my own beliefs or ideas, but through the powerful energy of God that filled me on this side, the "Side of the Spirits". The weight of my pain left me, replaced by His peace; like a tender hug from father to child, assuring all is well.

I surrendered myself completely to God. He held my entire existence, His light flooded out of me: exuding from my bones, pouring out from each strand of hair, even my eyelashes were aglow with His light and vibration.

God's love was drawing me back to His core, where I had belonged all along. I allowed myself to move closer and closer to His centre. Then suddenly, it was no longer external, it was internal, the bright light's source dwelling at the deepest part of my being. The Holy Spirit living inside me, residing in my heart, my spirit, my soul! For the first time, I understood that

God was vast and personal, and at my invitation long ago, had taken up residence inside me. I felt as though I might burst with joy, and explode into light, the rays from the blast reaching the farthest expanses of the universe. I dove into the light, wanting never to return to the earthly realm.

Then, suddenly, I was stopped. I knew I couldn't continue on this path ... not yet. I longed to stay, to make it to the spark of my existence, but it was not to be. I remembered this was a decision I'd already made; before I had ever got to the point of making it, as though it had been preordained, though that isn't the right word as the decision was of my own choosing.

The light grew dim and distant and I became fretful, crying out to God, "Please! Grant me at least the memory of this! Let me store within myself this time with You, so that I never forget. I will lose all hope if I cannot at least have that." I woke in my hospital bed ... the memory of my experience held deeply within.

I have experienced significant changes since my NDEs, and I see life in a whole new way. The most important thing I've learned since my experience, the message I want to share with the world, is that we are all connected. Life, at least in Western culture, teaches us to be independent. From the moment we draw our first breath, we are cast into a society of individualism. We build fences and walls, both literally and figuratively, to keep others out. As we grow into adulthood, those separations become battlefields, dividing us further ... even from the Source that created us.

This independence is confusing and contrary to what our spirits need and desire. It engages us in a lifelong struggle with our very essence and becomes the source of all conflict. If we, as children of God, are ever to make a real difference, we must first come to the recognition that we are all linked to each other by the Creator. I am linked in spirit with the criminal, the beggar, the infirm. It is by recognizing this truth that I realize I too could have gone the way of the thief, the impoverished or the afflicted.

I came back from my NDE with a true understanding of the strength and power that each of us possesses to help the hopeless and weary. We needn't sit idly by staring up at the sky and waiting for God to fix the problems here on Earth. He is right here with us, equipping us with His love so we can get the job done!

This knowledge has given me a sense of peace. Worry no longer makes sense, as I know that all things work together for good, if we choose to love God. Anger is so far from me, as is hurt. Why should I be angry or hurt? When someone wrongs me, I feel compassion. I understand that I once lived a life consumed with self, and unintentionally hurt others because of it. I walk taller and my smile is finally genuine, not just a mask I wear. I remember God's love when I move to speak, and gauge my words so they don't bring pain to others.

I thank God for my time in the void and in the light. I feel "real" now. I feel the connection, and I'm not afraid of it. The walls have come down! With the Spirit of the Most High, I stand upon the rubble ... ready to fulfil God's great and glorious purpose in my life.

This is quite an extensive NDE that has encompassed many aspects. Penny experienced the void, but went beyond it. Since her NDE, Penny experiences the world in a different way. I find it interesting that Penny has commented on her previous way of living being a self-constructed prison. I guess this applies to many people (I know it does to some aspects of my life!), which is why it can be such a revelation when it is actually experienced rather than merely intellectualized or considered in an abstract way.

Lovetta communicated to Penny that her body was close to death, but that her spirit was still connected to the body by a cord. There have been many reports of people actually seeing this cord during their NDE or OBE, so it is perhaps unusual that it wasn't seen here, but Penny was informed about it. Lovetta's communication also appears to reinforce many aspects of the experiences of others. Indeed, many other things that Lovetta communicated have also been alluded to by others, such as the explanation that consciousness does not die but changes form.

Particularly intriguing was Penny's description of when her brain apparently stopped thinking and she was left with the awareness of just I AM, which has been described in many sacred texts.

Maybe the most powerful aspect of Penny's experience was when she reflected on previous situations that she had previously felt sadness and anguish about. She was suddenly filled with a deep knowing that those situations were nothing like the way she had perceived them. My question is: are there any ways of developing techniques that can provide such a positive effect? I'm sure everyone has had life experiences that leave them with a sense of guilt or torment. Imagine if there was such an instantaneous way of reframing those experiences. Wouldn't everyone be living a much happier life?

Let's stay with Penny's understanding that we are all connected, even if we don't see the connections. The deeper implications are that whatever we do to others ultimately comes back to us.

Wouldn't we all live our lives very differently if this was instilled in us from a young age?

8

LIFE HAPPENS BUT YOUR JOURNEY NEVER ENDS

Michael Moon is a 64-year-old from Florida, USA, who connected with Kelly through social media. They were both members of an online NDE forum and Mike had been reading Kelly's posts. He reached out to her privately as he felt he could share his story with her. Mike's experience occurred at the dentist's. I have gathered hundreds of cases of NDEs that occurred while having dental treatment under gas. Most involved people who were children at the time of their experience; it is less common to find a report of an adult having one. Nitrous oxide was commonly used in dental work, but its popularity appears to have declined over the past few decades.

In May 1979, I was 26 years of age and my personal life was in turmoil. I was in my third job since being discharged from the army and my wife and I were separated. Also at that time, I was disillusioned with religion and possessed no true religious or spiritual beliefs.

I visited a dentist that spring and was told my teeth were becoming crooked. He suggested one of two options; either he could put me in braces or extract four teeth. I couldn't afford braces at that time, so I decided to have the teeth pulled. He was to pull the top two teeth in the first appointment and the bottom two at the second appointment. I arrived for the first appointment late in the afternoon and I think I may have been the last patient of the day. The dental assistant led me into a room and told me to sit in an old green dental chair that looked to be about 50 years old. She loosened my clothes and wrapped a cloth around my shoulders. The chair was reclined back and a mask placed over my nose. She instructed me to take deep breaths as she turned on the gas. I felt my body start to go numb and my eyes became very, very heavy. I tried to keep them open and stay awake for as long as possible, but, finally, they just couldn't stay open any longer. My eyes slowly closed and I started to sink into sedation. When the dentist came into the room, I was still fully aware of what was going on around me. Even though I could hear him talking to his assistant, I couldn't open my eyes and, thankfully, couldn't feel anything he was doing.

He started joking with his assistant about her boyfriend and their sex life, which I thought was quite inappropriate. I wondered what they would think if they knew I could hear everything they were saying. I felt the dentist open my mouth wide and put some kind of clamp inside to keep it open. I could, painlessly, feel a couple of needles being administered and he proceeded to put some cotton or gauze in my mouth to absorb the blood. He then wedged an instrument into my mouth and began prying and pulling on the first tooth. I was aware of everything he was doing, but thankfully, again, there was no pain. I felt my head being pulled up and down as he pried and twisted. Suddenly, I heard a loud SNAP and the first tooth was out. I began feeling as though I was sinking deeper and deeper within myself, and I don't even remember the extraction of the second tooth. After the first tooth snapped, I felt my jaw muscles begin to contract and I could hear a loud oscillating buzzing sound. I remember wondering why my jaws were contracting and what was causing the noise.

I continued to sink deeper and deeper within myself and thought my consciousness must have sunk way down into my chest. I could see a light far away in the distance and assumed I was seeing this through my eyes. I felt a rush toward the light and found myself in another room of the house. I seemed to be against the ceiling in the corner of a room, looking down at the dentist, his assistant and two other couples as they sat drinking and laughing.

They didn't notice me as I watched them. The room was a light greenish-beige colour with two couches, a chair and two dimly lit lamps. I couldn't understand why they were drinking and socializing while I was in the chair in the other room. The exact sequence of events at this point became a little blurred and, at one point, I was walking with someone down a road and into a city, the sky a dark red. The buildings were very dark and I remember being somewhat fearful. I assumed it was a bad place and didn't understand why I was there. However, we went into one of the dark buildings; I don't remember why or what else happened while I was there. I just knew it was dark and I was afraid.

The next thing I knew, I found myself standing in front of a misty grey wall. I looked in every direction and the wall was the only thing I could see. On instinct, I guess, I stepped into and through the wall. It felt like a cool veil as it touched the tip of my nose, then slid past my face and off the back of my ears. Once the mist slid, I was instantly on the other side. I was standing in the shadows and could see a soft horizontal light in the distance. The floor looked like it was made of a polished tile, giving a soft reflection of the yellow light. Someone took my left hand and said, "It's all over, you're home, don't worry about anything; it's all over, you're home."

I didn't recognize the person or entity but I've always retained the impression it was female. She just kept repeating those words over and over again. I sensed others in the shadows and one man in particular was waiting off to my right. He was facing me and appeared to be watching. I couldn't forget him because he wore a fedora hat that was popular back in the 1940s and early 1960s. The hat looked like the one my grandfather wore when I was a child, and he died in 1963. However, I have no recollection of who the man was.

A feeling of extreme peace, love and joy came over me as I realized my earthly journey was over and I was home again. I was where I belonged and was not interested in returning. My head cleared and it was as though a veil was lifted from my mind. Finally, I understood everything I had ever wondered about. All of the answers to the mysteries of the world were right there in my mind. I didn't ask about nor was I told anything, I just remembered! I thought to myself, "Oh well, I just forgot everything while I was there" (here on Earth).

I turned and looked behind me to see a large circle, and within that circle were smaller circles or bubbles. The small bubbles contained the faces of all the people who had been in my life. I looked at each face and sensed a rush of emotions and experiences with each. I don't remember anything specific, just the rush of the experiences. The smaller circles didn't fill all the space inside the larger circle; they only took up about one-third of the space. Years later, after learning about NDEs, I concluded this was probably an indication that there would be more people in my life before I left this Earth.

Meanwhile, my friend continued to hold my hand, and told me over and over again not to worry about anything, it was all over and I was home. I looked around again and it was as though I was standing on the moon or out in space somewhere, looking back at the Earth. I could see scattered white clouds covering the deep blue Earth. It was very beautiful and I felt happy and peaceful. I was home again and I was loved, regardless of the bad things that had happened in my life. It was in this moment that I realized I had wasted my time on Earth. I don't remember why I felt this way, but it was an intense feeling. Even so, I was still glad to be home!

I have always been a very protective person when it comes to my loved ones, especially my children. But at that time, I wasn't concerned about anyone. I knew they were okay and would all be with me soon. Oddly, though, I knew "soon" wasn't a time, but rather a "knowing" that they too would be coming home once their journey came to an end. With my friend at my side, we turned and began walking toward the light, back toward home. However, after only a few steps, I felt myself being sucked backwards, losing the grip of my friend's hand. I was pulled back through the misty wall and the next thing I knew, I woke up in the dentist's chair, alone and confused. The dentist never mentioned anything about what happened that day and I never asked.

I knew something profound had happened, but at that time I didn't realize how profound! I had no knowledge of near-death or out-of-body experiences. A few months afterwards, my wife and I divorced and the kids remained living with her. However, despite our divorce, we've always maintained a good relationship and worked together for the sake of the kids. For a few years following the dental appointment, my life was still in turmoil and I remained confused about what had happened and its significance. I wondered how to make sense of it, but had no frame of reference.

It wasn't until a couple of years after the experience that I watched a movie, based on a true story. The woman and her husband were in a car wreck and, unfortunately, her husband was killed. The woman was critically injured and rushed to hospital, where she was pronounced clinically dead on the operating table for several minutes. Thankfully, and to everyone's surprise, she started breathing again and was revived. The movie portrayed her experience in great detail during the several minutes she was clinically dead. As I watched her go through the tunnel leading to the other side, it was like reliving my own experience from a couple of years earlier. It was really exciting! It was as though someone had made a movie about my own experience.

In 1998, I had an allergic reaction to anaesthesia during a minor surgery. The doctor said my body and jaw muscles became rigid and contracted. He struggled to insert an oxygen tube down my throat so that I could breathe, and said he was afraid he was going to lose me. After I spent the day in recovery afterwards, the doctor suggested I be tested for a medical condition called malignant hyperthermia (MH). MH causes a reaction to certain inhaled and injected anaesthetics. In 2001, I finally had a muscle biopsy at Wake Forest University and all test results came back as abnormal or morbidly abnormal. After reviewing the symptoms related to MH, it was clear that I'd had at least three previous reactions to anaesthesia, including my trip to the dentist that led to my NDE.

MH causes muscles to contract, including the jaw muscles. I didn't have another NDE as a result of the other MH reactions, but I've always wanted one. If for no other reason, just to refresh my memory!

Since my NDE, I've become fascinated with ancient and theoretical history, and love nature in every sense, including every living thing. All life is energy and all energy is connected through love and caring for each other. My spiritual journey has been a bit like a rollercoaster, with extreme spiritual highs and lows. I still fear the process and the pain associated with death, but not death itself. A large portion of my life since that time has been spent searching for my purpose and making sure I don't waste the rest of my life. I'm retired now, but during my career I had a good job, earned a fair wage and helped many people. However, it wasn't the kind of help I really wanted or needed to provide. In the years following the experience, I started volunteering with the local hospice, wherever I've lived. I discuss NDEs with any patients, family members or others who will listen. I don't recall for sure how I started with volunteering, but it probably arose from the inspiring books I read in the years after the experience. I know hospice patients are going to die and I feel the need to help ease their fears as well as those of their families. I've visited many hospice patients over the years, and have many meaningful memories of each, but a couple stick out the most. There was a 12-year-old boy – for reasons of privacy, I'll call him "Toby"– who had lived with brain tumours since the age of four. I started working with him during the last couple of months of his life. After getting to know him better, often with much difficulty in communicating, I managed to let him know that there is a life after this Earth. At the request of his parents, we didn't talk about death per se, but he seemed to understand what I was saying.

When his condition worsened, his mother asked me to come to his home to say goodbye. He was in a coma at that point and I sat alone with him on the bed, telling him again about the peaceful and loving place where he was going. I encouraged him to go to the light and assured him that he would be home again. He passed a few hours later. His family honoured me by inviting me to be a pallbearer at his funeral. The large church was filled with several hundred people who came to say goodbye.

"Craig" was another hospice client who left a lasting impression on me. He suffered with motor neurone disease (also known as Lou Gehrig's disease). When I was first assigned to visit him at home, I was advised that he was a gruff and hard man who could be difficult to deal with.

He was a big, hardy man, but by the time I became involved, he was in a wheelchair and had limited movement below his neck. After gaining his trust, I shared my NDE and he listened intently. Craig was not a religious man, but he was pleased to hear my story and gain an insight into what to expect when he transitioned. He thanked me for sharing, and for the rest of that visit he was quiet and contemplative.

He later went into a hospice end-of-life facility, and one night they called to let me know he was in a coma and near death. I sat with him for a couple of hours, wiping his forehead and holding his hand. I told him it was okay to let go and reminded him that he was about to go home again. A few minutes later, he was gone.

Although many years have passed since my experience, I still struggle with my inner self-growth and to understand the meaning of life. At times, it has been a difficult journey. Life happens and it has sometimes been a terrible distraction from my journey. I am still an average person with normal everyday problems, and I'm no better than anyone else because of my experience. However, being given a glance at the other side has been a great gift. I know there is life beyond the one we live on Earth, and I strive to remember that nothing here is as significant as we think.

In the last couple of years, through the internet, I've connected with many good people who've also had NDEs. While every NDE is slightly different, the core elements are basically the same. Just as there are slight differences in each experience, I've learned there are slight differences in each experiencer's life thereafter. Some share their NDE and its impact on their lives in every form of media available. Others, such as myself, try to live simple and reflective lives, hopefully as an example of how the NDE has affected them. Neither is wrong, it's just what each needs on their individual journey.

I think, above all else, the most important gift I received from my NDE has been compassion for those in need during times of crisis, especially the loss of life and/or loved ones. As I've said before, we use our experiences in different ways and according to our abilities. The main thing is that we all come away with our own unique abilities.

My brush with mortality has been a source of comfort in recent years when I have had health problems. I know what lies on the other side of the veil and that, when I leave this Earth, I'll return home again. I live one day at a time and try to be the best person I can be. I'm not always successful, but I continue to try. I still volunteer for hospice work and I'm a better person for it.

Many people would conclude that the nitrous oxide used in Mike's dental procedure caused his brain to create his NDE. However, in light of other cases of NDEs and altered states of consciousness, it would be better to consider the possibility that nitrous oxide can in some way facilitate access to an altered state of consciousness rather than create some sort of hallucinatory experience.

Mike had never heard of NDEs prior to his experience. It was years later before he finally realized what he had been through, when, by chance, he watched a movie that featured an NDE. To this day, he still struggles with adjusting to his personal development. Integrating the experience into life post-NDE is not easy, which is why I believe it is essential that, as a society, we have a deeper understanding of NDEs.

Following his experience, Mike developed a love for nature and an understanding of the interconnectivity of life. Despite his previous well-paid job, his NDE led him in the direction of what he feels to be the more satisfying work of volunteering in local hospices and helping those who are dying. After an NDE, many people feel that their interest in material possessions and earning money disappears. This is replaced with a deep desire to be of service to others. Mike is no exception: he felt he could use his NDE to help others who were fearful of death. It is apparent from the examples Mike describes in this chapter that his work with these patients has helped enormously at the end of their lives. His NDE has also given him the strength and ability to cope with his own recent health problems. What is it about NDEs that motivates people so powerfully to be considerate toward others? If we could understand how this change occurs, there is the potential to develop highly effective therapeutic interventions.

9

NATURAL TRANSFORMATION THROUGH THE GIFT OF LIFE

Kelly was on a group holiday in Machu Picchu, Peru, and got chatting to one of the ladies in the party she was assigned to. When Kelly mentioned her experience, the lady asked if she knew Jeff Olsen, a public speaker, who has written books about his NDE. Shortly afterwards, Kelly connected with Jeff – now 53 years old – via email and Skype. Jeff's NDE occurred following a fatal accident, yet despite the tragedy he experienced he has been able to find peace. Jeff has appeared in many YouTube films and spoken at many conferences.

In 1997 I experienced a horrific car accident, the most difficult part being that the cause was me dozing off at the wheel. I overcorrected and lost control of the vehicle at 75 miles per hour. The car began to whip and roll, not off the road, but down the road propelled by the hard concrete.

Both of my legs were crushed, the left being amputated above the knee. My ribcage was crushed, my lungs collapsed and my right arm was nearly torn off. The seatbelt also ripped through my lower abdomen, rupturing my intestines and tearing through my hip. The most devastating part of the entire ordeal was the loss of my wife and youngest son, who were also in the car and were killed instantly. Our entire family was in the car. My oldest son was not seriously injured physically, but endured the emotional trauma of losing his mother, little brother and, in many ways, his father too. I spent nearly six months in hospital and had 18 operations in all before I recovered physically, but the emotional recovery took years more.

I blacked out for most of the rolling, but when the car came to a stop I was fully conscious. The first thing I heard was my oldest son, then aged 7, crying in the back seat. My initial reaction as a father was that I had to get to him. I wanted to comfort him and see that he was all right. That's when I realized I was unable to move. I was pinned. I couldn't see and I was struggling to breathe. All I knew was that I wanted to get to my hysterical 7-year-old son. That's when the brutal reality hit me that no one else was crying. I could not hear our youngest, who was just a toddler, and in that moment I knew that both he and my beloved wife were gone. I felt it deeply, not only in their silence, but in the overwhelming feeling of their actual passing.

It's the worst kind of Hell a man could ever be in. Being pinned immobile, hearing one of your children crying uncontrollably and not being able to get to him, while knowing also that the other half of your family is already gone, killed instantly, and that you were driving the car. Words cannot describe what that was like. It was the worst nightmare I could ever imagine. I laid there attempting to breathe and maintain consciousness, knowing what had just happened. I wanted to comfort my son and get out of that car, but I could not move.

Intense panic filled me that everything was slipping and there was nothing I could do to control it, but it was at that point that things drastically shifted. In those moments of horror, a strange thing happened. In complete contrast to the nightmare I was experiencing, a peculiar calmness came. It was the darkest moment of my life, yet I actually felt an embrace of comfort. It felt as though a warm blanket of light came and wrapped itself around me, creating a bubble of pure love. I began to rise above the entire scene and marvelled at the feeling that everything was actually all right. Or at least it felt as if it were in this beautiful bright bubble of comfort and love. I began to realize that I was actually okay. In doing so, I became aware that my wife, who I knew was deceased at the scene, was miraculously there in the bubble of light with me, and that she was okay too, except she was insistent that I could not stay, that I could not come with her and that I must go back to take care of our son.

I learned a lot about choice in that moment. There I was, looking into the eyes of the woman I loved more than life, so relieved and joyful that she was okay, yet I knew I had a son left alone crying in that back seat of the crashed car. "You've got to go back," my wife continued to insist. I looked at her, into her very soul, and knew I was not meant to go with her. In that moment I chose to go back, and it was as simple as the very thought of it. I realized how powerful our thoughts are. As soon as I looked at her, knowing this would be our last goodbye, I made the choice to go back. I left her side in that bubble of light and was suddenly transported to the scene of a busy hospital setting.

I had no concept of time while in that light bubble. I later learned that people arrived at the scene of the accident, one actually being a doctor. They could do nothing for my wife and youngest son, but they rushed me and my 7-year-old to a small local hospital. They then called for Life Flight to transport both of us to a large hospital that was equipped to handle my critical situation. My son was sent to a children's hospital to be observed overnight, while I was sent to a nearby trauma centre.

I had no knowledge of any of that. All I knew is that I had wrecked the car and said the most poignant goodbye I will ever say. I then found myself wandering around the hospital encountering all the patients, doctors, nurses and families of patients in the most profound way. Except this was different. I was wandering in spirit, not in physical form. I moved freely from room to room with no effort at all. I was not conscious of any physical pain at all. I simply moved wherever my thoughts took me, while being in very close proximity to the doctors, nurses, patients and families of patients all around me in the busy Emergency Room (ER) trauma facility. As I would get near every individual, I seemed to know everything about them. I knew the love, hate, joys and struggles of everyone I saw. I knew them as if they were me. I felt a literal connection and oneness with them in a way I had never experienced before, yet it felt intensely familiar. Everyone I saw I loved, unconditionally, regardless of who they were, what they had done or what had happened in their lives. I felt their feelings. I was experiencing their life experiences and knew why they had made every decision they had ever made. I knew them as well as I knew myself, and I loved them. I wanted to embrace them. I felt in many ways as if I was them. We were truly one.

It was in that moment that I came across a man lying on a bed that I didn't feel anything from, which I thought very strange. I stepped closer to take a look. As I peered at this body, I realized it was me. Or at least my body. I was me, having this profound, connective experience, but I was now looking at what used to be me, or my body. In that moment I had the profound realization that I am not my body. It was simply the vehicle I had been driving through my life. A literal skin suit. I felt an overwhelming sadness looking at my body and how broken it was. I had always taken it for granted. I had been a division-one athlete. My body had always been at my command. I had prided myself on my physicality and now I was everything but physical. I was spirit, I was light, I was a profound part of everything and everyone around me. I was the true me, but outside of my body.

I knew I must get back into the broken mess that was my flesh. Again, the simple thought was enough. I chose to be in the body and there I was, back inside. Back into the pain, the horror, the confusion and the guilt. Trapped in the broken heaviness of all the results, both physical and emotional, of the accident. I was ventilated and could not speak. Both of my legs were immobile due to the crushing injuries of the crash. My right arm was immobile, being completely torn out through the rotator cuff, and my lower abdomen was gaping wide open from the belly to the hip. I was experiencing intense infections from my intestines having been ruptured and spilling into all my open wounds. The only body part I could move was my left arm, which they eventually tied down because I kept trying to pull at the ventilator, the feeding tube, the Intravenous Infusion (IV) and other medical devices.

I was in the Intensive Care Unit (ICU) for months and spent nearly six months in total in the hospital. Medical staff were doing all they could to save my life, yet I seemed to have one foot in this realm and one in the next for much of that time. It was like a crazy nightmare that would not end. I would only find relief when I repeatedly left my body again for brief retreats, which felt like lucid dreams and were infinitely better than the pain, guilt, grief and regret I was experiencing in my body.

I learned a great deal in those long months as I laid in hospital. I learned what true love is. I watched my brothers nearly lose their jobs to spend time with me. I watched other family, friends and co-workers do so much on my behalf. I felt the hearts of medical staff as they did all in their power to heal me and make me more comfortable. I connected with my surviving son in ways I thought I never could from a hospital bed.

I learned a great deal about myself as well. I learned about fear, doubt, faith and hope. In fact, my faith and hope were actually transformed into absolute trust. Trust was more powerful and more real. Faith and hope seemed like a wish. Trust was knowing. I shifted everything I knew and even what I didn't know into trust simply in order to survive.

I chose to stop asking the "why" questions and move my concentration to "what". What was I learning from all of this and what would I do to overcome it all? What would I do with my life and how could I possibly honour my deceased wife and son? I had so much grief. One thing I learned in a very powerful way is that life is so precious and can be so fleeting. I knew better than anyone that I may not always have tomorrow, so I resolved to do what must be done today. Don't put it off. If there was a letter to be written or a conversation to have, a text to send or forgiveness granted, now was the time to take care of it. Yesterday was gone and over, and I might not be here tomorrow, so do it now.

I was eventually transferred to rehabilitation. It was there that I had what may have been the most profound experience of all. I was off all heavy narcotics by that time. My body was improving every day, but my heart was still shattered from the reality of losing my wife and youngest son. I slipped into a deep sleep, feeling burdened by the knowledge that things would never be the same.

As I faded off into slumber, still dwelling on the fear of what my life had become, I felt a strange, yet familiar feeling. It was the same light bubble I had experienced at the scene of my accident. I felt its calming effects. I felt the love that made the light almost seem tangible. I felt the familiar pull – the rising above myself – that now seemed to be lifting me higher and higher above my hospital bed. I basked in the feeling, free from the pain and grief, except this time the bubble seemed to disperse and I found myself in the most beautiful place imaginable. The feeling was one of being home. It was so welcoming and embracing. I was alone there, but felt an overwhelming sense that I remembered this place, and it remembered me. I began to run, joyfully running in this beautiful place which I could only call home.

It was a very physical experience. I could feel the warm, soft ground under my feet. I could feel the energy firing up through my calves and into my thighs. I could feel the joy of my athleticism as I raced about without growing tired or winded at all. My body was perfect. My mind was clear. There was no pain, no grief, only joy and glory. I was elated, and that's when the message came to me that I was not there to stay. In that very instant I also noticed a corridor to my left, and I knew intuitively that I was to go down that corridor. I began making my way down it and could see that it came to an end. At the end of the corridor was a baby crib. I made my way to this and looked inside. To my joy, there lying in the crib was my youngest, toddler son whom I had lost in the accident, sleeping. Beautifully, peacefully sleeping. I swept him up in my arms and held him close, which was also a very physical experience. I could feel the heat from his little body. I could feel his ribcage expanding with breath. I could feel his breath on my neck. I could feel his soft head against my face. It was him. It was really him. I smelled his hair and skin. It was my little boy. And he was okay.

I began to weep as I held him, marvelling that we were together. It could not be real and yet it was real. In fact, it felt far more real than this life and the hospital bed. Holding my son was the reality. As I held him, I felt something completely overwhelming come up behind me. What I felt was so powerful, so cosmic, so wise and so ancient, yet it was so personal. I became fearful. I did not dare turn around. I knew I was in the presence of God. I held my little boy close, still weeping. As I felt this overwhelming presence come nearer, my mind raced. I could not allow myself to turn around and had the thought, "I hope I'm forgiven." It was then that I felt loving, Divine arms wrap around both me and my son and hold us. The knowledge came to me in that very moment, not by words but by an absolute download into my entire soul, that there was nothing at all to forgive. In fact, the word "forgive" and any notion of judgement became completely foreign. There was only love. I was so overcome by pure, absolute, unconditional love that words are inadequate to describe it. I had grown up believing that God was going to judge me. And that I was probably in trouble. I believed that life was a test and that I was most likely failing that test miserably in spite of doing my best. Yet in those loving arms, there was no judgement at all. Only pure unconditional love.

We seemed to melt into each other. My son became part of me and then we became part of God. Then all three of us became part of everything that is and ever was. I was astounded. The entire universe had transformed into me and yet there I was aware of it all, like an observer from a very high perspective. I saw my life. I saw the things I felt were mistakes, and yet in those loving arms there were no mistakes. I saw the things that I felt were wrong and yet I did them anyway. In those arms there were no wrongs, only love, wisdom and learning. It was communicated to me, and again not by words but with pure knowledge, that all the judgements I was putting on the events of my life were simply my judgements and had nothing at all to do with God and unconditional love. I felt that in those arms I was perfect. In fact, I was Divine and completely connected to the source of all that ever was or would be. There was no time. There was only that perfect moment in which the entire universe had come together to honour me and my silly little life.

I saw the accident and everything leading up to it, from my childhood and adolescence to adulthood and all the people who had been in my life, as the perfect cast to a perfect play, which was created only for me and my soul's growth. That's when the knowledge flowed to me that I had actually created it. That I had orchestrated the perfect experiences for my soul's highest good. It was strange; I had spent months in that hospital bed believing that in some strange way God had done this to me. That this was all part of a cosmic test that I had spent my life up to that point believing in and attempting to complete with a pass grade. The powerful knowledge flowed to me as I observed all the sacred moments of my life that it was in no way a test at all, but in fact a gift; that every day and every moment and every relationship, family, friend or foe, was all for me, for my perfect experience, and was put into motion somehow by my will. It felt as if the entire universe had simply said a resounding "yes" to what I had chosen to come to and learn by. Here I was in God's arms observing it all with no judgement at all, only gratitude.

I also learned a lot about choice. I learned that literally everything is a choice. It felt as if the only rule in the entire universe actually was "free will and choice", but without judgement, only in unconditional love.

I began to become aware of myself holding my son again in my arms, but still feeling the arms of our Divine Creator around me. I realized how much I loved my little boy. He was perfect to me. As those feelings flowed through me in an intense way, I realized that in God's arms I was that little boy. That those same feelings I had for my son were very real and cosmically universal, only magnified. I was perfect in the arms of God, and I therefore knew we all are. Each of us is unique, but perfectly loved by God. I realized that God is in all of us and we are all in God, like cells in one giant body of humanity. Each with our unique function in the overall process, but in perfect order as a whole.

I held my little boy, still fast asleep, and the knowledge came to me, in that powerful non-verbal way, that I even had a choice about him and what had happened. I knew my son had died. I knew I was only in this realm for a moment. But it was communicated to me that I still had a choice in all of it. I could choose to feel victimized by God, I could choose to loathe myself forever more because I had lost control of the car, or, in this perfect moment, I could choose to give my son to God, therefore exercising my free will in the entire situation. I could give my son to God and never have to feel as though he had been taken from me. I could let him go into the arms of God in gratitude for the time we had spent together in this life, transforming my pain and resentment into thankfulness. I squeezed my little boy close and kissed him on the forehead. I was able to give him back to God. Give him back to peace, comfort and home. Then I woke up, back in the hospital bed and all the injuries, both physical and emotional, but with an entirely new perspective. A perspective that felt as if I were remembering what I had always known, but had forgotten.

Please don't get the wrong idea from all of this. It's not like I had a horrific accident, then had some powerful near-death or out-of-body experiences, and then I was okay. It was not like that at all. I had a terrible accident, I experienced profound spiritual experiences, but it literally took me ten years to begin to put all the pieces together and transform in any profound way. For years I was lost, searching for all the love I had felt in those higher realms. I learned to walk again on a prosthetic limb. I made my way back to work. I had so many people around willing to assist me with all the mechanics of my life, but something was still missing. Even with all I had experienced, I was still searching for external validation in some way that I was okay. Even with the cosmic truth that had been downloaded into my very soul, it felt as if I were continually homesick to be in those Divine realms again.

It was not until I had additional spiritual breakthroughs almost ten years after the accident that things finally began to make sense and true transformation began. It was as if I had seen the sum, but did not know the equation, and until I saw how things added up, I would never make sense of all that had happened to me. I had experienced pure Divinity, but was still looking for it somewhere outside of myself. Only when I finally realized that all the answers were within me and remembered that I was actually Divine, did I become whole and healed. It was found not only in forgiving myself for all that had happened, but in truly loving myself. Only then did transformation take place. It was a big shift, and I had created it. By loving, forgiving and trusting myself, I created love and trust in the world around me. Only in loving myself did true love and true transformation materialize. Only in unconditional self-love could I heal the things that I was still searching for and truly love others and the world around me.

Transformation took place within me and by my free will and choice. It had come as a process. The process of life. And I had created it. I had the key the entire time. I simply hadn't used it. Now I finally knew what God was telling me while in those beloved arms, but it took a long while before I ever actually comprehended it. I still have challenging days. I won't pretend I don't. I haven't ever completely left behind my deceased loved ones, but I have let go of the pain. And in doing so I feel them near, often. I feel them in the small things. In dreams, in feathers miraculously left at my feet, in the breeze rustling through the leaves in the trees and in those quiet moments when I am open to the simple notion that they are near and may have a message for me. Transformation occurs in being open to seeing miracles in simple, everyday occurrences. The universe speaks to those who are listening. That is where true transformation takes place. It's in the quiet whisper and not necessarily in some cosmic out-of-body experience.

On those challenging days when life seems to throw me another curve ball, I remember to be still, to be still and know. And what I know is that everything is in perfect order. That I, with God, angels and the entire universe, have created my life for the expansion and transformation of my already eternal soul. There is nothing at all to lose, but everything to gain, no matter how painful, joyful, stretching, confusing or bland and completely ordinary any moment may seem. My life is perfect for me because I created it that way, and the entire universe, knowing who I am and who we all are, said yes. That's what unconditional love does.

I've learned to trust the process, to let it be and watch it all unfold, simply making my best choice in every moment along the way, with the knowledge that, in the end, I really cannot lose. There is too much love out there for it ever to let me down. I've also learned to find joy in the simple, normal things of life. The little things, in reality, are the big things. A sunset, hugging, laughing, crying, even in the quiet lonely moments is where I find the greatest joy. Listening to the wind or watching an insect navigate its way through its own transformational existence. Life is perfect in its simplicity. That's where Heaven is: in the little things, the ordinary things of life. Look for them. Notice what you notice and you will see miracles and blessings everywhere. I do. And nothing really changed at all, except me. That is what true transformation is all about. Change your perspective and you truly will change the world.

This is a very powerful example of how Jeff's experiences gave him a radically different perspective on the tragic losses he underwent because of the car accident. To recover from such an accident and overcome such life-changing injuries is a feat in itself, without having the additional heartache of losing his wife and son. Yet his experiences seem to have equipped him with the strength and understanding that have been an integral part of his healing. It has taken Jeff ten years to find that peace, but his experiences appear to have initiated the very powerful change in perspective which was key to his healing. Just what is it about these experiences that delivers such a shift in perception?

It is interesting that his most profound experience occurred when he was off narcotics. In my hospital research, I found that those who were administered strong painkillers and sedatives were less likely to report an NDE. It's as if the drugs reduce the likelihood of these experiences occurring, as opposed to the popular misconception that drugs cause these experiences.

I wonder whether Jeff would have coped and been able to make a recovery, let alone find peace in his life, if he hadn't experienced an NDE. There is still so much to learn from NDEs, and unless we look at cases such as Jeff's and engage with them, we will disregard the benefits that can be gleaned for others.

10

A MID-COURSE CORRECTION

Kelly made the connection with our next experiencer through social networking. Diane Goble, aged 76, lives in Sisters, Oregon, USA. She is the author of several books and has appeared on many radio shows and YouTube. What started out as a fun day nearly ended in tragedy and was to change Diane's life.

In 1971, two months before my 30th birthday, I drowned and had, what I now understand to be, a near-death experience. Religion didn't play a big part in my life until I was 10, when my 8-year-old sister was accidentally killed. My parents didn't handle their grief well and I was lost in a fog of unresolved grief for several years. As a teenager, I began seeking answers by attending various churches ... Presbyterian, Lutheran, Methodist, Episcopalian. I didn't find any. When I was in high school, a friend invited me to mass at his Catholic church. There I began to find some peace of mind, if not the answers to my questions. I can't say that I ever actually believed in any of their biblical stories.

Still, I married in the church, had our three children baptized there, then left after a priest told me I had to make my own decision about birth control (I had to take it for medical reasons). I never went back, never gave God or religion a second thought ... until two months before my 30th birthday when I drowned in a raging river and had an out-of-body experience in another realm where I was shown the truth about who we are and why we are here. I chose to return to my body with a message to share and a mission for my life, which I promptly forgot upon my return.

The experience changed me so profoundly that within three years I lost my husband and my home, and my ex temporarily took my children away, implying that I was an unfit mother. He pretty much thought I was nuts. On top of that, I had been a stayat-home mum who hadn't "worked" for ten years. No one would give me a job. Alone and afraid, I turned to alcohol, drugs and sex as I searched for answers that weren't out there to be found.

When I was a child of 11 or 12 growing up on Long Island, New York, I would catch caterpillars and keep them in a cage so that I could watch their amazing metamorphosis take place up close. I found it fascinating that a creature could transform from a worm-like pest into a puddle of mush, then emerge as a graceful, colourful winged butterfly. Today, that's how I would describe the transformation process I went through during and since my NDE. Everything I had been was melted into a soup and reconstituted into a more evolved human being than I was before.

I ran into a good friend I hadn't seen since high school in Coral Gables, Florida, 20-some years after my NDE, and after a dinner spent catching up on each other's lives, she asked me, "Who are you and what have you done with my old friend Diane?" I'm not the same person I was before my NDE. Some personality changes were evident right away; other effects evolved as I made life changes. It seems to take a person about seven years to integrate an NDE into their physical life experience – as though the fog begins to lift and the path ahead becomes more clear, and the person discovers their ability to act on what they learned on the other side, and do it consciously. After going through hell, completely changing my life and pretty much losing everything I had, I returned to education within a month of that seven-year anniversary. I was guided to study psychology to try to understand what the hell happened to me. I still hadn't heard of such a thing happening to anyone else, so I still wasn't talking about it. I was just trying to survive, alone in a strange new city (from Chicago to Los Angeles) with three small children.

Even my return to education was guided, not planned. I threw my back out lifting heavy food containers at a fast food restaurant I was managing, lost my job and was unable to return to work full time for a year. When I could stand upright for more than a couple of hours, I started volunteering at a battered women's shelter to give me something to do. This helped me realize I wanted to become a counsellor to help other women who were trapped in the cycle of abuse.

I was able to get enough financial aid – student loans and work-study jobs, and clean enough houses every week – to support myself and my children over the five years it took me to earn a BS in Psychology and a Master's Degree in Community-Clinical Psychology at the age of 42. I had dropped out of college aged 19 because I didn't think I was smart enough. Now I was on the Dean's List every semester – and, except for a few classes, I hardly needed to study. I seemed to know everything intuitively.

For many years I had an intense interest in physics, subatomic particles and astrophysics, having had flashbacks of my NDE just looking at the images of the *Powers of Ten*. I'd read books on theoretical physics while my kids played on the beach. Years later, I realized that I received all this information during my journey through the Hall of Knowledge during my NDE. I was just stepping it down into human language, but I understood it from a higher perspective ... I could see the bigger picture.

I get the big picture quickly when I enquire into any subject because I have access to a larger knowledge base than people who haven't had an NDE, which includes a download of universal knowledge. The experience may activate new brain cells or a little-used area of the brain – perhaps a DNA switch was triggered that opens the window to the soul – mind connection. It was a huge Aha! moment for me as I travelled toward the light with a beautiful Being of Light by my side. I remember laughing at myself for forgetting this, and I recall also thinking how great it would be if we realized while we were still alive that when our body dies, we don't! Maybe then humans would be more compassionate toward each other and make peace a priority. I would call that higher-consciousness thinking.

In 1979, while volunteering in a nursing home, I wrote an article, which was published in a journal, in which I suggested the need for a little blue pill that would allow dying people to have control over their own death. It was based on conversations I had with elderly residents. In 1992, I became a hospice volunteer and continued to volunteer off and on for over 20 years in Florida, California and Oregon. I am a member of Compassion & Choices and advocate for a National Death with Dignity law in the US. I write a blog called "Let's talk about death and dying..." in which I discuss the pros and cons of this argument.

During my graduate programme, I was able to intern with a group of psychologists studying Family Systems theory, and partnered with a former minister presenting and selling personal growth and motivational programmes. I also studied Transpersonal Psychology and later earned another Master's Degree in Clinical Hypnotherapy, specialized in past-life regression and became an ordained minister. I opened The Stress Management Center in St Petersburg, Florida, in 1986 (before anybody knew that stress was such a problem), then my sister and I opened a mind – body – spirit integration clinic the following year (before anyone realized these all work together). We were way ahead of the curve. Some of the work we did 30 years ago is only now entering the mainstream. I realized I was a pioneer, a change agent, even then, and it has continued to this day.

In 1987 I had a spiritually transformative experience during a deep meditation at a Harmonic Convergence gathering that brought my NDE back into full consciousness. I later picked up a book by Ruth Montgomery, *Strangers Among Us,* in which she described similar unexplained experiences, and I suddenly realized I wasn't alone. I wasn't crazy. This has happened to others. And I began talking about it ... telling my story as if it had just happened yesterday. I could still see it all clearly, and I realized how it had changed me and my life course.

It wasn't just some random thing that happened to me. It was meant to awaken me to my higher guidance as part of my soul path, because my soul's purpose for coming into this life was to assist in the awakening of human consciousness to our spiritual nature. As I, Diane, continue to awaken, I become aware that what I am working on for my own spiritual growth is manifesting in the physical world, spreading exponentially across the planet.

I'm not suggesting that makes me special; unusual, maybe, but there are actually millions of people around the globe reporting NDEs and all of us together are trying to let everyone else know that this is who we humans really are: spiritual beings with the ability to exist independently as biological beings in an environmentally stable physical environment. We are all here to learn to love, not to kill each other off in as many ways as possible. There are no evil forces or angry Gods or predator extra-terrestrials lurking out there, wanting to destroy us. We are rising above our animal nature and developing into fully integrated spiritual-human beings. I see these times as that of a great awakening of humankind to its Divine Nature and an opportunity to bring peace to the planet. First, everything has to turn to mush and then the beautiful fully realized butterfly emerges.

If I hadn't had an NDE, I might have continued along my path as an unfulfilled, dependent housewife in the Chicago suburbs stuck with a philandering husband whom I had fallen out of love with, and I certainly would never have taken the path I did. On my own, I continued to study the world religions, philosophy and physics to reassure myself that what I learned on the other side was in sync with knowledge discovered by earlier humans. I began speaking at Light Centres, churches and personal growth conferences and became a spiritual teacher.

While doing this work, the message I was given by the light to bring back to share with others came back to me: *There is no death! We don't die!* Yes, our bodies die, but we are not our bodies. A physical body is the form we wear so we can experience life as a physical being in a physical dimension. Who we really are is the spiritual being that never dies. My experience of my conscious awareness shifting to a higher perspective, and observing the search for my body going on from above, happened simultaneously as my body was taken by the river. There was no time lapse.

The last thing I remembered was very calmly deciding that drowning was the better way to go and, with my last breath, yelling for the man holding my wrist to let go ... my body was sucked down into the violent turmoil beneath the big yellow raft that was trapped by the churning hydraulic action of the water and everything went black (which was exactly what I expected, having dismissed religion and become more of an atheist ... just lights out!).

Then, as if I just blinked my eyes and opened them again, I was looking down from above the treetops at the raging river below, the raft trapped by the hydraulic with the two men still in it, the other woman from our raft struggling in the rapids moving downstream. I could see my husband and my then 16-year-old sister, and other people running back upriver from the calm pool below the section of rapids to find out why all our equipment was flowing downstream.

When my husband jumped out onto a rock to look for me, I found myself at his side trying to tell him it was no use trying to save me. When I put my hand out to hold him back, I realized I didn't have a hand, I didn't have a body, and I thought, "Oh my God, I'm dead!" And with that realization, I was pulled away from the river, away from the forest, away from the planet as if speeding through the universe toward a brilliant, welcoming, white light far, far in the distance.

The feeling was awesome, exhilarating, amazing. I was filled with peace and joy, and an overwhelming feeling of being loved and completely accepted as if I were being welcomed home. It seems that in death, the soul learns it is not a body. I instantly knew where I was going and that I had done this before – left my body and returned home, thousands of times. Reincarnation, which I had dismissed previously, suddenly made complete sense. The Bible, which I had read but thought of as no more than a storybook, suddenly made complete sense – they just left out a few significant details.

I sensed a presence beside me and realized I was accompanied by a beautiful Being of Light, whom I sensed was my guardian angel. I instantly knew this loving being had been with me all my human lifetimes. It wasn't any identifiable religious figure, had no gender or form ... it was pure radiant light-energy. We communicated telepathically. Every question I had was answered before I could ask it, but it was more like I was remembering everything I had forgotten when I took on a body and now it was all coming back to me. I understood how it all works, everything made perfect sense, all the missing pieces fell into place. I promised myself I would remember all this in my next life.

Together we travelled through healing centres where I was shown how arriving souls were welcomed and comforted by their spiritual families, guided through their life review process, and healed from any traumas caused by misunderstandings about the life they had just experienced. We also visited several areas where these beings were being rehabilitated before they moved on to other aspects of spiritual life in other dimensions.

All of this was familiar to me because my soul has lived so many lifetimes; it was therefore just about remembering. I didn't know it then, but I was being given information that would be helpful to me upon my return. I did not have a life review, but I was assured that I was completely loved and accepted by the Being of Light.

We travelled at a high rate of speed through a warm, velvety darkness toward a sparkling light that intensified as we approached. It appeared to be a crystal structure, a group of spires that appeared to grow larger as we approached. It felt refreshing, cleansing, calming, smooth. The Being of Light and I communicated telepathically about going back into Diane's body and continuing my this-life journey. I was quite fine with where I was and eager to continue exploring more of this dimension. I was told I could choose to stay with the love I had already experienced during that lifetime and let that life go ... or I could accelerate along my spiritual journey by making different choices and taking a different path for that life by going back to Diane's body.

The Being of Light conveyed that we were in front of the Hall of Knowledge and that, if I chose to go back and resume this physical life as Diane, I would be given higher-consciousness knowledge about the transformation of humans to spiritual-humans, and a special gift from the light to share with humankind to awaken others to higher-consciousness thinking. I would become one of many light workers arising on the planet, sharing our inner wisdom with other humans about who we really are and why we are here ... and, by the way, bring peace to the planet.

Wow! My first thought was that this sounded like a mighty interesting mission, and before I could consider the consequences, my energy was pulled into this now-gigantic crystal structure so tall that its spire reached into infinity. Inside was like a hologram:

nothing solid, images floating, emerging, fading. It was like being in a really ancient library; there were shelves of books and scrolls with historical events rising and falling in space. I sat at the feet of the masters ... Aristotle, Plato, Socrates, Galileo, Jesus, Muhammad, the Buddha. I listened to them speaking. They listened to me. It seemed to go on for a thousand years and yet there was no time, it was all happening at once. Aspects arose from the ground of being and dissolved as I continued to spiral upward, absorbing knowledge and expanding my consciousness as I went.

I sensed that I was approaching the pinnacle and wondered what would happen next, when my energy suddenly crashed through the top and it looked like shards of broken coloured glass went flying every which way in the darkness ... and at that exact same instant, my head popped out of the river about 100 yards downstream from the raft.

I had no memory of my physical body being in the water after I went under the raft; of struggling to get out from under it, fighting the rapids, avoiding the rocks, getting slammed into rocks, struggling to breathe, fighting the current, until my head popped up in the calm pool below the rapids – a span, I would guess, of three to five minutes (estimated after recently viewing a video of a kayaker navigating that same section). I grabbed onto the nearest rock, coughed up a little water, and waited until my husband finally figured out where my body had ended up and ran back down to help me out of the river. They all thought I was dead. I didn't need to be resuscitated. I had no bruises or broken bones or concussion. A good thing, too, because we were miles into the forest on dirt roads in the middle of nowhere and this was before cell phones and search-and-rescue helicopters.

But I could hardly speak about it because I didn't understand what had just happened to me. I'd never heard of this happening to anyone. I couldn't find any other words at first other than "I went somewhere else." The local river people suggested I survived because I surrendered to the river.

It seems I had to lose everything my ego thought was important in the years to follow, but I came to find meaning in seeing the world from this higher perspective, and being able to share that with others to help in the awakening of humanity to its spiritual nature. It has been an amazing bonding experience. I learned to identify less with my ego, my body and the physical world, and to follow my soul path, not my insatiable human desires, and that's what brought me peace of mind and the ability to live my soul's purpose for becoming Diane.

Also, by coming back I didn't have to wait until my next lifetime to remember that I'm a spiritual being experiencing life through a form in the physical dimension, which gives this life a whole new meaning once one comes to terms with that. I didn't talk about my experience for 15 years, but, once I got started, I couldn't stop.

In 1989, I began writing a book I called *Through the Tunnel: A Traveller's Guide to Spiritual Rebirth* (1993) based on the Egyptian and Tibetan Books of the Dead and offering an NDEr's perspective on the art of conscious dying to help others realize that death is a transition rather than an ending. While I was writing it, other information continued to come through that had nothing to do with this book. I finally realized that several other non-corporeal beings were communicating information to me telepathically for another book, so we made an agreement that I would transcribe their book if they would then help me finish mine, which we did. Theirs is available as an ebook titled *Sitting in the Lotus Blossom* (2010).

In 1996 I started my first website, which became www.BeyondtheVeil.net. I wrote about my NDE, included similar stories people sent to me, and provided resources for spiritual seekers and seniors seeking information about end-of-life care. Since I was one of the first people to go online with this information, I was inundated with emails from people all over the world (140 countries) who hoped an NDEr could answer their existential questions about God, death, the afterlife, reincarnation, paranormal experiences, the meaning of life and spirituality. It became a full-time (non-paying) job that went on for over a decade. I posted their questions and my responses in my Seekers Open Forum on the website and recently included some in a book, now titled *The Hitchhiker's Guide to Cosmic Consciousness* (Kindle, 2016).

In 2008 I created an online training course to teach the art of conscious dying to holistic practitioners, yoga teachers, nurses, hospice volunteers and so on, to help them in their work with patients nearing the end of their lives, and I trained a number of practitioners around the world to carry on this work. After the US economy collapsed, no one could afford to pay for a course for which there were no jobs, so in 2015 I put the course into a workbook for caregivers and patients to learn the art of conscious dying together, titled *Beyond the Veil: Our Journey Home.* Now there are doulas and death midwives and transition guides galore, and I'm hoping the workbook will become a training textbook as well as a guide for those living with a terminal illness.

I put my spiritual lesson about reincarnation from my website into an ebook titled *Reincarnation and the Evolution of Consciousness* (2013), which describes my understanding of birth, death and rebirth, as the path to becoming Divine-humans. It is through experiencing the many aspects of love through relationships with others and, really, all of nature that we are learning to express unconditional love at all times, in whatever dimension we exist.

I realize now, looking back over the 46 years since my NDE, that my mission was to be a catalyst for change based on what I experienced during my NDE, which played out in the twists and turns my life took back on Earth. I was always the pioneer ... stress management, holistic healing and integrative medicine, NDEs, past-life regression and reincarnation, spirituality, conscious dying and transition guides/death doulas/spiritual midwives, Death with Dignity (DWD). Now we have DWD laws in four states in the US and in many countries around the world, while filling out Advance Healthcare Directives is becoming the norm. I activated the energy field and used my writing skills to spread the information through books and the internet, which serendipitously came along at the right time to accelerate the evolution of consciousness among humanity. If you think about it, I had millions of visitors to my website mostly from 1996 to 2010 ... I planted a lot of seeds over the past almost half-century.

I never made a living or received any support for my work, and I don't travel or follow the speaker circuit to promote my books either, so I've recently turned the marketing over to the universe. I'm just the writer, you folks do the marketing! And after decades of thinking that I was computer-literate, I can no longer keep up with the changing technology, either cognitively or financially, so I just need to heed my own advice to *let go and let God.*

Since my NDE, my values have changed. My beliefs have changed. My personality has changed. What I will tolerate from others has changed. My attitude toward life is different. It took off in a completely different direction. I'm smarter, more adventurous, more open, more forgiving, more aware, more alive. I swear like a sailor. I have no fear of death because I know we don't die.

I had lived life unconsciously, waiting to be told what to do, what to think, who to be, where to go or not go, what is true and not. But in the light, I saw face to face and my spiritual nature was reawakened. I was no longer afraid, no longer alone, no longer incomplete or unsure of who I really am. I know I'm not judged, but accepted completely and filled with unconditional love. The veil dropped away and no longer was it just a reflection or wishful thinking or some religion telling me what I should believe or how to please God. I knew fully that love is all there is and that we are all somewhere along the path to becoming that.

Over the years I've come to think of my NDE as something of a mid-course correction. I had strayed from my soul path. My soul decided to wake up in this life as Diane and be part of this awakening of human consciousness, but Diane wasn't paying attention. Diane was completely unconscious. I needed to be reminded of who I really was and why I was here so that Diane could use her spiritual gifts to pass that information along to others through the simple message that we don't die! This isn't all there is.

What a difference that would make in people's lives, in the ways we treat each other and our planet, if everyone realized just that. We're all one. We're all connected. There is no other.

It may have even been pre-planned. Something along the lines of: the first 30 years Diane gets to live her human life any way she wants, then she'll have an NDE to reawaken the memory of her soul mission and completely change her life for the rest of her lifetime to follow a spiritual path. I surely would not have done any of the things I did had this not happened to me.

Now, at the age of 76, when I think about what lies ahead for Diane, I feel that it's time to wrap things up here. I accomplished my mission. I'm at peace. I've done everything I came back to do in this life, though Diane still has a few things left on her bucket list. I live a peaceful aesthetic lifestyle in a small town at the foot of a beautiful snow-covered volcanic mountain range in northwestern United States. I spend more time in contemplation and writing than anything else these days, but I do still participate in activities with family and friends and continue to do volunteer work in my community. I prefer to live alone, not to be in a relationship, and don't like being in crowds or noisy places. I don't have a TV, but listen to the radio often enough to know that the world is deep in the mush. So I'm hopeful we are on the brink of the collective tipping point and that the awakening of higher consciousness among humanity will emerge from the soup as millions of fully realized Divine-human beings break out of their cocoons and spread light, love and peace all over the planet.

Diane's life drastically changed as a result of her NDE, and not all of these changes were easy. She was propelled from being a stay-at-home mother of three young children to literally losing everything. Despite her mothering duties, she was still able to excel in her studies. Interestingly, she remarked that her studying was more of a recalling of the information she was exposed to during her experience in the Hall of Knowledge. This information was then passed on by putting it into a practical form to benefit others. Diane is a classic example of a woman ahead of her time, whose NDE led to the innovation of many new practices which are beginning to gain momentum years after she first introduced them.

Like so many other NDErs, Diane was afraid to talk about her experience and tried to forget it. Incredibly, it took 15 years to realize that she was not alone in having had such an experience, when she happened to read a book that described other such cases. Prior to the experience, she was not particularly religious and didn't believe in God or an afterlife and had no reason to go to church. Her views subsequently changed and Diane is now certain that it is only the physical body that dies and "what we were before we were born is eternal".

Diane believes her "soul mission" is to assist in the evolution to a higher state of consciousness, which will lead to peace on Earth. Incidentally, this too is often declared by other NDErs. She has already contributed greatly to society and her work speaks volumes. She began teaching self-development to businesses and set up one of the first stress management centres where she taught meditation, personal growth and employed a massage therapist. She set up a website and now teaches about the art of conscious dying, which considers the acceptance of death as opposed to unnecessary prolongation of life through technology. This work is now becoming more widespread all over the world and is resulting in improvements in end-of-life care.

Diane wisely adds that had she not had an NDE she would never have known there was more to life than what her life was; she would have been content with that. So many people have benefited from Diane's efforts and revolutionary work since her NDE. Her life has been hugely enriched as a result of it, and this is something we can all explore further. Have you ever thought that there must be more to life?

11

THE GIFT

The first short chapter, written by me, transpired from the two emails I received as this book was nearing completion. The first one was from 43-year-old Barbara Ireland. I was in the unusual position of being able to respond to these emails immediately. Usually on a Friday, I get home from work and spend all my time with my two-year-old son, but on this particular day I was alone. I was staying in London in an apartment on the top floor of the College of Psychic Studies, where I was speaking at a conference the following day. I was reading a book, but was struggling to concentrate as I was aware of every creak I heard. This unnerved me slightly, as I was alone in a massive building that has such a rich history of psychic phenomenon. The emails were a welcome distraction for me, and I soon became engrossed in what Barbara had to say.

Below is a summary of Barbara's story and what she described to me.

Barbara is a successful professional singer and it was during a performance on stage with Stone Gossard from the band Pearl Jam that her story began to unfold. Barbara noticed a man in the audience who didn't appear to be enjoying himself. Instead of paying attention to the hundreds of other people who were having a good time and dancing along, she kept focusing on this guy, and consequently became overwhelmed with thoughts of self-doubt and self-criticism.

Barbara described the following to me: "I spent the entire show performing three tasks at once: (1) continuing to sing, dance, remember lyrics and cue with the band; (2) listening to a non-stop barrage of negative thoughts stemming from that guy in the front row; and (3) observing myself doing all of these things."

By the time Barbara got to bed that night she was exhausted. She analysed the whole evening and realized that she had to do something about this self-doubt. Out of desperation, shortly after that evening, she enrolled on an extreme boot-camp-style course that was designed to challenge her and push beyond her usual boundaries. She was determined to face her fears and overcome this self-sabotage.

Indeed, Barbara's confidence did increase as she took on challenge after challenge, the more extreme of which included climbing great heights, sleep deprivation and some other radical activities. Everything went well until the last hot and sunny day, when she participated in the final endurance challenge.

The first symptom to manifest itself was a seeming distortion in conversations going on around her; she could clearly hear people talking some distance away but the conversations of those speaking close to her sounded distant and echoed. Barbara's legs became wobbly and everything seemed to be enveloped in a glow. She persevered, but as she approached the end of the challenge, the movements of those who were cheering her on seemed to become distorted.

Although there was a medic as part of the team, he was totally inexperienced. Luckily, Barbara's friend had also signed up for the course and when she saw how sick Barbara looked, she stayed with her and took her to lie down in a quiet area away from others. As Barbara said, "I don't think any of us realized how serious a condition I was in; it wasn't something obvious like a heart attack. My doctor later said (when I got back and consulted her about what had happened to me) that she thought it was heat stroke combined with low blood pressure."

During the following four hours, Barbara believes that her life hung in the balance between life and death.

What happened next shocked Barbara: "Each of my limbs went numb and 'disappeared' until all that remained of me was a torso and a head. I felt incapable of moving. My life energy flowed out through the top of my head. I was terrified. I knew I was dying."

Barbara then experienced an extensive life review in which scenes from her life were not just remembered but actually shown to her. The review intermittently froze, while Barbara was asked a question by a voice. After each of her replies the scene would be erased, to be replaced by another scene from her life. This process was repeated for four hours, culminating in the voice giving her a choice of whether to continue with her life or move on and die.

While undergoing the life review Barbara was simultaneously experiencing pleasurable feelings of love and peace so it was not an easy decision and she had to ask the voice several questions in order to feel confident in her response. When she finally announced that she'd like to live, she could feel the energy rush in through the top of her head and sensation returning to all of her limbs. As she opened her eyes, she was aware of her friend praying over her and she felt an incredible sense of peace.

In the weeks that followed, Barbara lived in a way that was totally present to every moment. She took her time to eat fresh fruit and smell each flower she passed. Her listening to music was greatly enhanced and she was in awe of the various rhythms and tones she was exposed to – she felt totally alive.

Eventually this state of being passed and became infiltrated with her usual life routine. She walked past flowers without bending down to smell them, she rushed her food, and she began to let worrisome thoughts dominate her mind. She eventually experienced one of those "Aha" moments as she realized that these negative thoughts were constantly going around and around in her head.

While reflecting on her life review, she could see that, despite all of her success in her professional singing career and all her other achievements in life, she was still fraught with anxiety and that her troubled thoughts were manifesting themselves in her life. She'd been on antidepressants for years, was on an income that did not cover her outgoings, and – despite having attended the boot camp – was unable to change her negative mindset.

Driven by this sudden insight, Barbara intensely researched thought patterns, neuroscience, cellular biology, psychology and spirituality. She soon became aware of the way in which negative thoughts can become deep-rooted and continuously "loop" in the mind. Such thoughts then, in turn, create negative emotions that can impact on behaviour. Individuals often replay bad experiences in their mind repeatedly, which can lead to depression, low self-esteem, loneliness and anxiety. She was determined to overcome her destructive negative thoughts.

For four years Barbara explored various techniques designed to overcome such damaging thought patterns. She discovered how powerful human beings in fact are, and how we all have the potential to change our thoughts, thus redirecting the course of our lives. She devised a programme called "The 9 Ds of De-Looping", and the more she used these steps the more astounded she became by how her life changed for the better.

She had direction and felt she was living her true life's purpose. Her negative thought patterns ceased and she experienced good health accompanied by lots of energy. Her relationships healed and took on deeper meaning, her finances improved so that she was able to afford time for herself, and she was able to stop taking antidepressants. She still experiences challenges in life, but can now recognize them as soon as they occur and can thus change her thinking at the earliest opportunity.

Like many other NDErs, Barbara also described to me a feeling of interconnectivity and how her NDE has made her see the wider picture. She is no longer the centre of her little universe but perceives herself as part of the greater whole and lives her life being of service to others. This chapter is concluded in Barbara's own words:

The concept of dying is so abstract for most of us. It's almost impossible to imagine not being here, not being alive on Earth anymore. So coming face to face with one's own mortality directly, not as an intellectual exercise, but viscerally ... it can have unexpected effects on a person's life – such as a major switch in career paths.

One of the biggest perspective shifts for me was the clear understanding that it's not about ME. It's about US. I feel a sense of connectedness between every human, animal, and the Earth now – one that's mysterious and awe-inspiring. And I feel a strong desire to be of service to this grand matrix of life.

With all I'd learned about Mind Loops and how to change negative thinking, I wondered: was this what I'd been led to do? Everything that had occurred in my life certainly seemed to point to this. If so, it would mean I'd have to "go public" with my very personal and mystical brush with death ... and that scared me. But my desire to contribute was stronger than my fear.

Slowly, I began to talk about my NDE, and share the "9 D's of De-Looping". The responses were authentic and kind, and the transformations I witnessed as people began to awaken from their negative thought "hypnosis" astounded even me.

One woman released long-held shame and low self-esteem. Another person related how exhilarating it felt to attend parties again after "an amorphous sense of anxiety" had held him back from stepping outside his home for years. Many found the courage to speak up and express their needs in difficult relationships and work situations. Dreams that had been in the closet for years were finally dusted off and steps taken to fulfil them. People's potentials were being tapped.

I was elated. I imagined that every person who felt happier and more fulfilled was a step toward creating a happier planet overall. What more could a person wish for?

To spread the message further, I wrote a book: *How to Stop Negative Thoughts: What My Near-Death Experience Taught Me about Mind Loops, Neuroscience, and Happiness.* The book apparently hit a nerve, because it became a bestseller on Amazon in two categories the first week out, and is now being read in 12 countries.

I know the credit doesn't belong to me. It goes to my NDE, and the voice that asked all the right questions. If not for that experience, I doubt I would have even come up with the concept of Mind Loops, or healed my own destructive thought patterns so deeply

– let alone had the courage to reveal my story, work directly with others, and write a book about it.

Words can't begin to express the joy all of this has given me. How fascinating ... that the most terrifying day of my life ended up becoming the greatest gift I could ever have imagined.

This is a wonderful example of how the message of an NDE has inspired positive action to help others. Barbara has not only developed techniques to recognize and change unhelpful and negative thought patterns, which she has tried and tested on herself; she now offers them to others so that they too can be empowered. She describes the techniques in more detail in her book and has also provided further resources on her website that can reinforce them.

12

A LOST DOG, A VAST UNIVERSE AND A PRECIOUS GIFT

Deirdre DeWitt Maltby is a 65-year-old lady from Salida, Colorado, USA. Kelly became aware of Deirdre and her work via Rod Walton, a UK-based Christian priest, who has been studying NDE phenomena since 1975. He consequently set up the Bereavement Rescue Centre, a new paradigm in bereavement treatment that bases its approach on the evidence available for life after death. Deirdre has authored two books on her experience and has featured on the Biography Channel's series "I Survived ... Beyond and Back".

It is amazing how, in the blink of an eye, life can go from what one has always considered normal to never being the same again. Something as horrific as a life-threatening accident was the catalyst I needed to shake me out of my own personal box, so to speak; it would propel me on a journey of complete transformation of self – my inner self. Out of an unexpected and unfolding series of experiences, I was to receive the greatest gift of my life.

"Save my dog!" This wa**s** my cry after being involved in a near-fatal car accident, while travelling home from a routine shopping excursion on a warm November day in 2008. The next few moments produced what was to be the first of several extraordinary incidents that I would experience over the course of the following few weeks. I would be given the chance to see behind the curtain that separates this life from the next; a glance into the realm beyond ours. *And,* I would meet my Creator; what many in the world call God. These experiences happened to me both in and out of critical states. They happened in such a way that I could absorb them as truly having happened, and they would transform almost every aspect of how I now think, and live my life.

Trapped within my crushed vehicle, I was becoming quite frantic not only to free myself, but also to call back my dog that had just scrambled out of the overturned car onto the busy highway. Once they'd freed me from my car, the paramedics slid me into the ambulance. As they were working over me, I realized that my dog was still out there on the roadway – a busy highway – possibly hurt, or dying. Terrified, I inwardly pleaded to a God I had never really known, and, because of childhood circumstances, I had not much belief in: *please save my dog!* As I spoke those words, a very strange thing happened. No sooner had my plea for help been uttered than one of the bright lights from the ceiling of the ambulance seemed to shine down upon and warm my face. It felt as if it was being absorbed into me and, as it did so, it was warming me from inside myself as it pushed its way down the length of my body.

Accompanying this light was a great sense of peace; of wellbeing. In yet another instant, I felt I was also being given a silent answer to my plea for the safety of my dog with an unspoken promise that he would be fine, as would I; the situation I was in would just unfold as it should. My worries and panic vanished. Immediately I surrendered in complete trust to this strange yet comforting occurrence.

At the hospital it became imperative that I be placed into a drug-induced coma because the damage to my lungs had been quite severe. I was haemorrhaging into my lungs; my condition was critical. For 12 days my body was kept in this coma in the hope that my lungs might repair themselves. No guarantees were offered by the doctors that I would survive.

During this time, I would have another experience. Somehow I seemed to awaken within my coma. I found I was floating in colours. At first the colours were dark, menacing; there was pain, excruciating beyond anything I had ever known. I succumbed to this intense pain, and slipped into blackness. At some point I again became aware of being conscious within myself; any discomfort was now gone. Surrounding me at this point was the most beautiful vision of vivid colours, comprised of glowing pale gold, deep yellows and oranges. Brilliant beyond belief, these colours were shining into me and were also very calming. Within this state came the realization that I was without a body, shape or form. I was pure consciousness; effectively, everything that is actually ME: the inner me. At the same time came the recognition that I had separated from my own ego. There were no judgemental thoughts, fears or other detrimental dictates that the ego seems to drag along with itself.

At some point, without warning, my consciousness was whisked through a sort of kaleidoscope, consisting of hundreds of thousands of penetrating vibrant colours. Well beyond what we can perceive in this realm, the colours were now swirling me through their very essence, creating detailed patterns and shapes. My mind's eye could move in microscopically close, to view tiny details of each intricate pattern and colour as they formed, or could move away to see the overall pattern much like that of a mathematically constructed, computer-generated design. Each complex arrangement seemed alive; also three-dimensional. Each carried its own vibration; its own personal frequency. As well as this, there was music that seemed to me to be the perfect harmonic blend of a million voices, instruments and melodies; it penetrated the colours and me. I knew that, for some reason beyond my understanding at the time, I was being held within this beautiful realm for a purpose, but I didn't know what that reason might be, nor did I even care. I found I was unquestionably content in this unusual situation.

During my time in this indefinable realm, I did not see or interact with any religious figures, relatives or friends who have passed on. However, I did, at some point, come to the realization that I was being held or cradled by the very essence that created me; every cell of my body seemed to know this, much like an infant's awareness of being in its mother's arms. I *KNEW* without reservation this was my Creator; *this* was God. This parental energy was now holding the essence of *Me.* It was bathing me in the warmth of total unconditional love and an understanding of my being, certainly far beyond anything I had ever experienced. It was as if my soul was being stroked with what felt like a warm, loving, tender caress, by an unseen hand. As this happened, it was imparted to me to *stop thinking; just stop thinking – just BE.* How profoundly simple this was to do. As I did so, the colours melted away; I was now out in a vast realm of stars and galaxies extending into the forever-ness of a darkened universe. These celestial points of light were actually what I intrinsically knew to be the essence of living souls. I could feel them; feel every soul that had ever existed, exists now or will exist in the future. Myself as pure consciousness expanded out to meet and become one with all of this cosmic energy. I could feel the connectedness of *all* souls and the oneness of all with this great loving Creator. The realization of our connectedness resonated through me with full force. I also came to understand that nothing is hidden or tucked away from the universe; all is seen, all is known.

There was a filling up inside my soul of what I feel was complete universal knowledge. Understanding the universe now seemed so simple; it was as if I naturally knew all the answers to life itself. I saw that Love was at the centre of every answer. I also somehow knew that, by letting go in trust, a symbiotic flow would occur, bringing the ability to co-create in harmony and beauty with the force of this universe – our Creator – using this energy called Love. There was also the realization that how much or how little of one's self one puts into this process is what is then given back to the universe. That is how the universe operates. It was an amazing experience, beyond my ability to describe in full, yet one that garnered me many new insights; ones that I am sure to be processing for the rest of my life.

When I first became conscious in human form again, my mind instantly turned around inside myself to go back, as I so desperately wanted to return to where I had just been. But the wall to the other realm had closed; I was back in this world completely. While I was in my NDE, there was only this new realm I had found myself within; nothing else. I had lost the memory that I had ever occupied a physical body. I (guiltily admit) that I had also lost all remembrance of family, friends and loved ones.

Soon after coming back to the real world, I found that the promise made to me about my dog had been kept. After a long and harrowing midnight search by family members along that busy highway, where my accident had occurred, my precious black dog, in the black of night, was found safe and sound. God had kept him under His protection against great odds of being killed.

While I was still in the hospital waiting until I was strong enough to be discharged, a very interesting and strange occurrence took place. I was not on any medications or drugs that might have altered my mind; I was totally conscious as this incident took place in real time. From my bed, a flash of something caught my eye across the room. Looking over at the wall, I saw a strange flash of images that was playing out against the wall, much like a fast-moving silent film. It was a misty projection of people and events that were all interacting, then intertwining or overlapping with one another. Each action had an influence on the next. There was some sort of order to it all, but I didn't fully understand what I was actually watching. I saw that everyone was making choices about their lives, and those choices had effects on and were interweaving with others, who were also making choices in their own lives. I saw centuries of these cause-and-effect choices and actions; they were being interlaced within the history of time, one after the other; all of this happening since the beginning of creation. Then, at some point, while watching this admittedly bizarre vision on the wall, I saw images that were from my own lifetime. I was viewing my parents, then me, then anyone I had ever had contact with, and all these daily choices of life – both big and small – were intertwining and weaving until, finally, it came up to present day. Suddenly this hazy ethereal vision seemed to come off the wall and I watched as it bridged the span from wall to bed, where it was absorbed with a gentle soft *whoosh* into my chest. Immediately, I knew that I was precisely where I was supposed to be in the scheme of life itself. Life had woven itself into that moment; all was perfect! I realized that every choice made intertwines with everything else to make life what it is, no matter what those choices have been.

Yet my most transforming experience was yet to come. After a night or two back home, I was helped to my room to sleep and had a full night of intense dreams. I can honestly say this was far more real than any experience I have ever had, except for the recent NDE. Inside this dream I was in an operating room. I could see nothing, as everything was a deep impenetrable sapphire blue. However, with my mind's eye, I could perceive I was on an operating table and around me were several doctors. I was told that there was a procedure that must be done. I thought, *I don't understand.* Was I to have an operation of some sort? Everyone seemed incredibly expectant. I knew I was actually asleep in my room at home, so what the heck was happening now? There were several moments of silent anticipation and anxiety on my part. Then, following the gaze of where I knew the doctors to be looking, which was somewhere up above us, I observed a wisp of smoke drifting downwards. Softly, it swirled and very tenderly entered my body between my breasts. Quite suddenly, I was transported above myself and then came the realization that I was now viewing myself as I am seen from the eyes of my Creator. I was filled with such unconditional love for this form below me; this form that I had lived within my whole life. Yet in what must have been a fraction of a second, as soon as I experienced this unconditional love, I was back within my physical form again. Slowly, I felt arms encircle my body in a loving embrace. Immediately came the recognition that these were my own arms; and I was now loving myself the way I had just experienced being loved by God. I woke up and found I was sitting upright in bed, tears streaming down my cheeks.

I had been operated on not to take something out, but to put something in. I had just been given a beautiful gift – it was the gift of self-love!

Back in my daily life, I found that life was very different for me. Even though I had not had time to process much of my fascinating and quite inexplicable experiences, I did know that something very profound had happened. All of these experiences, I conjectured, had been tailored to fit my own personal way of processing and understanding. Also, as the days, weeks, months and years went by, I was slowly absorbing the deeper meanings of my experiences. I also came to realize that, just because one might be blessed enough to have what the world deems an NDE, it doesn't mean all one's problems are solved, that there is enlightenment or that one's understanding of life is complete, even though I now knew it to be there somewhere deep within my consciousness.

Like many other NDErs, I had a difficult time adjusting to being back within the daily life of the world. For some time, I could still discern a separation between my ego and my "self"; they had not yet merged back together. I seemed to have a foothold in both worlds for quite some time. I was me, yet I now knew, without a doubt, that I was so much more than just the physical body.

Slowly, of course, my daily life became clearer and the other realm I had experienced grew dimmer, yet something was intrinsically different within my inner being. I was thrust headlong into a new way of seeing this life. I knew without a doubt that we really do exist beyond these earthly shapes we inhabit for only so long; that what we have here is only a small part of what we will have and know *there!* I came to understand that what we are here (in our heart and soul), we take with us there when we cross to the other side; when we pass away. We *are* the sum total of that which we hold in our hearts. I learned also that my gift of self-love was not an ongoing self-perpetuating gift. It is a gift that I must accept daily if it is to be of value and worth. I had long hidden from others in my life my perceived lack of self-worth; I had actually spent a lifetime doing just that. Yet now I can feel daily how very much I am loved. It is sort of like having a life preserver around my soul. There are occasions when I may slip under with my own thoughts of self-deprecation, yet never as far or for as long as I have done in the past.

Somewhere within my experience the choice was given to me to accept all of this as genuine or not. With the choice of accepting the realness of what I experienced came the knowing that my life would forever be changed; changed because of the love I had been given, felt and accepted. Imparted to me also was the knowing that I would be loved just the same whatever decision I made. I realized that next to our precious gift of life, the gift of choice or free will is the next greatest one given to us. So, in a heartbeat, my decision was made. And, yes, my life truly has been transformed beyond what I might have ever imagined. It is still the same on the outside for the most part: same husband, same job, same friends, etc. Now, however, I have a new way of perceiving, and a new way of living: there is a new me. My life today is an ongoing relationship with a Creator that is no longer an imaginary force "out there" somewhere. It is an invisible relationship with the vibration of life itself, here in every moment of my life.

I have become more aware of my inner thoughts and the impact that even small ones have on the universe. Every thought ripples out; it is seen and felt. There are truly no hiding places for anything. So, this changes what I think; it also brings more awareness to the choices I make. I know that where I am in life now is a direct result of all my choices made within the circumstances I have gone through, as well as the choices made by others. I may not have had control over many of the circumstances in my life, but I have come to realize I DO have a choice over my own thoughts and feelings toward them. These are then woven together by God to make the tapestry of life. What came to me as well was the understanding that the higher the choices made, the more beautiful the tapestry of life that is woven.

Through my NDE experience I learned that I am loved totally and completely; not because of anything I have done, or not done, but simply because I exist. No conditions come attached to receiving this love, no matter what I hold to be my shortcomings or failings in life. My lessons included knowing I am truly a worthwhile human; and I do indeed have purpose in the universe. I was also taught that if I could learn to love others in the way I have been shown how much I was loved, my earthly life will unfold as it should: in the fullness of what I can be and give. I realized that it is truly the utmost of what a human can strive to do. Our life and how we live it becomes our gift back to God.

So many of what I had considered to be major priorities in my life have changed. Also, relationships with not only loved ones but even those I know casually have become more sacred to me. I see and experience the miracles that being present in the here and now are offering up to all of us. I see miracles where before I only saw a commonplace life; one that was too caught up in regrets of the past or worries about the future.

The first half of my life was centred on me: my career, my thoughts of a family, marriage, etc. After my experience, came the desire to serve somehow. What was to be my calling? I anguished over this for quite some time until, one day, during meditation and prayer I received my answer. My heart knew that I could only keep the gifts I had been given by giving them away. I also knew that I need not travel far or wide to find my calling; I could serve wherever I might stand. Within my daily life I could give love away even in the smallest of gestures: a smile to an unknown passer-by: holding a door open for an older lady struggling with her bundles; telling someone how much their friendship means to me; or expressing gratitude for the little butterfly on the flower outside my doorstep in the morning sun. Whatever is done, whether it is great or small, I know that what truly counts is only that it must be done with love, and by the amount of love put into it will the act be measured by God.

I share with others now in whatever ways I can do so, because all of this is so much bigger than what I can contain inside me. I know how many others are out there in the world who have held themselves in little esteem, holding onto feelings of being unlovable, for whatever reasons. Though many lead a life that, on the outside, is well and good in appearance, once alone they find it hard to love what they see in the mirror. I know, as I too was such a person.

The true journey of understanding our purpose in life, or of life itself, is not out there in a world seemingly obsessed with the outer trappings that build a false sense of self-worth and meaning. It is inside one's own heart, where this marvellous journey begins and ends. A journey that, when undertaken with true desire, will – like no journey ever before – take the traveller to a true discovery of who they are and what they mean to the Creator.

The lessons we learn here will most certainly be used in full when the time to leave this earthly playing field comes. *Because we do not die; we only go on to another way of living!*

I strongly feel that people need to know that what NDErs go through is very, very real. Yet whether one has had an NDE or not, I feel that there is a doorway of self-discovery waiting for each person on Earth; and one doesn't have to have an NDE to go through this always-open doorway. Also, I feel that each of us is spoken to in ways that we alone know how to understand and process. By learning not only about NDEs, but about other spiritual experiences as well, we can open the universal door just a bit further to learn about ourselves as a collective force of love, and about what is waiting for us in that love on the other side. If I had just one thing to tell anyone, it would be this: the journey you take inside of yourself will bear fruits much greater and sweeter than any taken without (outside of your own heart). You will be taking a magnificent journey to discovery of self-love; the Creator; and, the journey to our true home. With compassion and love shared between us all, we can help each other to do just that.

As spiritual teacher Ram Dass so beautifully put it, "We are all just walking each other home." Ah yes! What a home indeed!

This is another powerful experience that demonstrates the shift of consciousness that so many NDErs describe. What is particularly intriguing to me is that when Deirdre was recovering she had another vision, while very much awake and not under the influence of any medication. This appeared to be similar to a life review, and communicated to Deirdre the interconnectivity of everything in life.

Deirdre also described very intense dreams in which she felt reconnected to that state of consciousness. Interestingly, she described how she felt deeply loved and how this enabled her to feel self-love. This was when she woke up with her arms around herself. Kelly, too, described waking up with her arms around her body as she came out of her NDE experience, and she also felt self-love was previously lacking in her life.

Deirdre mentioned that previous events in both her childhood and her adult life had driven her away from God and made her feel unworthy of love, yet her experience totally turned this around. One of the biggest transformations she describes is a new way of perceiving things. Again, we could all benefit from doing this. Through personal transformation and renewed self-love, despite having reservations about being considered crazy, Deirdre now shares her message so that others, too, can be inspired to remember self-love.

13

THE CONNECTION

Erica McKenzie first became aware of Kelly and her vision via Robert Tremblay who features in this book, and Kelly simultaneously had become aware of Erica and her work through Amit Kainth, the presenter of a TV show by the same name. Kelly had been interviewed about her NDE on an episode called "Seven Steps to Heaven" and Erica had also been asked to appear on one of Amit's shows to talk about her NDE; he thus suggested that the two of them connect. Erica is a registered general nurse and was very receptive to unusual experiences from a young age. She hid a lifelong battle with body image and addiction until this ended in 2002, when she had an NDE that changed her life forever. Since having her NDE, Erica has worked with the States of Consciousness Research Team at Johns Hopkins University School of Medicine Medical/Neurology/Psychiatry and

Behavioral Sciences Department, where she is currently serving as the ambassador for their new anonymous, web-based survey study regarding near-death or other non-ordinary experiences that have fundamentally altered the public's beliefs or understanding about death and dying. She has also featured in multiple media articles and speaks extensively at conferences around the world.

We come into this world to find our way home. We are spiritual beings having a human experience. In fact, this is Earth school and we are here to learn. How do I know? Prior to my NDE, I recall my first Earth lesson. I was in kindergarten when my teacher punished me severely for being left-handed. As this event took place, I was desperately trying to make sense of why something so horrible was happening to me. The teacher's treatment made me feel different from my peers and, instantly, my heart flooded with the pain of separation. I heard a voice that clearly wasn't coming from anyone in my presence. The voice told me that it had created me and would always be with me because it loved me.

I looked around the room at my classmates and heard the voice tell me it had made them and loved them too. I received the knowledge from the voice that we were all unique; it was part of an important plan and love was the answer. At once, this love began to fill my entire being, like a life force. It circulated through me to each of my peers and back to me. We were all surrounded by it. This love was a connection so powerful I wanted it to last forever. In that moment, I realized where the voice was coming from – it was what I call God. The name didn't seem important; it was the connection that we had that was important. From that day forward, God and I were connected.

This connection opened the door to a life filled with a multitude of non-ordinary spiritual experiences that included encounters with the Divine, unexplained phenomena and the ability to communicate with the afterlife; each was accompanied by a lesson.

Growing up, I could feel this "love connection" between myself and my peers, and I realized how important it was. When I reached middle school, it seemed that many of the children who had once loved and accepted each other became spiteful and judgemental. They bullied me and others, excluding us for being different. At first, I felt compelled to try to change the way people were treating us, but the more I tried to help, the more my attempts failed. The bullying became so exhausting that eventually it deeply changed my ability to love and accept my unique self. I came to the conclusion that changing myself to fit in was the only answer. I began bingeing and purging my food – a dirty little secret that would last for 12 years.

Fresh out of medical school, I was introduced to the diet drug cocktail, Fen-Phen. As a nurse, I knew that the recommended maximum time to take the drug under doctor's supervision was three months. I also knew that the drug was a class-four narcotic and I understood its dangerous effects. However, despite this knowledge, I chose to replace my bulimia addiction with an addiction to this deadly cocktail. I took the drug for nearly nine years.

On 1 October 2002, I remember taking my last breath and being surprised that there was no pain. In fact, no longer bound by gravitational forces, my soul rose to the ceiling as it separated from my earthly body, which had collapsed to the floor, completely lifeless. The ceiling gave way and I quickly found myself in a tunnel filled with the energy frequency of love and light. I appeared to be on a highway leading to another dimension. I was a spirit vehicle, travelling at supersonic speed.

It seemed as though I went past the stars before I finally reached the end of the tunnel. As I floated around with infinite energy, I became aware of the fact that this was partially because there was no gravity. Human words cannot precisely describe the feeling that permeated each cell in my body, with more love than imaginable.

I was delivered into the hands of God. Immediately, I was aware that Heaven was right behind me. I was surrounded by its frequency field, and the most supreme love emanating from this place. God and I began to communicate telepathically, and instantly I recognized this voice. It was the voice I had heard that day in the kindergarten and throughout my life subsequently. God told me to look and, when I did, the stars parted ... and the life review of Erica McKenzie began.

As my life review came to an end, God turned to me and handed me a pair of spectacles. Once I got them on my face, God told me to look once more. The stars drew back like a curtain and a second life review began. For the first time in my life, I could see! I was blown away. This time I did not see the things I had seen in the first life review. Throughout both, I had a thought or reaction to an event in my life, then God answered it without judgement and filled me with unlimited knowledge of the universe.

On Earth I had been judged by people for my appearance. People were always concerned with the way I looked, and I could never escape the pressure of society's expectations. I thought about my first Earth lesson as a human. God's love flowed through me, like it had that day in school. It altered my energy frequency, eliminating all thoughts and feelings of judgement and disappointment. I never wanted to be separated from God again. I knew that I was finally *Home.*

Together, God and I shared a multitude of lessons: "The Rippling Effect", "The Gifts", "Eternal life", "Free Will" and the "New Earth", to name a few. As each lesson unfolded, I was filled with more Divine knowledge than imaginable and understood how crucial it was to share this knowledge with others.

When my lessons with God came to an end, we turned toward Heaven. I was blown away at the exceptional sight in front of me. It was miraculous, because Heaven was a golden planet. I felt connected to this sacred realm. It was so enormous that Earth appeared as a tiny speck of sand in comparison.

I began to run toward Heaven and never considered returning to Earth. I heard God's voice once more as he told me that until I learned to *love my unique self, I would be unable to complete my earthly mission.* Upon leaving Planet Heaven, God bestowed two more gifts on me. He gave me the gift of knowledge and the gift of wisdom. As I stood in the presence of God, I felt the top of my head open up and drank the Divine knowledge and wisdom being telepathically downloaded to me in enormous volumes.

Upon completion of this process, God told me He was sending me back for two reasons. First, my mission had just begun, and second, He reminded me that I worked for Him. He went on to share that, upon returning to Earth, I was to be quiet and listen to those who were put into my life. Then I would take this patience, beauty, new-found knowledge and wisdom, and speak to millions of people, whose lives would be changed. I felt compelled to argue my case to stay on Planet Heaven, but before I could, I felt myself being placed into a tunnel of total darkness. This tunnel was my vehicle back to Earth and my connection to God was what sustained me. I have no idea how long I was travelling in this tunnel before I came to a stop, finding myself at the Edge of Hell. This was the only time during my experience that I couldn't feel my Divine connection. I was beyond terrified. I can't articulate the degree of sheer terror I felt as a sense of helplessness paralysed me. The only thing I could do was to cry out telepathically, "Help me, God! Why am I here? Please help me! I was told I was here to learn." When my lessons were finished, I was returned to the dark tunnel, my vehicle back to Earth.

Connected to my Creator once more, I began my descent as I penetrated the Earth's gravitational frequency field. I felt an enormous magnet on my back that shoved me into my lifeless and primitive human body. I had zero access to my once highly developed blueprint of knowledge and scientific abilities. My body felt heavy, bound by the gravitational forces, and I had no energy. I felt confined and suppressed by all the feelings attached to my now sick and exhausted body, which conflicted with my spiritual one.

This was an enormous let-down from the Divine vastness of living as an immortal spirit with access to Divine truth that I had just experienced on Planet Heaven. In Heaven, I had lived as a multidimensional being with unlimited access to everything needed to sustain eternal life. I was home and in God's presence, only to be forced back into the stark reality of a limited-dimensional body of consciousness that would come with a multitude of physiological, social and environmental challenges. How could I fathom going back to that?

As I regained consciousness, my husband was sitting at my side. I was angry. The emotions and thoughts of my journey completely overwhelmed me. I tried to speak to my husband, explaining where I had been. But I didn't have a voice!

At this point, I only remember floating in and out of consciousness, unable to recall how much time had passed. I was quite ill, desperately in need of care, support and detox treatment. I needed to detox my body, mind and spirit from the numerous years I had binged and purged food while abusing drugs. I additionally needed healing from the physiological damage it had caused me.

I was desperately trying to make sense of the events that had unfolded, when my attending physician walked into my hospital room. I felt like I was going to throw up but realized that my nausea was my voice coming out of me as I described my NDE. However, as I tried to share this experience with my physician, I was medicated and involuntarily committed to a psychiatric ward. The doctor allowed his personal feelings to dictate his plan of care for me. Disregarding my physiological complications, he refused to listen. Instead, he completely dismissed me, diagnosing my trip to Planet Heaven and Hell, and my lessons with God, as psychosis instead of an NDE. Therefore, against my will, he implemented plans to transfer me to an inpatient out-of-state psychiatric hospital in an effort to treat me.

Looking back now, I find myself reflecting on the time I spent on a psychiatric ward as a nursing student, years prior to my NDE. I was told the patients were crazy and that medication was the treatment of choice. Yet several of those patients appeared to have an ability to communicate with something most people couldn't see. I thought about my own ability to communicate with the afterlife, which had begun as a child before I allowed myself to stifle that gift. I had believed that, in doing so, I would be embraced and accepted by others. Yet, here I was, years later, as a patient in the exact same position as some of those patients, being disregarded and medicated because I had an experience the doctor couldn't explain.

I realized through my own experience that patients need to be supported by an educated, empathetic and caring staff who embraces the reality of their experiences. I sensed that the drugs prescribed affected the ability of several of the patients to think clearly. Such drugs were changing these patients, and seemed to sever their ability to communicate with our Creator. This prevented them from accessing the transformational physiological rewiring process needed for total healing.

My NDE profoundly altered the course of my life. Having been both a nurse and a patient, I was clearly able to see how broken our healthcare system was. I identified the desperate need for education regarding the NDE and other non-ordinary phenomena. It is imperative that a healing protocol addresses the needs of body, mind and spirit.

As I reflect on the past 45 years of my life, I realize that the accumulation of my life experiences, the events which occurred during my NDE, and those that led to my death, began with my lesson in kindergarten. My trips to Heaven, Hell and the psychiatric ward were preparing me to help to give others a voice and create transformational healing in their lives. That being said, I could only begin to carry out the mission that God had designed for me after I healed myself.

I wish I could say that upon returning to my lifeless physical body I was healed in human medical terms. However, this is not what happened. It became apparent that my involuntary commitment to the psychiatric hospital for attempting to share my NDE was the reality check I needed to help me get real with myself: to become courageous, take full responsibility for my life and stop denying my capabilities.

My NDE enabled me to heal my eternal and spiritual self. I quickly realized that it wasn't productive to expect doctors, or anyone else for that matter, to know what was best for me, as this is Earth school – where we learn. Learning is different for each of us, and that is why "the work" is different for us all. Over time, I forgave both myself and anyone else who I felt had caused hurt in my life. I was able to achieve this due to the lessons I learned in Heaven, Hell and the in-between. I had to learn to survive and break the barrier of prescribed medical treatment, where I was assumed to be making progress only when I denied my Divine experience to my healthcare providers.

One of the most important lessons I learned was that our uniqueness is our value. Our value is our contribution here on this earthly journey. In addition, it is important to be quiet and listen to the people that come into our lives. At times, I feel it can be a challenge to do the personal "work" necessary to embrace these lessons, and sometimes we may even find ourselves scratching our heads searching for the purpose of such a task. However, if we choose to embrace this knowledge with the understanding that, in fact, these lessons apply to each of us, we are blessed with a multitude of learning opportunities that have the potential to create an outcome of Divine healing. Several of these opportunities come from some of our most unexpected teachers and can become our greatest gifts, so we must be mindful of replacing judgement with love.

While I don't have all the answers, I do know that we are here to learn to love ourselves and others, and that while residing on this planet we have the ability to learn. It's imperative that we embrace and empower each other as we work together in life.

My NDE instigated a deep personal change. I knew that I could no longer look to others for my value and wonder what people speculate about me. I had to refuse to let such feelings define me. Having feelings of ambiguity is actually ... okay. I have learned to acknowledge these, using them as tools that help me to trust there is nothing I can't get through. I have faith that God is at work in my life. He has all the answers so I don't have to come up with solutions. This helps me to be free to focus on my responsibility to be present for life's changes; not to try to control them, but to embrace them instead. I have finally found the courage to start listening to my feelings, intuition and God. I use these as a motivation for creating a healthy life. This is how my true "work" began.

When you read some of the challenging life experiences I've had, you may notice they all involve change, choices and exposing my flaws, imperfections and mistakes. Looking back now, I am confident that these experiences were not mistakes, but opportunities for learning. They originated – at different times in my life – as cancer, eating disorders, drug addiction, peer pressure, bullying, learning disabilities, endometriosis, early menopause, a career, being a parent, feeling judged and unaccepted, loneliness, heartache, anger, depression, challenging relationships, uncertainty, frustration, poor health, an NDE and more. From time to time, these experiences were mind-boggling and potential roadblocks.

Because of my NDE, I have become cognizant of the fact that these *potential roadblocks* are incredible learning opportunities. If I shift my perception of these experiences by implementing action (by embracing the lesson in each experience), they will never manifest themselves as roadblocks. Rather, they display an alternative for me to choose to change something that will result in powerful healing and awakening, bringing to light a profound personal transformation.

When I searched for the lessons in the experiences I went through, I found myself often thinking about my NDE. One of the most important messages I received then was that *your uniqueness is your value and your value is your contribution on this earthly journey.* It doesn't matter who you are or who you aren't. If you are here on this planet, *you are valuable!*

Through our connection with our Creator, we can heal our body, mind and spirit. We can grow our gifts and use them in the scope for which they were designed, and as we connect with God, we take our gifts to a whole new level. It is through this love that we will be able to accomplish this. I have come to appreciate the significance of this knowledge because now I finally understand that my uniqueness is my value, since it holds my unique blueprint and unique gifts that serve truly to fulfil my life's purpose. In fact, it is who I am and what it means to be me. The mind is an incredibly powerful resource, and the knowledge that dwells there is Divine power. If we choose, we can unlock the answers to our questions by looking within and reconnecting to God through our hearts. I understand it is through connection with our Creator that we remember who we are, and through this connection we can grow and cultivate unconditional love for ourselves.

This *unconditional love is the key* to light the power within. When we seek that power, we gain the knowledge needed to help us through every life experience, and we reveal our vital blueprint and gifts. Our blueprint is unique and by design: we are spiritual beings having a human experience. Any boundaries that may try to define our authentic life truly can't touch us when we choose to live without fear. We are also able to see that we can overcome all fundamental human limitations through our connection with our Creator. Additionally, we can access knowledge needed to overcome and heal ourselves from everything we face, no matter how challenging or unimaginable it may seem. We can surmount challenges, grow and become fearless because our blueprint contains the most crucial information needed for us fully to embrace change and achieve total health and wellness. We can acquire the knowledge needed to help us heal from our challenging life experiences.

I can honestly look back and say that I'm glad I was hospitalized against my will, since it meant I could experience the state of our healthcare system through the lesson of having been committed. It prepared me to see first-hand how damaged the system is and how it affects patients; I could then help change the healthcare protocol and support people, assisting them to become self-advocates. These experiences clearly disclose that there is a lack of knowledge regarding non-ordinary experiences and phenomena. From a medical professional standpoint, I'm determined to educate the public and healthcare community regarding NDEs and other non-ordinary experiences. In addition, I'm focused on raising awareness of spiritual crisis and the transformative potential of trauma within the field of psychiatry. This would enable individuals to become empowered to grow and heal from such experiences, not be repressed and pathologized. The presence of God and our ability to connect with our Creator is a miracle, not a medical issue. In fact, these experiences provide great healing for people, humanity and our planet.

My mission is to encourage people who have had related experiences to talk about them, because when you take a story, an experience that someone's had, and embrace it, using it as a learning opportunity, it has the potential to become a powerful tool of healing and awakening. Since sharing my story, people have been contacting me from all over the world with questions; many have graciously opened their hearts to me, sharing their own experiences and how it's changed their lives. I've been investigating these experiences by conducting personal interviews with experiencers and collaborating with experts who through their research are providing proof that these experiences are real, such as Roland Griffiths, PhD, from Johns Hopkins University School of Medicine, and Dr Claude Swanson, MIT/Princeton University physicist. Personally, I have been researching these non-ordinary phenomena for 15 years. My goal is to share these stories with the public regarding spiritually transformational experiences and other non-ordinary experiences, revealing the power of healing through the investigative television series that I wrote and now host. Through the show, my work with experts has taken me across the globe seeking answers to questions such as: are we connected? My journey reveals extraordinary stories of spiritually transformational experiences and other non-ordinary experiences as I explore on the show controversial phenomena and their after-effects. My experience of being allowed to visit the other side, bringing back lessons including powerful knowledge of a consciousness-based blueprint, teaches us how we can overcome any obstacles, which results in total healing and awakening in our lives. The show covers profound topics, with leading experts in science and medicine providing evidence that validates extraordinary experiences such as NDEs, shared death experiences, after-death communication, reincarnation, out-of-body experiences, premonitions, dreams, visitations, signs, messages, and how after-life phenomena are potentially changing how we view life and death, paving the way for humanity to take the next step into conscious evolution. Through the show, it is my hope to bring light, love and knowledge to viewers, so that all may feel and know that they are not alone but loved unconditionally the way they are meant to be – each one of us as our unique self. Knowledge is power.

Erica's experience has had a profound effect on the way she views and deals with life's challenges. Her new perspective has resulted in a deeper understanding of any challenges, and an ability to face them and embrace them as learning opportunities.

It always intrigues me how other nurses or healthcare workers are changed after their NDE. I was particularly interested in how Erica's views changed after she became a patient and how her experience revealed to her flaws in the medical system that must be drastically improved. She described receiving a download of knowledge and wisdom, and she is putting that to use in her work of sharing her experience and educating others about these experiences. Erica is very aware of the lack of knowledge concerning these experiences within the healthcare system and is striving to introduce them into the education of all healthcare workers.

What I found shocking about Erica's experience is that her NDE was misdiagnosed as a psychosis and she was transferred to a psychiatric hospital where drugs were administered to suppress the experience. This highlights a great misunderstanding in our current medical systems where doctors, nurses and other healthcare workers are not educated about NDEs and other spiritual experiences, resulting in a lack of psychological support for those undergoing them.

14

THE VORTEX CHILD

Kelly connected with 44-year-old Katherine Baldwin via social media. She lives in Melbourne, Australia, and was only 3 years old when she had her first NDE – one that greatly influenced her life, from such an early age. Later in life, Katherine had a second NDE, which also significantly impacted on her life.

I was only 3 years of age when I had my first NDE. I have no memory at all of my short life before the day I drowned. However, I remember every day since, clearly and profoundly.

It was a typical hot summer's day in Australia, one of those days when the sun beats down intensely and there is no cool wind in the air. My family were all having fun in my grandma's swimming pool, playing with a beach ball while laughing and joking with one another. My 5-year-old brother and I were in the pool, playing in a blow-up canoe.

The beach ball suddenly bounced up over the side of the pool, and my mum and dad both got out to grab it. In that split second, our canoe tipped over with quite a force. It happened incredibly fast and within a second I was under the water, totally upside down. My brother managed to swim to the surface and tried desperately to rescue me, but no matter how hard he tried, he couldn't pull me to the surface.

I know this may sound strange, but I wasn't scared at all; it was like I was just observing and feeling what was happening. I could see the sun rippling on the water, hear the voices and laughter of my family as I sunk to the bottom. I couldn't feel any pain and I had no fear whatsoever. It was a total surrender; a letting go until everything went totally quiet and then black. All of a sudden, an amazing peace washed over me and everything started to change around me. The darkness very quickly turned to a bright light, which felt so soothing and tranquil. The light was not just light, it was what I would now see as a moving energy all around me, swirling and moving about. I became as light as the light itself and felt an amazing rush, as I lifted off and floated through this exquisite energy. This felt totally different to where I had just come from.

I started to regain focus as I moved further and further away from where I had been. No longer was I back in the pool; I was looking down watching my brother. He was scared, trying to pull me up by my ponytail, while yelling for help. Thankfully my mum heard my brother's cries. She screamed and pointed as my dad ran over and pulled my lifeless body out of the pool and placed me on the floor to resuscitate me.

My family had no idea about the incredible experience I was having, and that it would change my life forever. I was once again immersed in the white, euphoric energy of light, when there before me stood the most beautiful, white, angelic, feminine figure. She was gentle and yet had tremendous power; she was peace. Well, that's how I would describe her energy. I had never experienced such love. I now know her as one of my main guides, Geraldine.

She held out her arms and wrapped me in love and peace. She then spoke with a mesmerizing voice, "Would you like to go back there or come back home?" I looked up into her white face and thought for a moment about what she was asking me. I nodded and said, "I'll go back." "Are you sure?" she asked. I was excited to go back to my family! "Yes! I'm ready!" I received a deep hug and the next thing I knew I was coughing, and back in my body gasping for air! I was alive! Cold and wet, but I was alive.

Since that day nothing has been the same. At the age of 3, my soul had been awakened and I had all this knowledge and wisdom that other children of my age did not have. I was now awake and had the realization that we are all one, all connected. I knew who I was. I knew that the place where I was hugged by Geraldine was my real longstanding home. I knew that life on Earth was short, and I was eternal. I knew that no matter what others did to me, they could not take that away from me.

As my confidence grew and I spent more time with the universe, it became very clear to me that every animal, person, plant – everything – was from the same place. The strength and love that comes from loving all others, from understanding we are not alone, that we are all endless and magnificent, was very comforting to me. To see every leaf on a tree, the patterns in colours, people's auras and the energy inside them, was so special. I would spend my days, just as I do now, seeing and talking to spirits, such as my passed grandmother, as if they were still alive. I started to sing every day. My beautiful, caring mum put me in a singing academy so I could express myself and learn to sing. I felt I could do anything! I started meditating and spending time with the universe. I was lucky to have such wonderful parents; they knew I was different, but loved me anyway. My mum was always telling me I was beautiful and wonderful.

A year on from my childhood spiritual awakening, life was about to get very difficult. My mum and dad had to start working two day-jobs to make ends meet, like most Australian families did. I had to spend a lot of time at my grandparents' house. My grandmother was a schizophrenic who was very tough to live with; I had to use my skills to avoid her discipline the best I could. Then there was Pop. He was an extremely mentally ill man who got away with much more than he should have. I had to protect myself while staying there. I would often run away from my grandparents. I would hide under my nan's bed to get away from her, sometimes for five hours at a time. I would just fall asleep under the bed. I made sure that I never ever talked back, and I stayed as quiet as I could. I only spoke when I was spoken to. I hated it. Thankfully, no matter what my grandparents did, I never let them stop me from knowing who I really was. This is something I don't feel I would have experienced without the NDE.

At the age of 9, it all got too much to cope with and I ran away to my aunt's house – she lived down the road. I refused to go back. Shortly after that, we moved to the country and I never had to stay at my grandparents' again.

I was finally free, but needed to heal and forgive them for all the terrible things they had done to me. At the age of 14, I turned to alcohol to numb the pain, and by the age of 19 I had quite a severe drinking problem. I decided it was time to stop drinking and start working on myself.

I was trying my best to stay and feel connected, which was difficult after everything I had been through. I needed time to learn who I was again. I left home and moved in with my partner at 21. I got married, as you do, working jobs that my heart wasn't in. I always wanted to help people, but didn't know how to. I had a good life, but knew there was something more for me; in my heart, I knew I was living someone else's life. I needed a wake-up call to shift me, but what!? Well, the universe took care of that!

When I was 26, out of the blue, I had a severe abdominal pain. My gallbladder ruptured inside me, due to a hereditary disease I didn't know about, and I was rushed to hospital. The doctors were having difficulty figuring out what had happened and delayed my care until it was almost too late to operate. This is where I had my second NDE while under anaesthetic.

I had emergency surgery and stopped breathing three times on the operating table; my heart also stopped beating. However, this time I did not go back to my spiritual home. I only remember seeing my body from the roof, watching as they tried to get my heart beating again. As I heard all the noises, beeps and yelling, and observed everyone hurrying around my body, suddenly a surge of emotion came over me, a feeling of "No way! It does not end like this! I have something more I need to do in this life." I felt like I rushed back into my body and I wanted to fight for my life!

I was in hospital for a month, still touch-and-go for much of that time, and the doctors were worried I wouldn't make it out of there. However, I fought hard and knew I could not give up. My body was weak, but my mind was strong. I knew I was no longer going anywhere. I had a mission to accomplish. This was my last life here on Earth and I had to try to make the most of it!

I went home trying to figure out my life, knowing there was something more I was here for. I just had to find it! I went back to practising meditation, as I had at the age of 3 and 10. I needed to find what made me happy again. After struggling with my marriage, I decided I had to change my life. At the age of 31, I left my husband so that I could start my life over again and rediscover the 3-year-old me that I had experienced after my first NDE.

It was then that I was introduced to a lovely man online named Jamie. The moment we met, I felt he was my soulmate. He looked and sounded just the way I'd envisaged such a soulmate to be; it was love at first sight, or should I say first type. He lived in Essex, in England. Interestingly, when I was a child I used to say that my husband would come from England and his name would be Jamie.

He was my rock. Finally I had met someone who understood me. Jamie listened as I explained everything I knew about the universe. I told him, day by day, everything that I was learning and discovering. We were a perfect match.

After the second NDE, my psychic abilities came back in full swing and I was feeling everything again so vividly. At the time, I worked as a manager for a cosmetic company, so many women would come to me to talk for hours and hours. A lot of the ladies I looked after were cancer patients who had lost their hair, and they would sit with me as I drew their eyebrows back on. They would often come back and tell me how much happier and more energized they felt after talking to me. It was then I realized I wasn't just talking to these beautiful women, I was healing them.

I went home and spent some time talking to Geraldine, along with my other spirit guides, and asked how I was healing these ladies with my voice. I was told it was two things: the tone in my voice has very strong healing qualities, plus the channelled words I spoke were so soothing that the women could not help but feel better. I could no longer ignore the truth. I took a leap of faith and quit my job.

I practised meditation and healing techniques every single day for about eight hours at a time. I guess you could compare it to a spiritual boot camp for myself. I also started working online for free, 30 hours a week as a medium, to advance my skills and learn as much as I could. I didn't just want to work in the spiritual field; I wanted to be one of the best there was, so that I could help as many as possible.

I was offered a job as a spiritual teacher and learned many different healing modalities. I was beyond a natural. I started seeing one-on-one clients of my own. It was then that my company, Angel Soul Healing, was born. I worked from home and at any centre I could. When I wasn't working, I was healing myself. The more I healed myself, the more I saw and experienced the source energy in all that I did. This magnificent pure energy of light flowed through every part of me. As I learned to love myself and feel the light inside me, it felt more fulfilling. I believe everyone has the right to feel this way: to experience that same oneness and loving Source that looked after me during my first NDE.

Learning from my team of guides helped me release all fear associated with spirituality. I met one of my main guides, and what a shock it was. The moment I saw her I was flashed back to the day we met during my first NDE; she was the one that hugged me! She was the one who gave me strength to keep going! I was so grateful to be shown that this whole experience was real and true, and not just a memory from a dream. She was Geraldine!

I knew I was on the right path; in fact, I was moving so fast that one day when I was channelling, I was taken back to that exquisite place where everything once more became peaceful and calm. I could see the fabric of time, I could see pure white light and the universe again. Every day subsequently I could feel the deep peace of the oneness; that all are worthy, all loveable and all have the same ability to be connected if we allow it, if we practise it. It was as though I were back in my NDE, although not having to die to reach it. I have remained in this peace to this very day. Being in this perfect bliss and never going back to the negative is what has enabled me to live the loving life of enlightenment that I have now reached.

A large part of my peace came from Jamie being so loving and supportive as we developed our online relationship and shared spiritual experiences together. I had so much love in my heart and it was during this blissful time that it was revealed to me that I was finally ready to meet my team of healing guides.

I started to meet guides such as Jesus and Quan Yin, and five of the archangels: Michael, Metatron, Gabriel, Uriel and Raphael. They all reported that they were part of my main team and that they needed to teach me a new form of healing. I looked these masters up online and was shocked that they wanted to work with me and were part of my team! I felt so blessed and knew this was my chance not to let the two NDE experiences I'd had go to waste. I realized I was starting to live the life of passion I was always meant to.

I channelled with these masters every single day. I began to share my energy with them as I was asked to surrender all that I was, allowing six to channel with me, then 15, then 30, and so on. I was not afraid of anything to do with the spiritual world and wanted to surrender my services to Source, the Divine oneness of the universe. I understood I now had everything within me to be the light. In just 12 months, I could now channel with over a million pure non-physical beings, just like I do in all the Vortex healing sessions. I am now what many call enlightened, living my life in the tenth dimension and beyond. The concentrated energy of the Source in my body is like a freight train; it never slows down.

It became very clear to me that all the clients who came to me were the same: loving human beings who wanted to feel better. I knew I had to live a pure life and practise everything I taught, always remaining authentic so that I continued to be a clear channel for source energy to work through me. I was sent the most unusual cases. I was given an astonishingly wide range of subconscious clients who needed to release negative patterns from their subconscious. People with multiple personalities; cancer patients; people with physical burns, mental health issues, deep fears or patterns that were affecting their lives deeply. This healing modality that was being channelled to me became the fastest and most effective modality I have ever used. As dis-ease is vibrational, if we can go deep within and get to the cause of the dis-ease in the subconscious, in the mind and body, it is possible to remove anything. Right?

I worked on all these amazing cases, and it became completely clear that every subconscious was just as rare and unique as the clients I was seeing. Think about it. Five people can all have the same experience, and experience it in five different ways! One person can see the positive and another a negative in that same experience. It all depends on what deep chords are struck from one or more of their prior experiences while growing up, while forming their subconscious threads. My team and I find and target the neurons in the brain and gently track them down to the subconscious threads, then remove them; we clear them and teach people how to unlearn all of their conditioning since birth. Then to live life from this new vantage point, and rebuild their new belief systems.

We don't have to have an NDE to become all we want to be; we don't have almost to die and go back to realize that everything we thought we knew about ourselves is untrue. The truth is, we all have what it takes. We were all worthy before we decided to incarnate here on this Earth. We are all completely worthy when we are born, no exceptions; completely worthy right now, no matter what we are going through. All the faults we think we have. We are all just unlearning the conditioning we learned along the way.

When we decided to come here, we knew that with every breath we took, our universe and our guides would receive the benefit of our life. We knew that, with all our discovering of who we are, the non-physical would gain the benefit even before we did. We all said, "Yes, I'll do that – I'll live and learn and do the best I can," so that the Source can become more. That's how giving we are, that's how special and kind-hearted we all are. That's how strong and full is the light that lives inside us. We just need to remember. We just need to forget all the rules and the limited beliefs that our families so unwittingly taught to us because, when we do remember, we realize we are unlimited. When we see who we really are, we shine. We shine the light for many, so that they too can reach for their inner light.

I continued learning this very technical physical healing. I asked how far it could go. Well, the universe answered again in a way I didn't expect. Just as I was about to buy my plane ticket to fly over and see Jamie, I was sideswiped by a drunk driver, the impact shattering my right foot. I needed reconstructive surgery and was told there was a high probability I would not walk again on my own. I was sent home for six months to rehabilitate as the doctors were not sure what to do to fix me. I was told that whether I would ever walk again depended on what happened during that six months. I healed my foot using subconscious Vortex healing for hours every day. I meditated from morning to night, rebuilding my bones, nerves and tendons. My toes started to move and I could feel the bones under my skin moving all by themselves.

After the six months were up, I went back to the hospital and, to the amazement of the doctor who saw me, it was clear I was going to walk again. The doctor said to me, "I don't know what you did, or how that happened? But whatever it is, keep doing it!" I knew then that anything would be possible with this healing process, and now I have an unstoppable belief in the modality for every client I'm guided to help.

Now that my business was booming and I was walking again, it was time to take my final leap of faith! To buy my plane ticket and be with my soulmate. After six years of talking to Jamie online, we finally met in person. It was love at first sight all over again. Jamie proposed the day before we went on a holiday to Paris, just four weeks after being together. We applied for a visa for Jamie and, after just two and a half hours, it was approved that same night. So we flew to Paris caught up in a whirlwind romance. We then flew back together to my home in Australia, 12 days later.

We were married six months later, and have now been working together at Angel Soul Healing for the past three years. Having built our own house and healing centre, we can finally live out our dream of helping millions of people become the light. A centre full of love where all different kinds of healing modalities are offered.

After my first NDE, I found out who I am. Through my second NDE, I found my life purpose. I now know what my job is here on Earth, and I will always find a way to live out this incredible purpose! I will share what I now know with anyone who is ready for help. My post-NDE vision and life mission is about bringing the light and love to millions. We are here to help make this world a better place for all living beings that walk this Earth. I am so excited to be living out this wonderful, pure, heartfelt dream.

That is why I am proud to be the CEO and founder of Angel Soul Healing, and honoured to be the creator of the internationally trademarked Vortex subconscious sound healing modality and to run our healing school. Our new products help people to reach greatness. I am thrilled to be able to channel with many ascended masters who have guided me through the material on the happy sticks. Every note, sound and vibration in this product was guided by them. I know that this new healing product we have produced is an easy-to-use tool and a key to help everyone in the comfort of their own home, to help them on the journey to be all they can be. The happy stick is the first of its kind. A new affirmation, meditation and healing USB product that can reach anyone all around the world who has access to a computer. The happy stick has been designed to help everyone from all walks of life!

The people of Melbourne have already embraced this incredible new healing tool. As we branch out across

Australia and the world, our dreams are now a reality. We are also excited to have brought out the first children's happy stick: the first children's product of its kind. After all, why wait till we are grown to heal? We should start with our greatest gift: our children. We look forward to many more innovations, like our new "I am" range and movement. We are enjoying the impact that our new products and services are having on women in our lives and in our community. We are all in this together and Jamie and I are making it our life mission to share this.

I believe that once we know the truth about who we are, we have a duty to share this knowledge to help all others see how magnificent they are. We all have a special purpose to become our own loving light. The world needs more love, and you are the key. Once we reach love or enlightenment, it's time to help others find theirs.

My heart and soul is so full of love for humanity and I wish to thank every single being, both physical and non-physical, for co-creating with me in this life, and I look forward to the day we are reunited in our eternal home.

It is apparent that Katherine's NDEs have had a profound impact on her life. The fact that her first NDE occurred at the age of 3 appears to have greatly influenced how her life developed afterwards, because she wasn't conflicted by the usual societal views that are instilled as we mature. This has subsequently given her the confidence to act on what she learned during her NDE and not be deterred by the views of others.

Katherine describes meditating and "spending time with the universe"; both unusual things for a young child to undertake voluntarily. Many young people are frequently discouraged by others once they begin opening up about their NDEs. Well-meaning relatives and friends often try to stifle attempts to talk about the NDE, but this doesn't appear to have happened with Katherine.

Interestingly, her second NDE was different and had a slightly different influence on her. The first NDE reinforced that she is more than just a body, while the second helped her find her purpose in life and serve others. She also describes how, after her second NDE, her psychic abilities were rejuvenated and enhanced. This is very common after an NDE.

She continues to connect with the guide she met during her first NDE and the guides she has met since. This may seem like a bold statement for Katherine to make, as there is no way to prove (or disprove) if such guides exist. However, Katherine obviously has helped many people with her healing work. Many other NDErs have reported encountering archetypal beings such as those described by Katherine. Katherine's ability to encounter archetypal beings after her NDE appears to have developed through her continued spiritual practice. The fact that she consciously used these techniques on herself and believes that she healed her own foot is also very important. This encompasses treating the whole person, not just the physical. I have met other people who likewise claim to have healed a physical injury after their NDE.

Scientifically, a lot of what Katherine has described is unverifiable. However, rather than ignore the therapeutic intervention she has developed, it would be beneficial to investigate it further through research trials. This might pave the way for some types of intervention being used in conjunction with modern medicine, to enhance healing and recovery from illness – and that would have wide-reaching benefits.

15

THE SHARED CROSSING PROJECT

The second email I received while staying at the College of Psychic Studies came from William Peters. We arranged a Skype chat and William described the wonderful work he has been doing with the shared death experience that transpired from his NDEs. Below is a summary of our conversation.

In 1979, William had a skiing accident that left him with severe injuries. While he was unconscious, he experienced his first NDE. William remarked how, on reflection, the NDE guided his life subconsciously from that point on. The accident occurred when William was moving at high speed and, on impact, felt propelled out of his body, rising higher and higher above the scene where he viewed the entire surrounding environment, then the whole of the American continent, the oceans and all other continents.

Simultaneously, he experienced an in-depth life review. From this he intuited how each of his actions had affected every person he had ever interacted with. While enveloped by a bright light, he realized that he had died, but he also felt that he had wasted his life. He begged to be sent back to life to finish his work. With a rush of energy, the whole process inverted and he watched his life review in reverse order, while feeling himself getting closer to the Earth. He re-entered his body and was terrified that he was paralysed. He pleaded with God (the light) not to be paralysed and felt sensation return to his body. However, the spinal injury he sustained meant that he could no longer be as physically active as he had once been. This left him feeling increasingly alienated and isolated from his free-spirited college friends.

When William graduated, he promised himself that he would work with those in need. His life's path took him all around the world. He worked as a Jesuit International Volunteer in Belize and Peru. While doing this work, he empathically felt the suffering of those he was helping and, as a result of this, he himself experienced trauma. When he returned home, he studied theology and philosophy in an attempt to understand all he had encountered. He went on to become a social worker in San Francisco, providing end-of-life support to those affected by AIDS.

After contracting a rare blood disorder in 1993, William had a second NDE. He again left his body, and this time could also hear the conversations of the nurses. He witnessed the doctor standing by his bed and asking him a question. Knowing he was much more than a physical body, William willed himself back into his human form. The process left him exhausted. William recovered, but in 1998 he experienced another significant event that would shape his future work. While attending to his dying grandmother, he witnessed her having an animated conversation with an unseen entity.

Shortly after, William became deeply depressed due to a foot injury that left him incapacitated. To counteract the depression William began meditating, and eventually his injury began to respond to surgery and physiotherapy. His meditation practice, and his grandmother's passing, helped him realize the importance of being fully present around death.

While working as a hospice volunteer, William encountered his first shared death experience. As William sat at the bedside of a dying man, he suddenly left his body and found himself face to face with this man, who was also out of his body.

William then had a series of mystical experiences while visiting John of God during his travels in Brazil. After this, William and his family settled in Santa Barbara, where he has worked as a family therapist ever since. While attending a workshop about death in 2009, William heard Dr Raymond Moody talk about shared death experiences and, as a result of this, was able to put a label on what he had experienced with the dying patient when he worked at the hospice. William "knew" that he could facilitate the shared death experience. It was a big wake-up call, and he realized this was his life's purpose.

He returned home and set to work on drafting protocols on how to facilitate the shared death experience. He practised and developed these with friends and relatives, refining them as necessary, and now offers workshops and training as part of the Shared Crossing Project.

William has devised two programmes: The Life Beyond Death and the Shared Crossing Pathway. So far there have been over 200 participants. The Shared Crossing Pathway focuses on preparation for a graceful death – a conscious, connective and loving end-of-life experience that includes protocols to enable shared crossing experiences with an emphasis on the shared death experience (SDE).

I was curious to learn more about William's work, and he was kind enough to set aside some time and answer the following questions I had for him:

What sort of feedback have you had from the people who have learned and implemented the protocols?

Most people report that our protocols bring them directly into relationship with death – their own and that of their loved ones – in a very life-affirming way. They express that they are moved by the heartfelt connections they experience with loved ones both alive and deceased. They are surprised by the simplicity and clarity of the protocols when they learn them.

Over 80 per cent of our Shared Crossing Pathway participants who utilize the protocols report experiencing some type of shared crossing, and over 50 per cent report a shared death experience. Perhaps the most remarkable finding is that when our Pathway alumni enter a deathbed scene, other loved ones or caregivers often experience a shared death experience without having any previous training or knowledge of our protocols. It is as if our Shared Crossing alumni carry with them the knowledge of how to enable an SDE and the capacity to do this seemingly creates a field of awareness that other loved ones tap into, thus gaining access to the SDE.

What is the Shared Crossing Project showing you? What is it teaching us?

We have learned that we can teach or train people how to have a shared death experience and other shared crossing experiences. People who have experienced a shared crossing, report that a deceased loved one is attempting to communicate with them across the veil. These Shared Crossings refer to end-of-life phenomena that are highly relational in that they are personal and deeply meaningful for those who experience them. Surviving family members, friends or caregivers often feel they've received a gift or transmission that was crafted specifically for them. A shared crossing is a central component of "The Graceful Death".

Shared Crossings typically consist of four common elements that their experiencers report:
1. Deep heartfelt connection between the dying and their surviving family members, friends or caregivers, often at the bedside.
2. Expanded awareness or heightened consciousness. In the midst of such

loss, many express a deep sense of trust or knowing that "everything is okay just the way it is".
3. Uplifting emotions of gratitude, kindness, humility, love, peace and bliss.
4. Life-affirming thoughts and feelings, expressing a greater appreciation, empathy and wonder for the gift of human life.

How can individuals benefit from participating in the project?

The most noticeable outcome is a reduction in anxiety and fear around death. These experiences are very powerful in helping others to have a different perspective and understanding of death. Participants also report feeling more comfortable being around friends and loved ones who are facing death and dying. This can result in a deepening of relationships, especially when doing the programme with a loved one.

Many participants also describe a refocusing on one's purpose in this life. It can instigate reflection and re-evaluation of how the individual is living their life.

Participants also find that there is an increased propensity for accessing shared crossing experiences for themselves and their loved ones. The project also provides community support and training, which is ongoing, as well as authentic connection with like-minded people. Many feel an increased openness to or increased belief in a pleasant afterlife.

Shared Crossing Programme alumni who have experienced a shared crossing express the following:

1. A feeling of peace in knowing that their deceased loved one who has died is actually alive and well in the afterlife. A common refrain is: "I know my beloved is OK." There is a sense of confidence in this knowledge that departed loved ones are well.
2. Elimination of their fear and apprehension of death. There appears to be a rather simple letting go of anxiety around death. Shared death experiencers (SDErs), like NDErs, report, "I am not worried about death." There is also

great "Peace of mind, settledness about death".
3. Refocusing on one's purpose in this life. A new frame emerges for this human life; people often feel that they need to do their work here because they know they are not here for long. There are often changes in relationships and career, and people often undertake personal growth. For example, one participant pursued a profession as a psychic intuitive.
4. Certainty about an afterlife. There is an assuredness about seeing departed loved ones again. We get comments such as "I know I will see my beloved again", "I know life goes on." As with NDEs, the SDE left experiencers with a *calm certainty about a benevolent afterlife.* They report that their SDE was *far more real* than their human experience. From the SDE perspective, the human realm is like a dream.
5. There is also a great reduction in grief. I've found that those who have an SDE undergo a greatly

reduced grieving process and heal from losses more rapidly. They still grieve, as grieving is a natural and healthy process, but their grief is held in a larger context that comprehends human death as part of a human life. Most do not see human death as the end, but rather as a transition to another state of consciousness that is pleasant and desirable. This being so, their grief tends to be less intense and easier to deal with.

William's work is incredibly important. I have spoken to many people who have experienced an SDE and they too have been changed in ways similar to those that William has discovered in his work.

When I worked as a nurse, I frequently tended people who had not been able to get over the death of a loved one. Many had turned to alcohol or had simply been so consumed by their grief that their health had begun to suffer or they'd fallen into self-neglect. If programmes like William's were more widely available, this could greatly influence how we can help those who experience difficulties in their grieving process.

I feel passionately that this sort of work should be embraced and developed further. Unfortunately, because there is no scientific explanation or understanding of such experiences, they are simply overlooked and not considered a viable avenue of pursuit. Consequently, there is no funding available for such developments and those struggling to come to terms with their grief are left to suffer alone. Thankfully, recent years have seen a shift in attitude and understanding, and increasing numbers are becoming more receptive to investigating these experiences further. Thanks to people like William, who are continuing to develop protocols like the Shared Crossing Project, I think there will be a deeper understanding of death, which will result in a renewed attitude to life and in the grieving process being easier to endure.

16

THEN THERE WERE WORDS

Kelly connected with 49-year-old Robert Tremblay through social networking. Synchronistically, when Kelly mentioned her idea for this book, Robert replied, "I think the book concept is a clever idea. It's sure to reach many. Penny's book was the first I ever read serendipitously upon my awakening. I love that." Robert's NDE had a profound effect on him. Subsequently, he lives his life in a totally different way. He was given a terminal diagnosis, admitted to a hospice, and was approaching death when his NDE occurred. His chapter opens with a description of what happened subjectively as he lay on his bed near death. Robert has appeared on numerous radio and TV shows, including CBS, Turning Stone and MMTV to name but a few, and has recently made an appearance in the documentary "Back from the Light", *which highlights how people deal with the after-effects of an NDE.*

There was no speaking, as the figure's lips never moved; nor did mine. But there were words that were crisp and clear. The voice was deep and loud and what I would describe as raw. It was a question – "Are you ready?" I felt no ambiguity in its meaning. I replied, although my lips didn't move and I have no memory of actually speaking, but I remember my voice booming and clear. I simply said, "No, I'm not ready yet." This seemed odd because I had already given up and was ready to die in my awakened state and body. Evidently, I was not ready, though, in whatever place this was; that was beyond doubt, certain.

The next and last words were haunting but lined with hope and purpose: **"There is something important you still need to do."** These words came with a smile beginning to form on the man's face as more rays of light began to shoot out of nearly every part of his face. Like rays of the sun peeking through the leaves of a tree. Without thinking, and with a desire unmatched in my life, I reached for his face, unafraid but exploring. Unhesitatingly, I placed my hand on his cheek. I wanted to touch this peace. I had originally thought he would have been well out of my reach, suspended over the expanse, but he wasn't. I realized that the red ribbon of light I'd previously seen was gone and all that remained was the white radiant light from the orb, continually increasing in brightness and vibration. The face of the man encompassed its mass ... leaving me in awe.

As I reached out slowly and deliberately and touched his cheek, my body quaked and the light flourished in intensity and brightness while his smile expanded. There was a tingling in the touch and warmth that is indescribable to this day. It was a numbing, painless vibration, but on the other hand it was warm and almost saturated. In all honesty, I felt everything release, including my bladder, and I didn't even care. He was golden like the sun but not yellow. He was pure white and gaining radiance. I began exploring the variations of textures in his face, and this touch lasted for what seemed like forever. I then realized it felt as if I had been here before. I experienced several moments of *déjà vu.* It's hard to find words to describe the sense of time, or lack thereof, that I experienced. As the light became vivid and intense, so did the hum and the pulsation, and his smile widened until it distorted the image of his face. It almost seemed as though there were other faces evolving through the image I touched, yet seemingly similar to the original face. Like a billion faces all in one, I remember thinking. As his smile expanded, it dissolved the image of his face and again the light became more vibrant. I felt as if I were falling but I hadn't moved and wasn't scared.

Suddenly, I was surrounded by valleys, mountains, streams and small spots that appeared to be people and even animals in the domain below me at a great distance, yet defined. It felt too brief in retrospect, but it was a complete vision of a peaceful place of indefinable colour. Greener than any green I had ever seen, bluer than blue. To this day, I just can't explain the colours I saw. They did not exist in my memory prior to the experience. The entire field of view became this white light and I felt weightless as it engulfed me. There was a whitewashing of my retinas, like when you look into the sun, but without any pain, and it revealed even further layers of a spectrum of colours that I had never seen before. "Colours without names," I said to myself. There was a sense of speed somehow as I felt my body travelling and my view blurred. The bright light was similar to being in a blinding snowstorm while driving, except it was faster and more furious.

Within seconds, I was in my hospital bed. I was scared, yet peaceful. There was none of the pain I had felt previously, but an alertness that was confusing to me. Like I wasn't sick at all.

Within minutes of this experience, I requested to see all of my doctors urgently. There was something important I was supposed to do. It was like they all appeared effortlessly and seemingly instantly. There were exactly 12 of them. I affectionately called them my disciples and asked each to speak their mind and explain "my options" and "chances". Each doctor did so with fluent quick responses and I looked into the eyes of each of them as they spoke. I was focused and attentive. I felt things coming from each of them, it seemed, but I could not understand it all. They all looked at me oddly, as if wondering where all my control had suddenly come from considering my nearly comatose state since my arrival. The changes were already evident. I heard nothing but positives from each and devoured all of it.

I spoke to them as a group and told them I was supposed to live. I told them specifically that there "was something important I was supposed to do." This day marked the beginning of life-saving treatment that would go on intensely for the next year, full of challenges that actually continue to this day.

Prior to my experience that day in the hospital, I had been a fast-paced and adventurous, if not ego-driven, man in a world where all I knew was work. I had spent time as a soldier, a policeman, and a trainer and instructor in management and sales. I had been full of myself with only two speeds: 1,000 miles per hour or a dead stop, and nothing in between. Fourteen-hour workdays were a common occurrence. When I wasn't working, I was playing just as hard.

My NDE changed me altogether. The effects were immediate and my contribution was effortless. Suddenly I found beauty in everything and everyone in this world. This was a completely different scenario for a man previously always in a hurry and full of judgement upon others. I found myself childlike. I was curious about things I had seen thousands of times, but with a different kind of passion and insatiable curiosity. If I spent enough time concentrating, I would be flooded with ideas on the working function of whatever it was I was looking at and, more importantly, its role in a "oneness" that seemed so certain to me. The light I saw in the hospital that day allowed me easily to download accessible information that was universal in nature, which seemed vast, if not endless.

During that first year after my NDE, as I began the long journey of countless medical interventions, I remember laughter becoming a regular part of the routine. Rarely feeling frustrated or in a bad mood became the new normal. But there was this haunting I felt from the experience due to a lack of being able to identify it. One thing was clear from everyone who knew me – I was different in nearly every aspect and, quite honestly, it frightened them. I could sometimes feel their fear intensely. That was another change that troubled me. It seemed I could feel others' emotions clearly and concisely. I experimented with it often. It seemed as if I knew people down to their very core, as if we were all related.

After a year of toxic medications and treatment, I found myself at great peace with one of the most painful decisions that a man makes. I gave up the medical treatment. I surrendered with great peace and a certainty that it was the right decision. I had lost over 100 pounds, and was weak and tired of the treatments. My intuition screamed at me to surrender, and surrender I did without ambiguity or fear of any kind. I still had at least eight months of toxic treatment remaining, had I chosen to continue with it, but, quite honestly, I had nothing left in my fuel tank.

I entered a hospice and stopped all medication and treatment. Thus began the most blissful period of my life. It seems odd to describe being in a hospice in such a manner, but the truth was I felt free and unencumbered by any perceived pressure other than each movement of each day – another wonderment since my NDE. It was truly a gift to understand presence in all things. Interestingly, in spite of my new hospice label. You couldn't keep me inside four walls. I was constantly enthralled with life of any kind and the sun became my God, it seemed. I walked every day, challenging myself to go further. I would disappear into the woods for hours and simply lose myself in the sounds and peace of the swaying tress. Everything spoke to me, and my childlike ways were full of curiosity yet with a defined understanding of everything I studied. After my NDE, I started to write about the changes within me, both psychologically and physiologically. The list grew to nearly 15 handwritten pages. My blood pressure had even lowered. I was having difficulty with electrical devices. They would literally malfunction in my presence. I started having visions, which later would come to life and, in all honesty, scared me to death. But every day I got stronger, and I ate everything I could get my hands on. After 60 days in the hospice, I had gained 60 pounds and had a glimmer in my eye and hope in my step that was definitive, yet confusing.

My intuition, which seemed never to leave me alone since my NDE, was louder every day, and on day 60 at the hospice, I finally listened. I went back to the doctors and explained that, with my renewed strength and weight, I thought it was worth going back into the toxic treatment as I was certain my body and mind could now tolerate the remaining eight months. There was something important I was supposed to do and it had been haunting me. We began testing to see how much damage had been done in the 60 days without treatment. To everyone's surprise but mine, nearly every infliction I had experienced previously had healed, without medication or toxic treatments. When I'd entered the hospice, I had numerous diseases and illnesses, compounded by my immune system being destroyed. From a blood infection related to tuberculosis, to bleeding retinas that left me technically blind, to hypocalcaemia that left me forever on the verge of a stroke, to insulin-dependent diabetes, just to name a few. They had simply vanished. I departed the hospital feeling on top of the world, leaving the doctors and nurses staring in disbelief. There was still one disease that lingered and it would be the fuel that would inspire me further into an avocation that continues to this day.

Two years after my NDE, as I neared what I hoped to be the end of medical treatment, I received a calendar at Christmas from my mother. The calendar had been a staple among our family for years, filled with pictures and memories each month. As I stood there scanning the pictures I noted one seemingly out-of-place black-and-white photo in the very month of my birthday. The picture was of a man whom I recognized immediately. My breath was sucked from me and tears poured from my eyes as, nearly hyperventilating, I staggered to a chair, stunned. Once I could muster the words, I told my family that this was the face of the man in that giant ball of light that I had seen in hospital. My family explained that the man was my grandfather, who had died years before my birth. I don't recall ever having seen pictures of him; his presence was never a part of my growing up. It was then that I realized my experience had actually been an NDE. This moment of realization seemed to open a floodgate of even more changes. Day after day, I was inundated with epiphanies on topics I had never had any interest in: physics, chemistry, quantum this and quantum that; mathematical equations and multiple downloads about connectivity and energy that I spent my days researching, only to find that all were scientific findings by clearly greater men than me. I was somewhat thankful for that.

I wrote a lot during those days, including starting a blog about my experience and the after-effects that continued to unravel every day. There is nearly 40 years of validated research today on the "after-effects", and I am near certain it's the element we are distracted away from by the drama of the experience itself. There is great synchronicity in the after-effects, right down to the timing for all of us. I think we need to pay attention to it so I often write about the findings on my blog, as well as having done so in my book *Twenty-Seconds.*

The blog went viral but continued to torment me for my lack of disclosure of what was the most remarkable part of the journey medically. The "oneness" I had was clear and present every day and I dove into it wherever and whenever I could. I volunteered everywhere or would just talk to complete strangers with such love and compassion that their life stories would unfold before me. I loved everything and everyone, and it continues to this day. But the one aspect that haunted me was full disclosure medically, which quite honestly was the most remarkable part of the story. It took time and a bit of courage finally to publish a book about the story where I finally told all. When I was first diagnosed as terminally ill, it was the shocker of a lifetime for a married heterosexual man. With my wife at my side, I was diagnosed on 16 February 2011 as suffering from END STAGE AIDS, a disease I had hurled into a drawer previously as a "gay" disease and not of my concern. The news took the feet from under me and my wife, who, by the way, miraculously never got infected. However, it did end our marriage almost immediately.

The book I wrote was raw and truthful. I included the medical details of my illness and treatment directly from my medical records. It spoke volumes about one aspect of my experience that continually comes up over and over again. The impact of fear on our bodies is drastic, all the way down to the cellular level. Fear and stigma of AIDS continues to a level of alarming proportions. This results in many people avoiding a test that could possibly prevent the spread of such a tragic disease. Because I waited so long to be tested, it resulted in a diagnosis of End Stage. Had it been detected in its infancy, my life could have been much more normal because new medications have changed the face of the disease. Today, the fastest-growing population with new HIV infections is in WOMEN, aged between 13 and 24. Right before our eyes, the disease has evolved and is attacking our children. It seemed obvious that the book wasn't just important for me, but for everyone who lumps this disease into the same drawer I did. It was my intuitive calling, courageously to tell the story and advocate for education and changing targets concerning it.

The story contained other anomalies that needed a voice. Many report miraculous healings after NDEs, and these have sparked great debate about the power of the human body and our miraculous immune system. But there was something about my story that was screaming for attention. How do you heal any of the things I had when you don't have a functioning immune system? It has baffled doctors from Vermont to the Mayo Clinic, but it doesn't baffle me. Because of my late diagnosis, my immune system today is still only about a tenth of the norm. But I continue not only to survive but to thrive as I tell my story around the world. I have brought new light not just to the NDE but to HIV as well.

There was one aspect of my journey that multiplied every single day, and that is the love I have for myself and everyone along my path. It remains to me the biggest change in my persona and for that I am forever grateful. I make a point to see every sunrise when I wake up each morning and then conclude my day by catching every sunset. As the first light of day warms my face, I simply say, "Thank you for one more day." There is something important that should be noted, something I truly do believe in. My life today, not unlike my journey while I was ill, must always consist of being surrounded by the people who love me. However, the forgiveness and love for myself was the catalyst to allowing it. There's something important I am supposed to do and I do it every day. It has become clear to me from my research and direct experience. It's not just our choices that lead to a healthy life. What matters is how much we love and are loved.

Every day I set out upon my task of connecting others to educate them about the changing face of AIDS, the infection rates for which remain nearly unaffected over the past 35 years. It brings me great joy to do this. The disease has clearly been targeting a different group in our society lately, as if reminding us it takes everyone to effect change. A portion of the proceeds from my book are donated to an HIV awareness charity, and this fuels my continual healing every day. It was my encounter with my grandfather during my own NDE that made the experience real for me and resulted in my personal transformation. It is hard to comprehend until you have your own experience. In this spirit I tell my story whenever and wherever I can. Doing so, fills my heart with HOPE which is, quite simply, everything to everyone. There are many "important things" I do every day. However, one of the most important is giving back more than I receive, which I will continue to do this until my last breath.

Many people tell me that I am the most positive person they know. It seems to confuse them, considering all the body and mind trauma I have endured. My body remains on a very fragile edge virtually every moment of every day. Remaining positive, however, seemed to be one of the strongest messages from my experience. The defined essence of loving ourselves is in our choice of attitudes. I barely have an immune system, yet I choose to remain positive. My body agrees and responds accordingly every single day. If I get stressed, unbalanced or negative, I feel an immediate physical effect. Remaining positive isn't just a gift I received in my experience; it's a daily necessity that I am reminded of always.

My journey has not been without its trials. Thank God; it's sometimes the only way to learn. I have become, in no uncertain terms, sensitive and loving in a world not exactly streamlined for it. My most important discovery, while with the man in the light, was my vast potential for love and forgiveness. It fuels my ability to overcome anything and shapes my life and the lives of those around me. I live in continuous gratitude for this gift.

I had been writing cheques with a love that couldn't be cashed honestly. Today I love with great passion and emotion. I just don't know another way. It can confuse people to live with such vibrancy, but there's one thing I've learned in my life – never apologize for being authentically awesome. I just don't have time for anything else. My greatest act of courage, and one I see every day in others, is the ability to be vulnerable. That's courage to me. Opening yourself, being spiritually "naked", and loving as though nothing else matters. It's quite possibly the most important thing in life.

The man in the light, and a massive spiritual explosion, showed me that there is way too much fear in the world. We are definitely more magnificent than we've been taught. This is quietly whispered to us through miracles around the world every day. Millions have reported NDEs and the changes that come with them. But at some point, miracles stop being miracles when they happen all the time. And it's happening.

The world is waking up, albeit slowly, to the single most common aspect or lesson given to all of us who experience an NDE – A ONENESS. This is the number-one after-effect of any NDE. A oneness of awesome potential, but just out of reach for most. Therein lies the beauty of the journey. After a year as a bestselling author, I can vouch for one thing: most will never understand something completely, until it happens to them. So, when in doubt, I say one thing: PUT SOME SKIN INTO IT! SHOW UP and do enjoy the ride. Love like there's no tomorrow and apologize for none of it. Today is really all that will ever matter; the rest is just junk.

One day, I will once again stand before that light and I will be ready. There is no fear of death any longer.

My experience taught me volumes about death, but there was something else. It taught me to live ... to truly and freely live ... and love like most have never imagined ... And oh, how I do live!

Thanks for one more day.

This is a great example of how radically someone's thoughts and views of life can change. Robert saw beauty where he had never seen it before. He found solace in nature for the first time and began to appreciate things that he had previously taken for granted. Every morning Robert is thankful for one more day.

It is interesting that Robert, when he saw the photograph of his grandfather who had died 22 years before he was even born, suddenly had an "Aha moment", recognizing the man he'd met during his NDE as this grandfather. Again, this is something that has been reported by other NDErs. Is it possible that Robert had previously seen this photograph and that the image was stored in the depths of his subconscious? But why would a person he had never met be part of his NDE experience rather than someone he had met?

Robert now totally embraces life and lives it in a way that has the greater good of mankind at its heart. He is constantly raising money for AIDS charities and is a great support to the wider community.

The fact that Robert has remained so positive and grateful since his NDE may be the key factor in maintaining his health despite living with full-blown AIDS. Previous studies appear to indicate that those living with AIDS, who succumb to apathy and depression, tend to have a lower life expectancy than those who have a more positive attitude. It appears that the NDE is responsible for Robert's elevated positivity. How did the NDE facilitate such a renewed attitude? Is there some way this can be replicated in others? These are all potential avenues for further research that could result in developing techniques conducive to good health.

17

GOD'S BOOT CAMP

Kelly connected with 56-year-old Paul Ammons via social media following an introduction from Robert Tremblay. From a young age, Paul appears to have had a deep connection with nature. A close brush with death strengthened that connection and now Paul is doing extremely important conservation work with bees.

I always felt different from others. I felt alone – a loner. I would go to school, come home, go to my room and sit in my closet making model aeroplanes. I was very creative and always looking for new things to make or do so that I could feel a sense of accomplishment. I had few friends by choice, hiding the learning disabilities that I was labelled with.

By the time I was about 8 years old, I had created a number of safe places where I could go – whether it was a deep, dark hole I'd dug in the damp, cool earth, a hidden tree fort in the woods, or a cubby in the closet. One day when I was crying and feeling quite hopeless in the closet, someone or something came in on my right side. It was an intense feeling that resonated clearer than any voice. It said, "Paul, you are a special child, we have chosen you; you are safe, you are loved. Keep the animals and nature close to you; there will be a time we will need you. I promise we will be back." I remember wondering what that was all about. Then I took a pen and wrote on the back of my plastic ring – "the animals".

High school was a daily struggle. I was picked on because I did not mature physically as quickly as the other boys. As I grew older, my memory of that secret visitation with "the animals and with nature" began to fade. I never had a girlfriend until I was 21. After dating for three years, we married. My wife was a diehard Catholic, while I was an agnostic if not atheist. Unfortunately, the marriage was short lived due to my workaholic behaviour. I was never around. By the age of 37, I owned several successful businesses. I sold them and retired. I had arrived, so I thought. As I sat in one of my homes, I realized I was empty. I had given up everything – family, friends and my wife. All I had was a large bank account to make me happy. Soon I was drinking and taking drugs. After every blow-out, I would wake up and wonder what had happened.

This behaviour landed me in an inpatient rehab centre in Arizona. I liked it. It felt safe, and I didn't want to leave. Finally, I had friends. We had something in common. Soon afterwards, I went into aftercare in New Mexico and, after three months, was released. Having spent well over $100,000, I thought I was fixed. I bought a cabin in the Sangre de Cristo Mountains near Pecos, New Mexico. My dog Sheba loved it as much as I did. I had raised and trained Labradors since I was 16. Sheba was an exceptional dog. We connected on a level of understanding beyond that of my closest human friend.

In June 2002, on a return flight from a trip to Africa, unbeknownst to me, I developed a blood clot (deep vein thrombosis). Upon landing, I went to my cabin to pick up Sheba from a neighbour, who had been caring for her during my trip. I confirmed to him that I would be leaving on Monday; it was Sunday, Father's Day to be exact. On that eventful day, the blood clot broke, giving me a double pulmonary embolism. The following Wednesday evening my neighbours were walking along the upper road. Sheba had broken through the cabin screen door to get help. Wondering why Sheba was there, they came to my cabin and found me lying on the edge of my bed in a coma. I was all but dead. I had septic shock blood poisoning, a significant drop in blood pressure that can lead to failure of organs, respiratory and heart failure, stroke and death. My body temperature was 107 degrees; I had jaundice, a kidney infection and double pneumonia; my blood oxygen saturation level was 72 per cent (hypoxemia); and I was hyperventilating due to the thin air at 8,700 feet. I was bleeding from every orifice of my body due to sepsis and my organs were shutting down. I was so severely bloated from the decomposition of my body that my clothing had to be cut off. No one knew at that time that I was paralysed on the right side of my body from lying on my femoral nerve for more than four days. After two hours, an ambulance came to take me to the nearest hospital (an hour and a half away) since it was too windy for a helicopter to land for an emergency evacuation.

Lying on the gurney in the ambulance, everything came alive. I sat up, placing my legs off the edge of the gurney. (Later, I was told that this was physically impossible, given the condition I was in.) There were "people" in front of me. I heard a muted humming sound. I was looking through a light grey fog and could only make out the outlines of the people. A young man from the volunteer fire department was shocked to see me wake up, and even more shocked to see me sit up. The ambulance crew tried to get me to lie down, but I wouldn't. I felt lots of fear, panic, anxiety, sadness and confusion, but it wasn't mine. Evidently, I was feeling the emotions of those around me. I know this to be true because I had an indescribable feeling of love that had no pain, worries or anxieties; all I knew was that moment. The weird thing was, I had the sense that there was no time. I was experiencing the highest level of bliss that one could imagine. I was living in the now.

Given my sudden consciousness, one of the crew began asking me questions. I felt obliged to calm them down, as if I needed to help them with the panic state they were in. I was filled with compassion for them and, since I was feeling more than fine, I began to joke, hoping it would relax the situation. One of them grabbed my hand, and my sense of his fear and anxiety doubled with his touch. He said, "Paul, you need to get serious with us now. You are dying." Without hesitation, in a calm and understanding voice, I said, "We are all dying." You see, I was in a state of timelessness. The moment I said those words, things began to accelerate in many different ways. As I sat there, I could suddenly see through the ambulance walls. I saw my cabin and the details of the front porch. The Pecos River and large Ponderosa Pines lined the edge. Everything grew quiet. I detached from my physical body and my soul became one with the universe and all that is.

It's very difficult for me fully to express what I experienced, but the nearest analogy I can give is that I started to become everything and everything became me. As I felt this happening, my surroundings started to break down into particles – zillions of them – including the ambulance, the cabin, the trees and everything around me. I no longer felt the people in the ambulance or their fears, anxieties, panic and confusion; I felt something much greater. All at once, everything stood still. I found myself hovering in a place that was mostly darkness; the glow of star-like objects illuminated my surroundings. I was in a series of multiple dimensions, on what seemed the edge of infinity. I remember wondering why I was not able to move into the lights, which were moving clockwise into the white core. I had a strong sense of spirit-beings all around me, holding me in a loving and nurturing embrace. I was being cared for by a sense of unconditional love. At the same time, information was being downloaded into me, as though I were a super-computer. My experience was the complete opposite of fear and everything it represents. It felt like untainted, pure love, made of bliss greater than one can ever humanly imagine. It was surreal.

I observed a swirling abyss of infinite lights that I perceived to be souls moving in sequence toward the distant vortex. I felt drawn to the vortex and wanted to follow them in, but there seemed to be a boundary that I was not allowed to cross. It quite simply was not my time to join these other souls. I did not hear voices or see anything that looked familiar. We were as one and communicated, not through words, but through emotions that were louder than words, mixed with all the other senses.

Again, I wanted to join the star-like bliss activity, but a strong intuition told me I was not to move. I just watched and took in all the beauty; it was like a painted canvas of all the love and connection possible – one that kept me in a state of heightened awareness and bliss. I felt the presence of what seemed to be angels behind me as I continued to watch the wondrous array of lights. Some of the lights were far away, moving in a clockwise motion, until condensing into the solid white core, while others stayed close, communicating with me. To this day, I truly believe what I was experiencing could only have been the gathering and sorting of souls in Heaven.

I was then returned to my body. I was in intensive care in isolation – ironically, the same place I'd been living most my life, by choice – and had been placed on the highest level of emergency status. The hospital called my parents and told them I was not expected to make it through the night, and that they should arrive as soon as possible if they wanted to see me alive one last time.

By morning, my parents arrived. I was still breathing, thanks to a ventilator, and had made it through the night. The doctors indicated that if I didn't die, I would most likely be a vegetable on a dialysis machine. They told my parents that a decision might need to be made about continuing life support. The diagnosis was unknown, and my condition remained very critical for the first few days. The doctors were having difficulty determining what had caused my illness. What they agreed on, however, was that no one should have survived what happened to me up in the mountains; laying in a coma in desperate condition, in rarefied air, and for over four days without food or water.

Coming back to consciousness – as we understand that term – I felt the worst pain and fear of my life. Medical personnel were running around in their yellow full-body suits used for quarantine. At one point, I thought I was being tortured by aliens! I tried to pull out my ventilator, so they strapped me down to the bed. My brain told me they were wrapping firecrackers around my arms and lighting them. This, and more, went on for days as I slowly returned to consciousness. I was hardly able to talk to the first person who spoke to me. My voice was so weak that, when I received my first visitor, I had to whisper in his ear, "Get me out of here. They're torturing me and will kill me." I was told, "Everything is okay. You are safe." I cried uncontrollably and said that I was being punished for all my sins. At this time, I did not remember the message I'd been given when I was eight: "Keep the animals and nature close to you." Could that mean my Labrador Sheba and my cabin in the mountains?

After a month in the hospital, I was discharged and sent home in a wheelchair holding a cocktail of painkillers. I had no idea how hellishly challenging the next 13 years would be. For the following few months I felt different, as if I were experiencing things for the first time like a small child. On occasion, it felt as if I was not even here; as though I were disconnected from the reality that I once knew. I attempted to talk to family and friends, but got little understanding and many strange looks. Out of frustration, I soon went back to my old ways, becoming self-centred with no concern for others. I was essentially in survival mode and operating mostly from a place of fear, not love. I went to physical therapy to rehabilitate my paralysed leg, but the process seemed too slow. I felt like I was back in the special education classroom being treated like a child, so I decided to do it myself. I worked hard seven days a week, from pool therapy to the weight room. In eight months, I was able to progress from a wheelchair to extreme snowboarding. I healed very quickly, to the surprise of the doctors. I had, however, become chemically addicted to painkillers due to overmedication. My addiction haunted me for many years, until I finally managed to heal and overcome it.

In 2004, I got re-married, and my wife soon had our first child. On 20 June 2005, Father's Day, exactly three years after my pulmonary embolism and NDE at my cabin, I was infected by a flea bite from a wild rabbit. I developed tularaemia, an extremely rare but severe infectious bacterial disease. It began with flu-like symptoms that quickly spread throughout my body. Suddenly I lost my eyesight and, once again, saw that grey misty fog. I was rushed to the emergency room, where doctors told me that I would have died within six hours if I hadn't sought treatment. Thanks to powerful antibiotics, I recovered quickly and regained my eyesight.

Very little seemed to be going well, including my marriage. The blood clot in my leg, which had been treated with blood thinners, never completely dissolved, unknown to medical professionals. I was not checked out after the blood thinner treatment, so for 11 years I was a walking time bomb that eventually blew up.

After going through my second divorce, I became very tired emotionally, physically and spiritually. Taking care of my son left little time to take care of myself. All my efforts toward getting healthy soon dissipated, leaving me in a place that was very dangerous. In March 2013, a blood clot, of which I was unaware, gave me another pulmonary embolism, and put me back in the emergency room. When I was finally discharged, I was a weak, broken man, who had to remain on blood thinners for the rest of my life. The blood clot was said to have calcified. In a short amount of time I gained 35 pounds. My whole body ached from the severe nerve damage that had once paralysed my leg, and the tissue damage from the tularaemia. I started to self-medicate. Swearing that I would never take another painkiller, I instead turned to alcohol (totally unaware of how this would interact with my prescribed blood thinners). My blood was already three times thinner than that of a normal person, and the alcohol exacerbated this, so when I fell and hit my abdomen, I suffered severe internal haemorrhaging. Back to the emergency room I went, where I had my stomach pumped and several blood transfusions. For the next year, such types of accidents were quite common. I was committing a slow, unintentional suicide.

In December 2015, my son and I went to Texas for Christmas to visit family. I was at the lowest point in my life, with little to no hope. Conditioned to hiding my feelings since childhood, I concealed them as best as I could. During my visit a miracle happened – everything came together for me when the dream that I'd had after my NDE was confirmed.

Back in 2002, a few months after my release from hospital, while I was still walking with crutches, I went up to my cabin with Sheba for the first time since the coma. That first night I had a dream that was intensely real. I woke up at 5.32a.m. in a panicked sweat. In my dream, I was forewarned of the death of three close family friends. One death would be imminent, but I guess I didn't realize at that stage how soon, and the other two deaths would be years later. These premonitions all came true. The dream was one of many unexplained mysteries in my life. I tried to rationalize all that was going on, but no answers came. I was left feeling more alone than ever. Not wanting to look like some sort of freak, I let it go. However, during my holiday visit, I met up with someone who confirmed the details of the deaths in my dream. What astounded me was that the first death happened at 5:32a.m., the exact time I awoke in a state of panic from my dream. In that precise moment, I said to myself, "This is real. No more trying to say it's merely coincidence." There were just too many so-called coincidences.

I started to Google NDEs, and this led me to Facebook, where I connected with a few people. Soon things started to shift dramatically. The more I engaged and spoke to other NDErs, the more I received in the form of synchronicity. At the same time, I allowed myself space to reflect and understand all I'd been going through. As I did this, I became overwhelmed with a sense of God's presence around me for the first time in my life. I suddenly knew that God was real and always with me. I had been so wrong in the past when I did not believe God existed. Then it occurred to me that what I had been told as an 8-year-old boy – "there will be a time we will need you. I promise we will be back" – had all been true. God had kept his promise and come back – I know now that he never left me, I left Him.

My spiritual awakening had once again intensified. I was filled with deep compassion, love, hope, patience, awareness and a positive attitude. I now do what I can to enhance my new qualities on a daily basis, and every day my life gets better and better.

My experiences led me to explore alternative medicine. I had a Doppler test done to check the status of my blood clot. The technician looked at me and said, "You don't have a blood clot." I just smiled. This is all new for me. Or more accurately, I've finally become aware of what has been going on all along. I brought back from the spirit realms the belief that our purpose is to help bring "Heaven" to Earth and into our everyday lives. It seems that the God of creation put me through his boot camp. He schooled me in the truth, and gave me the courage to share what I've learned with others. I have beaten all the odds, and I know now that I didn't do it alone.

There was another positive aspect that transpired after my NDE. I started taking a keen interest in honey bees. This began with photographing them, but it soon evolved into an obsession. I watched the bees, saw them work in harmony and get along as one. It struck me that we have a lot to learn from the disappearing honey bee. In 2004,

I became a hobbyist beekeeper, with four hives occupied by colonies. I quickly taught myself how to manage these so that they would yield honey. By 2006, I had eight hives with colonies, and my interest went beyond garnering honey. I felt a profound connection with and love for the bees. I had a personal relationship with each colony, as if I were connected to them. However, unbeknownst to me, during 2006, some of the first cases of CCD (colony collapse disorder) were showing up in apiaries all over the world. Over the next few years life got hectic and I faced more life-threatening issues with my health. That did not stop my passion. In fact, by 2011 I took the hobby and went commercial with it, calling my new company "Enchanted Honey". I had over 350 hives and colonies. My working life was no longer just about making money; it was about my soul's purpose! This is where I find value.

The impact of CCD was devastating. In 2013, I lost 95 per cent of my colonies, but I kept rebuilding. Each year I would try to better my losses.

In the fall of 2015, I sold my company due to continued colony destruction and ongoing health issues. The Honey Bee is still a big part of my life. I kept my Facebook page and turned it into an information and conservation/environmental site that is quite popular. Today I am back as a hobbyist beekeeper with a few hives. I'm very excited to be collaborating with a team of PhD and citizen scientists here in Texas. We are developing a revolutionary beehive designed specifically to monitor – and hopefully determine and solve the mystery of – the disappearing Honey Bee "Colony Collapse Disorder".

A famous quote: "If the bee disappeared off the surface of the globe, then man would have only four years of life left. No more bees, no more pollination, no more plants, no more animals, no more man" (Albert Einstein).

I continue my work with bees to this day. I intend to solve this devastation of the Honey Bee so that I never allow Einstein's quote to become reality and humanity's worst nightmare.

Today I can say that all I went through was for a Divine purpose; to prepare me for my purpose here on Earth. Each day brings a new beginning. I look forward to sharing my experiences with others in the hope that they are meaningful to their own life's journey.

Paul describes being a loner as a child. At a young age he suddenly became aware of a reassuring voice that told him he was loved and special. It felt significant to him, but he didn't understand it so kept it to himself and eventually the memory of the voice faded. Does the fact that Paul had few friends and sought seclusion from a young age predispose him to being more sensitive to anomalous experiences or having an NDE? With fewer external distractions, was Paul able to cultivate an ability to be more in touch with his intuition?

It is apparent from his testimony that Paul struggled for 13 years with the changes that went with his NDE. He tried to discuss the experience with his family and friends, but no one understood. This is very common;

unless you've had an interest in NDEs, it can be very difficult to relate to something that seems so beyond comprehension. It was only when Paul scoured the internet and explored NDEs that things began to fall into place for him and he started to gain a deeper understanding of his experience. I suspect he will discover many more things now that he has connected with people who do understand.

It is fascinating to hear of Paul's work with the preservation of bees. There have been many articles published on the importance of bees to the ecosystem. Paul has intuitively been drawn to this cause since his NDE. As he has stated, he is now living his life purpose.

18

LITTLE GIRL SOLDIER

Kelly connected with 34-year-old Jessica Harper via social media and developed a friendship and deep trust that allowed Jessica to open up about her life. Jessica resides in the United States, is educated with a bachelor's degree and works as a business professional. She is a veteran of the United States Army, who served in the Iraq War during the invasion in 2003, when she was 20 years old. Most of her life she struggled with her identity, but she eventually became her true self: a woman. She always felt she was a woman. However, despite having faced the hardships of war, she lacked the bravery to face societal struggles relating to her identity.

It was dusk; I could hear the distinctive sound of the radio break in the background. I laid against a bare wooden building we had constructed months before that we used as our command headquarters. I could feel every muscle in my strong, powerful body, as I had just finished a five-mile run hours beforehand. I ran every day because I was scared; I knew my ability to run, my ability to stay physically stronger than the opposition, would help decide if I was going to live or die. I saw the war as senseless, but grew to hate the enemy. I didn't hate them because I was an American and they were of different national origins, or because of mindless patriotism. I grew to hate them because of the things I had experienced and the stories that my fellow brothers and sisters in arms told me.

The constant roadside bombings, the guerrilla war tactics, the shooting down of our aircraft and killing of our crews, seeing body after body of American soldiers, being bombed, being rocketed, having to face a child in the streets and decide whether to kill him or not. All this bloodshed, and it wasn't just a story you watch in the theatres, it was real. The strain of six months of war had taken its toll on my mind, although it had not yet become apparent.

Lying back on the wooden building felt like a rest for my soul. I stared off blankly into the abyss. No more memories of my childhood home and the abuse I endured that led me to run away and join the service. I couldn't feel anything. I had no emotions. I felt disconnected from the world around me.

I remember leaning forward and seeing a stick on the ground. Grabbing it, I began drawing in the sand, the face and body of a man. Then, slowly, I cut away his harsh, jagged features, making the figure appear like that of a beautiful woman; giving him soft, sensual lips, a pretty nose and upturned eyebrows, long hair and a curvy body. Looking at what I'd created sent chills down my body. I felt something and then I brushed it away.

God and I had made an agreement before I left to go to war. I wasn't going to talk to him, and that was okay as long as I didn't beg for his help when in need. I felt developing a foxhole relationship would have been dishonest since I didn't wholeheartedly believe in God. I knew I was in this situation for a reason, and that someday, I would face something in life much harder than this war. I had always felt different on the inside, ever since my earliest memories at about three years of age.

Closing my eyes, I imagined a far-away place, where I stood in a wheat field, surrounded by rolling hills, beautiful trees, and bright blue skies. Adorned in a flowery dress, I saw myself dancing and spinning in the sunlight. At that moment, I was free for the first time; then I heard the radio break.

I spent the next six months fighting alongside brave men and women, enduring some of the Earth's most terrible conditions. Assigned to night-shift operations, expected to be resting, I spent my daytime hours wide awake, baking at up to 135 degrees in a vinyl tent. Unable to fall asleep naturally, every third day I would pass out from heat exhaustion. If the heat didn't get you, the flies would, as we lacked proper sanitation.

The sandstorms and dust devils scoured my lips and hands until they cracked and bled. I began to grow hair in places on my body that I had never grown hair before, and it certainly wasn't because of lack of puberty. It was as if my body somehow knew to return to a primal state when living in such harsh conditions. The dirt had filled my pores; I looked aged. Our home, this place, rested well with the scorpions, camel spiders, wolves and vipers.

The war was anything but beautiful, but the sunrises and sunsets in Iraq are some of the most stunning examples of God's work. Every morning when my shift was complete, I sat patiently waiting for the sun to rise. It gave me such peace knowing I had made it just one more night, and that another day would come. It's funny, even in the worst places, God shows his beauty and magnificence to wretched men. When we left for the invasion, they told us we would be gone for a few months; now a year had passed. Much of our lives back at home had changed. We had changed.

I returned home, injured from war. Gone was the sweet, soft-hearted, smart-alec kid with big dreams and ambitions. I faded away. I was cold. There was something inside me that was triggered. I knew how to kill, and I knew I could kill. It felt disturbing, like I wasn't me anymore. While on active duty, my mental state had declined, and no one around me saw it. I showed early signs of Post-Traumatic Stress Disorder (PTSD) and bulimia, a severe eating disorder. My time in the Army came to an end in the middle of 2005, and I started college later that year in the fall.

For many young people, college is a time of self-exploration and discovery. For me, walking back into a classroom for the first time seemed like a surreal paradise of lollipops and candy canes. There I was with a bunch of bright, happy, cheerful, recent high school graduates, listening as they spoke fondly of home-life and dating. My reality had substantially changed; even though my hometown was 30 miles away, my mind was still 6,000 miles away. My thoughts bounced between combat and severe gender incongruity.

To survive and control my obsessive thoughts, I buried myself in academia, excelled at school and moved to the top of my class. I convinced myself that my gender issues would resolve themselves when I joined the military, but I was wrong. The feelings of being a girl had hardly gone away. The slower pace of civilian life and the freedoms of college allowed for a wandering mind. Denial of combat trauma and gender dysphoria caused my depression to grow.

I came to a point where I would not talk about my military service with anyone. I believed people would not understand. I felt they'd be angry and judgemental, determined to see me only as a man; so I kept quiet. I continued to focus on school and buried my trauma. This fed a veiled eating disorder that consumed the next ten years of my life.

I made it into the sophomore year of college, spending many nights in the library, my head laid down on the books, praying that somehow I could wake from my nightmare. I felt like I was born so wrong. On the inside, I felt innocent and beautiful, but on the outside I was anything but. I was so depressed that I attempted suicide several times.

I was born a twin. My sister Sarah, born six minutes after me, often reminded me that I was the middle child. There were two boys and one girl. One of my earliest memories at the age of 3 was when I first discovered I was a boy. My father and I were showering, and I saw we matched. I was so confused. "How was I a girl yet I looked like daddy?" I thought to myself. I remember begging my mother to let me be a ballerina, telling her I wanted to wear a pink tutu; she would reply that boy ballerinas don't wear those things. I insisted I could. I played with dolls; I rode a pink bike; I would even wear my sister's clothes. I thought I could somehow grow up and become a girl.

The turmoil of being transgender, a poor college student, and a closet veteran suffering from PTSD, caused a desperation that led me down a very dark hole. In 2008, feeling I had no other choice, I began the process of transition. I felt if didn't do it, I would die.

By twisted luck, the eating disorder had destroyed my once robust body; I had become fragile, losing over 100 pounds of muscle mass, which gave me a feminine physique. I grew my hair long and had extensive surgery on my face. I was becoming me. By the time I left college, I was a woman.

My family had deserted me, they didn't understand. Their son, the soldier, was gone. This woman had killed him, and they didn't want her. With nowhere to turn and the economy in shambles, I packed what few things I had, bought a cheap car and headed to Texas, where I heard there were job opportunities.

I spent the next year in Texas living hand to mouth, making the hardest decisions of my life. Dark and lonely times over that next year left me wishing I was back in Baghdad. My time on my own, and the accumulations of all the hardships I had faced, made me doubt the existence of God even further.

I felt completely abandoned by everything in my life. I wondered, "Why would God allow me to have the thoughts and feelings of being so genuinely female, but be given no way to express it? And, when I finally tried to do something about it, it nearly destroyed me?" This question killed me, as I felt all the good had left me. I felt broken. I hadn't found a job in nearly a year. I had no money, little to eat and the banks were calling me. I hit rock bottom.

As my depression grew, my anger boiled on the inside. I was rendered powerless by my situation. How could God allow his creation to endure such pain and suffering? I developed a deep hatred for God and religion and became an atheist. I spent my free time reading atheist blogs, watching videos, and finding fellowship among other disgruntled non-believers.

As time went on, the economy finally started to pick up, and I found a job. I worked there for six months, until I eventually found something better. As life goes on, we go on. It lifted my spirits. I started to feel value in myself again. Now that I had a job, and income, I needed to address some health issues. I sought out an ophthalmologist.

I was scheduled for a Friday morning procedure, eye muscle surgery. Over the years, I had experienced numerous issues with double vision, so I finally decided to have it corrected. Having been through two complicated, yet unrelated operations, I felt relatively at ease regarding this shorter procedure. When we arrived that morning, I faced all the standard hospital questions and initial checks, and was whisked off for the 15-minute operation.

They wheeled me into the operating room and I remember feeling anxious and tired, as I'd had a long stressful week. I recall feeling the cold air of the room, and as I looked up without my spectacles, how blurry the ceiling appeared. The anaesthesiologist stepped in and asked, "How many margaritas are we giving?" I said back, grinning, "A lot." Smiling, he secured the breathing mask to my face. As I looked up, breathing in the gas, I heard a female voice in the room count down as I waited to wake up in the recovery room later. With a couple of deep breaths, I was unconscious.

When I awoke, I found myself standing in a location where everything below me was of beautiful bright golden light, and a sky of blackness was around me. I felt touches of tranquillity and my soul was vibrant. It was like awakening from the most peaceful rest. Strangely, nothing seemed out of place. I was totally unaware that my reality had shifted.

Off in the distance, I saw a group of four people standing together in a circle, conversing among themselves. Looking around, bewildered by my surroundings, I moved toward them. As I approached, they stopped communicating and seemed as though they hadn't expected me.

Confused, still assuming I had somehow awoken from the surgery, I looked up at the tallest of the spirit-beings, who gave off an essence of masculinity, and asked, "Are you Dr Smith?" The tallest spirit-being stepped forward from the gathering of others and peered down at me, standing silently. I did not recognize this person, as its body appeared to be made of white light surrounded by a golden aura. I looked back at them. Growing frustrated, I asked again, "Are you Dr Smith? I am having surgery with Dr Smith."

As I demanded answers, still not understanding the gravity of my situation, the beings switched my visual perception so I could see all four of them and myself from afar. When this happened, the being's golden auras changed to a deep dark electric blue with a thin line of golden light. Their bodies had turned from white to black. Towering over me, the tallest spirit-being transmitted rods of white light beams from my head to his.

From this perspective, I could see my appearance was that of a young girl. I had long, beautiful, soft, curly hair, and delicate facial features. My body was not human, but similar to that of the spirit-beings with whom I was communicating. Wearing a white silk dress, my small delicate frame was surrounded by an aura of golden, white light. I finally understood I was not in the recovery room waking up from surgery. It was a moment of clarity.

Mesmerized by my new reality, I gazed at the spirit-beings in astonishment. I studied every element of them. They had no definable gender and no faces. They were made of pure white light and still had a humanoid shape, but without arms or legs. Golden particles surrounded their bodies. Each particle was definable, as if you could touch each of them.

As I gazed upon them, one of the other spirit-beings stepped forward and mentioned something regarding a nurse to the tallest spirit-being. I did not understand what was said. As the two spirit-beings stood before me communicating among themselves, without words, I looked around and saw something in the background that caught my attention, which I had not seen before. Off in the distance, in the darker sky of the realm, was an alluring white sphere of circling light. Part of me felt drawn to it. It was like meeting your first real love and locking eyes, but I still looked away.

As this happened, the spirit-being surrounded me, cuddling me, like a father or mother would hold a child. It felt very calming and euphoric. It was as if we had become one and the same. When they did this, all the memories of my life were washed away as I stood, looking up, gazing at them. My emotions intensified to feelings of pure innocence. I felt so childlike and safe with them.

As they took away the memories of my life, the beings appeared to debate among themselves. I knew they were talking about me and what had happened in my life, but I was not allowed to understand what they were saying. As their conversation intensified, the shifting of their graceful dance-like movements mesmerized me. Their auras that surrounded their bodies changed from golden to an intense orange. Amused by this, I looked up at them happily, watching their bodies interacting with each other, as the light swirled around and the colours became a mixture of light.

From their appearance, it seemed as though one of the spirit-beings was very upset about the things they had seen in my life. This appeared to cause a marked difference of opinion among them as to what to do with me. While their conversation intensified, I grew fatigued of waiting. I looked over to my side, and saw five broad Roman-like columns assembled in a line, with arches connecting them.

Taken over by my curiosity, I moved away from the spiritbeings. I felt drawn to explore. The ambience was serene and harmonious. The realm was made of golden light and hues of white and ivory, but everything was clear and translucent at the same time. Everything projected light. The surface was cloud-like but firm. Where we stood had boundaries of darkness surrounding it. Instinctively, I knew not to go near the darkness; it was like being on the edge of a void.

Focusing back on the wall, I recall standing, looking up and admiring the magnificence of the columns. I was curious to learn what the columns were made of. My eyesight zoomed in and I saw what the crystal-like structures consisted of.

As I looked back up to study the columns further, I saw the sphere of light again. Drawn to its grasp of love, I quickly flew up toward it. Instantly, the light grew until it engulfed me. Everything had become piercing bright-white light. Abruptly, the four spirit-beings moved in front of me, surrounding me in a u-shape, holding me back. They then pushed me back further, until everything was dark. The only thing visible was their dark bodies, outlined by a thin line of gold surrounded by blue auras.

The spirit-beings stood sternly towering over me, forming a straight line, and I knew I was not to go forward. As I looked at them, I felt as though I were being scolded, like I had done something wrong. As I was pushed away, I gazed back at them in that final moment and saw their bodies relax, like they were relieved, and their auras turned back to gold.

Awaking in recovery, I felt so peaceful and beautiful. I didn't understand what had just happened. Heads were popping in and out of the recovery room, and I sensed the nurse was shocked by the amount of energy I had, as I stood up right away, trying to put my clothing back on, saying I was ready to leave. The car ride home was the strangest thing; I had one eye full of blood and sutures, yet I felt so happy.

It took several weeks to process everything. I felt connected to the Divine Source. Any thought or question I had about anything regarding the universe would be answered, even before I could think it. On many occasions, I fell into unelected deep meditative states in which I kept repeating the words, "I want to be God's Love."

I felt like I was losing my mind after what I was experiencing. I started my search online, and it ended with a conversation with my doctor. When I approached him on an unscheduled visit, I was blunt about it. I asked him, "Was there anything unusual that happened during my surgery. Were there any complications I was not told about?" Caught off guard, he blushed and answered, "Yes there was a problem with the anaesthesia, and you had an airway blockage that would have resulted in your death if we had not intervened quickly. I had only seen this twice before in my very long career." I told him what I had experienced, and he openly and warmly listened.

I returned home relieved, as my suspicions were verified. The meditative states continued for about another week, but this would not last. I was soon left spiritually cold again, as I felt the deep connections of the initial after-effects of the experience as they were wearing off.

As the years passed, my ideals and beliefs about God and the eternal world would yo-yo back and forth. It was difficult to reconcile the pain of being transgendered on Earth with my recollections of Divine connection and beauty on the other side.

After my atheistic beliefs died, I still struggled to understand why I had suffered this pain in my life and prayed for an answer. After losing a transgender friend to suicide, I was in great grief. This was now the second time in a year and a half that I'd lost a friend like me to suicide.

One night, after falling asleep, I awoke back in Heaven. You would think this was a dream, but it wasn't. It was more real than real. I had no body; I was a speck of light. A beautiful young girl was standing before me, with her back turned to me. She had long blonde hair that came down to her backside. She was slightly taller than the girl I had seen in Heaven. Her body was closer to Earthlike reality, but was of vivid light. To my right side, I felt a great, warm male presence; it was the being with its beautiful bright, white brilliance. Immediately, I entered into her little body, which I realized on reflection was actually me. I could not see my face, but I finally saw how God saw me. The only words I spoke were, "I am perfect." With those words, a flash, a piercing bright light overcame me, and it was over. It was like taking a deep breath back into eternity.

I sat up in my bed, and felt completely at peace and full of warm love. For the first time, I felt healed. My anger with God was washed away. I understood, He loved me, and all of this had a purpose. It was about love.

My soul was completely transformed, as I no longer felt the dark bitterness of my past. Although my life had not physically changed, I now knew how much I was loved and that my suffering would always lead me back to love. I felt compelled to stop hating God and took the time to start getting to know God instead. I felt peace as I learned how to appreciate and love those who hated me. For the first time, I stopped allowing people to abuse me, as now I loved myself for the way God created me.

Individuals who are transgender are still souls. The little girl who claims to be a boy, grows to be someone like me. Some people try to claim being transgender is a mental illness. On the other hand, leading doctors understand that being transgender is an illness of the physical body. Like those leading doctors, I suggest that being transgender is someone opening the door to their soul.

My life has come with many challenges. However, I feel blessed to have had a number of spiritual experiences that opened my heart, mind and soul to God's infinite love for all of humanity, regardless of our many differences. If I had one wish to fulfil in this lifetime, it would be to open a real conversation with those who are fearful and lack understanding and compassion for people who are born transgender. Without my NDE and subsequent spiritual experience, I doubt I would have the courage to speak so openly about my life. I know the mission I was given was to bring about positive change in the world. It is essential to me that this be accomplished. I thank God for giving me this Divine purpose and the opportunity to make a difference.

This is a truly fascinating account of how empowering NDEs and spiritual experiences can be. Jessica has lived a life of adversity that has been laden with challenges since her childhood. I find it intriguing that her initial NDE was a precursor to transformation, even more so than the trigger for the transformation she described. The deep connections that she experienced during the NDE began to dissipate with time – which can happen. However, she appears to have maintained a spiritual connection, because she also described entering into spontaneous meditative states. Her feelings toward God fluctuated between love and hate as she dealt with a combination of wonderful memories of the NDE, coupled with a sense of rejection during it. Although other people I have spoken to have described similar feelings, this is far less commonly reported.

The turning point of Jessica's transformation came a few years later, when Jessica underwent a spiritually transformative experience that occurred shortly after the death of her dearly loved friend. Such experiences are very common following a period of grief. The significance of this experience was that it totally transformed her thinking and perception of herself, to the point that she feels that all previous hardships in her life have been healed. The bitterness and darkness of her past have been totally transcended, and she has been empowered to love herself for what she feels is God's purpose.

Subsequently, Jessica is now compelled to speak about her life *publicly. She feels passionately about helping others and being an advocate for raising awareness about transgender issues. Her new perspective on life has resulted in her finding meaning and purpose. She now understands this could only have been achieved through loving herself exactly as she is – perfect. The courage Jessica has demonstrated will be a beacon to others facing similar issues. We feel honoured that Jessica has allowed us to include her story in this book, as this is the first time she has publicly shared it.*

19

COLLECTIVE CONSCIOUSNESS

Dr Bernie Siegel is a retired paediatric surgeon, who lives in a suburb of New Haven, Connecticut, with his wife Bobbie. He has written many books on the relationship between the patient and the healing process, including Love, Medicine and Miracles *and* The Art of Healing. *Bernie has been named as one of the top 20 spiritually influential living people on the planet. We feel honoured and privileged that, when approached to support our project, he not only offered to endorse our book, but also kindly proposed to share his own NDE that he'd experienced as a young child. In addition, he gives his professional opinion on collective consciousness.*

When I was 4 years old, I was at home in bed with one of my frequent ear infections. I took a toy telephone I was playing with, unscrewed the dial, and put all the pieces in my mouth, as I had seen carpenters do with nails they were going to use. The problem was that I aspirated the pieces and went into laryngospasm. I can still feel my intercostal muscles and diaphragm contracting forcefully, trying to get some air into my lungs, but nothing worked and I was unable to make any sounds to attract help. I had no sense of time, but suddenly realized I was not struggling anymore. I was now at the head of the bed watching myself dying.

I found it fascinating to be free of my body and a blessing. I never stopped to think about how it was that I could still see and think while out of my body. I was feeling sorry that my mother, who was in the kitchen, would find me dead, but I thought it over and found my new state preferable to being alive. Intellectually, I chose death over life.

Then the boy on the bed had an agonal seizure, vomited and all the toy pieces came flying out. He began to breathe again and I was very angry as I returned to my body against my will. I can still remember yelling, "Who did that?" My thought afterwards, though, as a 4-year-old, was that there was a God who had a schedule and that presumably I wasn't supposed to die now. The way I would explain it today is that an angel did a Heimlich manoeuvre on me.

On the basis of my later life experiences, I really do believe we unconsciously create a schedule for the future. Twice I have had my car written off by people driving through red lights and once I fell off our roof when the top rung on my wooden ladder snapped off. In none of these incidents did any significant injury occur to my body. Someone told me it was because I had an angel and he knew his name. I asked what it was, and he asked, "What did you say when the ladder broke?"

"Oh shit!" I said.

"That's his name," he replied.

I should add that this angel always shows up when I call him in an impassioned way.

My next experience was with the healer Olga Worrall. I had injured my leg training for a marathon. It was very painful and not responding to rest or therapy. At an American Holistic Medical Association conference, Olga was a guest speaker. My wife told me to ask her to heal me. I was embarrassed to ask and, quite frankly, a non-believer. Nevertheless, my wife pushed me forward and Olga sat me down on a chair and placed her two hands on my leg. The heat from her hands was incredible. I remember putting my own hands on the opposite leg to compare the heat sensation. There was no sense of warmth from my hands coming through the dungarees. When Olga was done, I stood up and was completely healed. The pain was gone and I could walk normally.

Another time, Olga and I spoke at the funeral of a mutual friend. After the ceremony, we were standing in a deserted hallway when she asked, "Are you Jewish?"

"Why are you asking?"

"Because there are two rabbis standing next to you." She went on to tell me their names and describe their garments, which included their prayer shawls and caps. Her description of them matched exactly what I had seen in my meditation and imagery sessions, during which I had met these figures while walking on my path.

Another evening, I gave a lecture, but it felt as though I was simply verbalizing it for someone else. A woman came up to me and said, "Standing in front of you for the entire lecture was a man, and I drew his picture for you." Again, exactly the face and features of my inner guide. I still have the picture hanging in our home.

My next experience came when I was telling a friend about how busy I was, and she said, "Why are you living this life?" Her intention was to get me to slow down and travel less, but her question sent me into a trance and I immediately saw myself with a sword in my hand killing people. My first reaction to this was that I had become a surgeon in this life to use a knife to heal, not kill.

I spontaneously went into a trance again a few days later and saw myself living the life of a knight – a knight who killed because he feared his Lord and what this Lord would do to him if he didn't carry out his commands. In this trance, I killed my wife and her dog, and was devastated by the experience. But at the same time, it revealed to me why my wife's face has always had a hypnotic effect upon me and why I am so involved in rescuing animals.

Ultimately, my NDE taught me about having faith in the true Lord and – like Abraham, Jesus, Moses, Noah and others – to understand that what our Lord asks of us is for the greater good.

I learned from this that if I had faith in my Lord, I would have been asked to bring families in conflict together and the solution would be for the young woman and myself to marry and be given the land that was being fought over to us as a wedding gift. Then we became one family with nothing to fight over.

Most recently, one of our cats disappeared when a door was left open. After several weeks with no sign of her, I was sure she must have been killed by a predator. A friend I had made, Amelia Kinkade, is an animal intuitive who lives in Los Angeles. We live in Connecticut and Amelia has never been to our home or near it. I pestered her to tell me where the cat was. She told me in an email, without my even sending her a picture of the cat, "The cat is alive because I can see through its eyes." Her message detailed the house, yard, other animals and people who were involved in the cat's life. The next day I went out and found the cat exactly where Amelia said it was hiding.

If that doesn't make me a believer in the collective consciousness, nothing will. I totally believe that consciousness is non-local and not limited to the body. I have experienced this also through the drawings and dreams of patients I have cared for, which help them to know their diagnosis and what the future holds for them. As Jung said, "The future is unconsciously prepared long in advance and therefore can be guessed by clairvoyants."

I have also had communication with the dead through a friend who is a medium, mystic and former patient. In addition, I hear a voice speaking to and advising me at times, and the words have had an enormous impact on my life. I believe it is this unconscious awareness that we are each impregnated with when we are born. I do not believe we literally live many lives; rather, that we bring with us the experience of previous lives. Thus, the wiser we get, the better the future will be for those who follow us.

It is so interesting to read of Bernie's experiences, beginning with his NDE at the age of 4. It appears that his NDE may have influenced how his career developed, giving him an openness and understanding of spiritual aspects of patient care. Bernie shaved his head 40 years ago, when it was considered by others to be an abnormal thing to do. He learned from Jung's work that it facilitates the uncovering of one's spirituality, as monks do, and being like a newborn child again. Bernie is a trailblazer and has led the way for physicians exploring the mind – body connection.

He developed a therapy for cancer patients in 1978 called Exceptional Cancer Patients, which focused on group therapy incorporating patients' drawings, dreams, feelings and images. The therapy facilitates lifestyle changes through loving, therapeutic confrontation leading to personal empowerment and healing in a supportive, loving environment. Bernie strikes me as being a man ahead of his time in instigating such therapeutic processes, which are becoming increasingly more popular as further research confirms the importance of addressing spiritual and mental aspects of disease, as well as the physical.

Bernie has predicted that, in the coming years, research will begin to focus on spirituality, consciousness, non-local healing, body memory and heart energy. Already those changes are beginning, as many exciting research projects are being embarked upon. As Bernie's website states, he "embraces a philosophy of living and dying that stands at the forefront of the medical ethics and spiritual issues our society grapples with today. He continues to assist in the breaking of new ground in the field of healing and personally struggling to live the message of kindness and love" – the ultimate message of NDEs.

20

THE GIFT OF BEING

(In dedication to Dr Barbara Mango's father, Melville Pollak)

Kelly connected with 61-year-old Dr Barbara Mango via social media and they quickly became firm friends. During the early stages of the writing of this book, Barbara's father was diagnosed with a terminal illness and he sadly passed a few months later. Despite this especially traumatic time for Barbara, she has continued to be enthusiastic about this book and has contributed this chapter. We are indebted to Barbara for her dedication in continuing to work with us, despite the emotional difficulties she was facing at the time.

Dr Mango is a graduate of the American Institute of Holistic Theology, with an MA and PhD in Metaphysical Science. She has published blog, web and print articles, and has appeared on radio and TV.

One of the most powerfully transformative encounters of my life occurred as I sat with my father as he lay dying of terminal cancer. During the last weeks of his life he underwent an extraordinary series of experiences, known as an NDA, or Nearing Death Awareness. As the foundation Eternea (The Convergence of Science and for Personal and Global Transformation) explains:

When people dying ... of a terminal illness are approaching death, they too, have remarkable experiences ... and seem to develop an expanded awareness. This is called Nearing Death Awareness (NDA), and these experiences bear distinct parallels to NDEs (Near-Death Experiences). In fact, dying people seem to be able to drift from this reality into another and back with relative ease. Their attempts to share the wonders of these experiences by words or behaviours are often thwarted by our lack of understanding of the symbolic language they use. Yet, they are talking while the experience is actually happening.

It is all too common for family members to dismiss this figurative language and instead label it as the "ramblings" of a dying mind or drug-induced hallucinations. However, it is precisely *through* this dialogue that the dying communicate with us. Deciphering this seemingly mysterious language requires listening with our hearts, rather than logic. Messages of the dying typically describe what they are actually experiencing or requesting. If we truly listen, we share in the journey of our loved one's transition, while simultaneously helping to facilitate a peaceful, comforting and reassuring transition. Sadly, this communication is usually viewed as patient delirium or agitation, requiring sedation.

Somehow, I easily understood my father's symbolic references/other reality. I attribute this "knowing" to a lifetime of spiritually transformative/anomalous experiences. Many components of my experiences share characteristics found in NDEs/NDAs: communication with spiritual beings and deceased loved ones, experiencing a profound and peaceful love inexplicable in human terminology, and a knowing that consciousness exists after physical death.

From these collective experiences, I was healed emotionally and physically, and they facilitated my spiritual growth. In retrospect, each occurred at precisely the "right" time in my life – when I most needed a particular message, Divine inspiration or loving assurance. Synchronistic in nature, they gently and repeatedly guided me toward becoming the person I am today. Combined, they have cemented my belief that NDEs and STEs provide a glimpse of a realm we move to when our physical body dies; one of Divine existence, oneness and indescribable love.

The depth and breadth of my experiences could fill an entire book, let alone a single chapter. Throughout my lifetime, they have transformed the way I view life. I am no longer interested in materialism or superficial pursuits. I have no patience for divisiveness, self-absorption, prejudice or superiority.

Living as an empathic, tolerant, open-minded, compassionate and loving person is the only way I know how *to be.*

My life dramatically changed in May 2007, during which time I was working as a pre-school teacher for low-income and high-risk children. I absolutely believe synchronicity and our shared passion for working with/helping underprivileged children later connected me with Kelly Walsh.

On 15 May 2007 a particularly active 3-year-old had scrambled to the top of a very high play structure. I climbed as quickly as possible to retrieve my energetic student when suddenly I slipped and fell seven feet flat onto my back. I was very lucky I was not paralysed. I was, however, in excruciating pain. Two months later, and after numerous scans, I was diagnosed with a traumatic sacral fracture with severe damage to my left SI joint (a joint connecting the sacrum to the pelvis).

I have always been physically fit and extremely active, yet I could no longer work or do any physical activity. The sacrum supports the weight of the upper body; thus, I could not sit or stand for more than five minutes at a time, as both were agonizing. Merely walking short distances was challenging.

This injury was a huge turning point in my life. I became depressed, both from chronic, unabating pain, and from grieving the loss of the physicality I once possessed. I wallowed in self-pity, trying my hardest to understand why this "terrible thing" had happened to me. "Why is life so unfair?" I screamed to myself. The answer came to me like a lightning bolt ... rather than fight my pain and physical limitations, I decided to embrace them, realizing there was a Divine reason this accident had occurred. My injury served as a lesson to guide me further toward my path of spiritual development and life's true purpose. However, I still remained unsure exactly what that was.

Physically limited, I turned my energy inward. Due to my lifetime of anomalous experiences and interest in metaphysics, I enrolled in a Master's Degree programme in Metaphysical Science. Because of unrelenting pain, I was unsure if I could complete one class, let alone a two-year programme. However, I was mesmerized by my course-work and, despite my physical challenges, I completed the programme in 11 months. I immediately enrolled in the PhD programme. Fascinated with NDEs, I wrote my doctoral thesis on them, entitled: *Divided Minds: The Spiritual and Scientific Debate of the Near-Death Experience.*

Of course, my mind and heart were not divided. I knew without a shred of doubt that life did not end with physical death.

Because of my lifelong experiences and spiritually based education, I was able to be at my father's bedside during the final weeks of his life, lovingly and without fear. He was diagnosed with stage 4 metastatic pancreatic cancer in March 2016. He bravely underwent both radiation treatment and chemotherapy, but to no avail. I took a leave of absence from my job, and travelled back and forth to Florida (my parents' home) several times. I flew down for the final time in August 2016. After a long, hard battle with this vicious disease and numerous hospitalizations, my father was placed under hospice care at home.

As Elisabeth Kübler-Ross, Swiss psychiatrist, pioneer in NDEs and author of the ground-breaking book *On Death and Dying* has stated: "Death is not a medical event. Death is a spiritual one."

How true these words rang for me. I was about to embark on the most profound spiritual journey of my life. I would not have been able to be a calm presence in the face of terminal cancer without my belief that life does not end with physical death. In fact, death merely releases the glorious eternal essence confined by physical being.

NDErs clinically die, transitioning **away** from their Divine experiences back to physical being. However, I was given the gift of sharing my father's progression **toward** this Divine state of existence. I suddenly realized that these two seemingly distinct phenomena are actually two aspects on the same continuum. This is beautifully summed up by French novelist, Anais Nin: "Life is a full circle, widening until it joins the circle motions of the infinite."

Watching the deterioration of my father was heart-breaking. Each day his frail body seemed to shrink and shrivel further into his hospital bed. I felt helpless, overcome with sadness and, at times, absolutely overwhelmed. I sobbed for hours and was mentally and physically exhausted. Yet spiritually, I always felt calm and centred.

I sat by my father's side, holding his hand, stroking his arm and gently rubbing his feet. I gave him manicures, applied cold compresses to his forehead when he spiked fevers, and applied balm on his dried and cracking lips. I kissed and hugged him, played his favourite classical music and helped feed him. These were acts of pure love.

My father always described himself as an "atheistic Jew", which is actually a complete oxymoron. He believed death was THE END, period; no afterlife whatsoever, only an eternal, deep and dreamless sleep. Throughout his lifetime, he remained absolutely unafraid of death. Because of this, we were able to talk openly about aspects of dying, the afterlife, and his wonderment of "hovering" between the physical and non-physical worlds.

Knowing that my father was returning to his "real" home brought me great peace. We spoke of special moments, memories and our love for one another. Although he had hurt and let me down many times throughout my life, I was able to see past these imperfections to the beautiful, spiritually perfect being he truly was. None of us, while in physical incarnation, understand our life's "grand" plan or purpose. I certainly did not fathom what my father's was, nor my own, so how could I pass judgement of any kind?

My father's hospital bed was placed in our family room, which I quickly dubbed "operation central". The hospice team worked in 12-hour shifts, with at least one hospice nurse always present. I cannot speak highly enough of the staff and, most especially, the critical care nurses. Many had over 35 years of hospice/critical care experience. They were loving, patient, compassionate, knowledgeable, kind and always accessible. I spoke in depth with most of them.

Many days, I sat next to my father's bedside glued to my laptop, working furiously away on this chapter. Several nurses asked me what I was doing. I hesitated to tell them. Obtaining a PhD and researching, writing and speaking about NDEs has not, unfortunately, made me immune to strange looks and lost relationships due to my perceived "weird beliefs". I have been called crazy, ungodly and numerous less kind words. Traditional science ridicules the idea that consciousness survives death. Medical staff commonly dismiss the validity of survivors' NDEs, insisting instead that they are mere hallucinations. Family members and friends struggle to understand the NDE phenomena. The majority of individuals fear experiences which are imperceptible to our five physical senses. Unfortunately, fear often perpetuates judgement and narrow-mindedness.

My father's nurses were especially open, non-judgemental and accepting. They truly *listened* to him, neither rejecting nor discounting his experiences. Thus, trusting they would understand my own perspective, I talked about my lifetime experiences, education and the purpose behind this book. They were actually eager to talk about STEs/NDEs. What a relief! From that point on, we talked in depth about death, dying and spirituality. I asked nearly every nurse if any of their patients had undergone an NDE and, if so, approximately how many? Their answers were nearly identical. Each responded, nearly verbatim, "Yes, quite a lot – approximately 40 to 50 per cent."

I was shocked – blown away, actually. Current statistics report approximately 15 per cent (although it has been suggested that the number is indeed much higher) of the US population has experienced an NDE. Of course, the hospice figure is approximate and could not, in any way, be considered scientifically valid. The nursing staff, however, proposed two reasons contributing to their high estimate.

First, hospice nurses, except for short breaks, spend 12-hour sessions of not only caring for, but *observing* each patient. Thus, unlike a hospital environment, they spend the vast majority of their shift with a single patient. Second, this one-on-one setting allows patients to become comfortable with, even close to their nurses. A hospice is a unique medical setting, in which patient and nurses experience the dying process together. In this loving and supportive environment, most patients feel safe sharing their spiritual occurrences. My father was one of these patients. He experienced two STEs and one OBE (out-of-body experience); they all occurred a few weeks before his death.

I must emphasize again that my father was a complete and total atheist who did not believe in spiritual experiences, period. Thus, his scepticism, made these occurrences especially wondrous. One morning I awoke and stumbled blearily into the kitchen. My father called my mother and me to his bedside with frantic urgency. He insisted I get a paper and pencil and write down EXACTLY what he said. This is what he told us:

Earlier this morning I saw a being, not a person. It definitely was not a human being. Together we hovered above the foot of my bed. We were looking down at myself on the bed. The glowing being told me it was time to stop giving away my things. This Being of Light told me a party was going to be given in my honour, and I was to be the special guest. However, because mom (my mother) was unwilling to come, it had to be cancelled.

I found this compelling for two reasons. First, Dad was extremely lucid and not medicated at the time. Second, dream psychology (or psychology of the unconscious) tells us that the giving of gifts or "offerings" indicates that one is on his/her path toward spiritual fulfilment. I knew, without a doubt, that my father had indeed undergone his first spiritual encounter.

I firmly believe that my mother *had* to deny the validity of dad's conversations because she was emotionally incapable of accepting his impending death. Although I completely understood her deep-seated need to reject his poignant messages, it broke my heart. Dad desperately sought her acknowledgement of his last remaining wish – to "let him go with love". Lacking this support, he felt trapped in his physical body – unable to attend the glorious homecoming party awaiting him.

Days later, he once again insisted on speaking with us. This time he described several Beings of Light smiling with joy and kindness as they prepared him for a Jewish ritual cleansing ceremony. The Jewish ritual cleansing bath, called *mikvah,* is the purification rite of a male Jew before he is laid to rest and his soul ascends on high. The beings next told him they were unable to finish the ritual cleansing, as again my mother chose not to be a part of it.

The third incident occurred in the early morning on the day I was flying home. Before her shift was over, the night nurse grabbed my arm. She told me that in all her years of hospice work, she had never experienced such a beautiful and transformational evening. In the middle of the night my father awoke and insisted that she play a particularly beautiful hymn, one that she had never heard before. She found the song on her cell phone and played it for my father. He rarely sings and, as far as I know, doesn't know the words to any hymn or religious song. Yet, he placed his weak and trembling hands in a prayer position and, while looking intently toward the ceiling, sang every word clearly and correctly. (In Judaism, spiritual hymns are called *Nigunim,* or "songs" of joy. They are sung to give one profound peace and closeness to God/Source.) Immediately afterwards, he saw his name "written" above him, and was at utter and complete peace. The "beings" were waiting for him! The nurse said, "I knew there was a purpose why I was chosen to come to this house tonight. It was the most peaceful, beautiful evening I've ever had in my 35 years of hospice work. The energy in the room was so serene it was palpable." Coming from a long-term hospice nurse, that's saying a lot.

Being by my father's side during his final weeks on Earth was alternately heartbreaking, overwhelming, and both mentally and emotionally draining. However, it was, without question, the most loving, gentle and transcendent experience of my life – a profound gift. I always loved my father, yet now, my love was deeper. We forged a stronger, more honest and meaningful relationship during the last weeks of his life.

I have been dramatically changed by this experience. Likewise, Dad transformed in ways previously unimaginable. His anger and passive-aggressive behaviour were replaced by a calm gentleness. Previously unable to express affection, he began saying he loved me and showering me with constant hugs and kisses. A man who always found it extraordinarily difficult to discuss inner feelings now openly shared his deepest fears, wishes, regrets and hopes for the future once he was gone. He developed expanded spiritual awareness, deeply comforted by the transcendent nature of his journey. I equate my father's NDA to peeling an onion. Each layer represents an aspect of ego. As one peels away the seemingly endless layers, the inner core, or soul, is finally exposed.

Countless individuals question the significance of sitting with a loved one during the final weeks of his/her life. Why is this so important? It is because of the meaning we give to being present. Perhaps the best gift we can offer our transitioning loved one is to let him/her see that we are sharing this experience *together.* In other words, the simple but powerful gift of loving presence, or simply *being.*

However, it is critical that care-takers and family members provide unconditional love, understanding and empathy to NDA experiencers. As difficult as it is, we must listen to our beloved ones with open hearts and minds. Nearing Death Awareness is not a black or white experience. Instead, it is a transcendent encounter filled with a thousand shades of grey. We must understand that although the figurative language of the dying is unlike that of the living, it doesn't make it less real. We must not assume these conversations are merely the result of medication, lack of oxygen or hallucinations. The presence of an informed caregiver is invaluable, and can ultimately provide both care-taker and patient with a wondrous opportunity for growth and healing.

Any experience may be considered spiritually transformative if it causes a person to change in a profound and different way, forever altering his/her beliefs, priorities and sense of self-purpose. Such experiences may be triggered by various occurrences. These may include (but not be limited to) NDEs, out-of-body experiences, after-death communications (ACDs), and, as demonstrated by my father, Nearing Death Awareness experiences. Because, in the end, they all share the same universal message of Divine love, peace and interconnectivity with all.

Barbara has experienced many spiritual experiences throughout her life, which was one of the motivating factors in her studying NDEs at doctoral level. Some people experience an NDE, then have a second chance at life, while others don't experience anything out of the ordinary except as they approach death. Death is a natural process and something that awaits us all. It is when we begin to confront our mortality that our fears can begin to dissipate. Barbara had the gift of being able to be with her parents and attend to her father in the last few months of his life. It is not easy to watch loved ones endure the physical ravages of the body, but Barbara was also able to witness the spiritual experiences that were a part of her father's transition into death.

POSTSCRIPT CROSSING OCEANS TO LOVE

One factor that has been felt by every contributor to this book is love. Their experience opened them up to depths of love that, in many cases, had never been experienced before. As we draw this book to a close, we would like to add a short postscript from two of the contributors. During the early planning stages of this book, through a synchronistic connection, they fell in love.

Ainsley Threadgold

I want to take the time to share this part of my story. It is beautiful, poignant and filled with the most Divine unconditional love. This part of my journey has found me re-emerged. Before this point I was a caterpillar; I am now a beautiful, glorious butterfly. Krista is the wind under my wings and the many colours that they display. To her I have given my heart. It is through her that I have discovered true love and the ability to show it.

Our early interactions were awash with energies. I look back now and I feel that it was as if we were given the first tantalizing tastes of a connection beyond any either of us had known. Unfortunately, neither of us were in situations where we could immediately explore this. There was a 4,500-mile expanse between us, we were both married to other people, and I had become a new parent, but still I couldn't help but be drawn to her. I felt a Divine spark pull me in her direction and, like magnets, the closer we got, the stronger the attraction between us, the greater the friendship.

Though it was obvious that we cared deeply for each other, I found myself having to withdraw. I was plagued by a lifetime of emotional pain and for the first time had to take a long hard look at who I had been. This meant withdrawing from Krista; at the time I couldn't tarnish her with my pain.

Then, weeks later, through a series of synchronous happenings, Krista found a way to break through the barriers I'd created. She wrote me the most heart-warming message; one which, like a gentle warm breeze, permeated my being. It was immediately clear that our friendship meant as much to her as it did to me, and the universe knew that; it wasn't going to let our egos get in the way of something it knew was to become Divinely beautiful.

This was to spark off a huge wave of change for us both. I became increasingly aware that my current relationship had failed; worse than that, my continued presence was causing more pain.

I understand now that, while each NDE is unique, there are also key similarities. Likewise, there are also parallels in the transformative after-effects: I'm aware of a number of accounts in which people have re-emerged into their old lives realizing that they don't fit anymore. My situation was no different, and after a karmic kick up the backside from a Tarot reading, I saw the road I'd hidden from. For a number of years I'd been living in a relationship where both parties were denying a poignant truth: being together was tearing us apart. Sometimes the most loving act is to do what hurts the most, so at the beginning of July I left home. I had just a bag to my name and nowhere to go.

I was soon able to sustain myself as well as my wife and daughter, while having my own space to breathe. This brought up old energies that, like the seemingly destructive nature of a forest fire, needed to be cleared. I again found myself retreating. Opening up was too much; I erected my barriers again and closed down. Once more I found myself retreating from Krista. As much as it hurt her, with the grace of an angel, she gently gave me the space required for me to do what I needed to do.

After the fire has died, new life emerges. Two days later I received a message from Krista, wanting to move forward. I was later to learn something which, to this day, moves me to my very core. After spending several days suffering in her ego, Krista had an experience of being immersed in the most Divine feeling of unconditional love. She then knew that we were destined to do and be more; she also knew that she wanted to be a part of my life. She broke through my barriers, showing me that I could love myself and that it was okay to be vulnerable.

The many events that followed would prove beyond a shadow of a doubt that our friendship was turning into love and, to use the analogy of an alpine flower, growing in the harshest of circumstances. Our human response to it is to move the flower. The flower only knows it needs the sun. Krista was the sun I needed to open my delicate petals and, for the first time, see that my scars were beautiful because they were me.

There is so much I wish to share here about synchronicity – about pain through stagnation, pain through change – and also about growth but, at this time, I would like to delve into some of the more personal changes that my NDE has allowed me. After all, this isn't just about the experience itself, but about how I have developed since, how I have coped after having re-emerged again and again. I have made several leaps forward within myself and with the gifts I am developing to help all those Divine souls who I will be blessed to touch.

One of the immediate changes I felt was a need to understand more of myself. I was awakened into a life that was so closed off, so emotionally trapped, that I wondered how I was to move forward, and where I would start to make sense of my life to that point.

I had a number of hypnosis sessions with my therapist, Karen, dealing with present pains and finding that the root causes of a lot of them weren't all from this life but from many past lives too. The more work I did on myself, the more open I became and the more love I showed myself. I discovered that the key to my moving forward was to forgive myself, to learn for the first time to love who I was and not just to seek it from outside of myself. The KEY to truly showing love and compassion to others is to show it to yourself first!

This has been an ever-evolving and ever-healing part of my "self" work and that which I have done with Krista. We are intrinsically linked; what she experiences I feel and vice versa. Even though there are thousands of miles between us and a five-hour time difference, we each can feel the other. If Krista is upset or is healing from a particular aspect within herself, I feel it with her, often gaining healing of my own. Where before I would struggle to share how I was or what I was feeling, with Krista I can be completely open and I know that she can be completely open with me. She has helped me develop my intuitive skills; this, in turn, has opened me up to my ability to channel information. I am often inspired to write about a certain subject. I feel the words flow through me, as if the universe is using me to write its Divine melody: messages of love, hope and inspiration have come through and I have posted them. I have been met with the knowledge that it was exactly what someone needed to hear, or it spoke of how they were feeling and helped them to understand.

This has further developed with my ability to channel messages for people, either from the universal energies, guides and higher powers, or from deceased loved ones. This has proven very accurate; with me gaining knowledge that I couldn't have previously known for those I have channelled for. The process for this is usually through me opening myself up and allowing any inspirations to flow through me as I write. I have also spoken messages to people. I feel a subtle change within me, then have this feeling that the words I'm saying have an added power, and I know that they are serving a greater purpose.

I have rediscovered my lost memories. Regaining them has changed and enhanced who I am; it has taught me that we are all connected by love, that love combines us, holds us all together. We are like individual cells in the body of the universe, each carrying the Divine spark and being miniature representations of it. We are each unique and uniquely connected; there is a common goal hidden in the common struggle. We are all here to relearn the love that we are made of, to be the experience of the knowledge of all that is.

My discovery of this has allowed me to express it within myself and it has also helped me to (re)connect with the love of my life. Finding her, discovering that this is a love that will not just define this lifetime, but has defined many, knowing that on a soul level we are here to share that love, is wonderful. I, indeed we, are truly honoured to share what we have to the world. We both want people to see that love IS the key to magnificence; it is the key to unlocking lives. We have co-created a number of very loving circumstances, where we have crossed the oceans to spend time with each other. We also know that we want to live, love and work together.

In closing, I want to say that everyone is love, even if their current incarnations show the opposite; they are still love because they help define it. With every world-changing event in which people have done some truly horrible things, or when natural disasters strike, the immediate aftermath is for people to unite in love for all differences to be forgotten because, in those moments, we are moved by our most innate natures. This nature is love.

Krista Gorman

Making the choice to move on from my marriage opened me up to new possibilities where, up until then, feeling disempowered and disconnected from my true self, I'd felt I had to try and make the best of my present one. My future, I thought, was what I had then, but I couldn't have been more wrong. One of the most healing, most beautiful experiences of my life has been through a Divine relationship of the highest order with someone I have met as a result of our mutual NDE. Ainsley and I came to know each other through a series of amazing synchronicities, and many subsequent synchronicities have followed since we've met and reconnected our souls.

The path to our connection began with Dr Penny Sartori. While researching publishing houses for my book, I came across one based in the UK and browsed through their list of books. Dr Sartori was one of their authors and I was immediately drawn to her subject matter. With Penny being an ICU nurse and studying NDEs, I felt an instant connection to her, so I sent an email saying hello. In her warm response she gave me the name of Kelly Walsh, who had also experienced an NDE and lived in the UK. After speaking with Kelly, I felt like I'd met an old friend, a soul sister. We had an instant bond and I became a part of her Positivity Power Facebook group. It was there that I watched a video Ainsley had posted. He spoke about how we all have our frailties, and how these frailties bring us together. In the coming together was the potential to initiate change for the better in the world, through love. It was a heartfelt call to action and I literally felt like I'd been hit by a freight train. Something shifted in me on a very deep level and I intuitively knew Ainsley would be someone special in my life.

Soon after that, Ains and I did become friends and had an almost instant, deep connection. We discovered how our lives seemed to have paralleled one another's and it felt like we'd been brought together for a greater purpose, one far greater than we were yet able to understand. Those synchronous events have no other explanation other than they were created and co-created by us with the Divine loving intervention of the universe. Since then our connection has deepened so miraculously, so Divinely, and continues to do so each and every time we are able to drop the barrier of ego and allow ourselves to give and receive more love. For Ains and I, it was through our finding one another and nurturing our connection that we have then both been able to heal a lifetime of emotional wounds and re-experience the same Divine love that we are. The receiving part has been the most challenging, as it is with all of us, yet as we move along in our relationship that barrier has weakened and my love for myself, my Divine connection to myself, has deepened. As my self-love grows, so does my ability to love more. It's a gorgeous dance of life that defines why we are here. I'm being given the gift of re-experiencing the love of the afterlife in this life and am able to know and appreciate what a Divine miracle it is. If I never take another breath, I can rest assured that, through this love, I've been gifted with the experience of what it truly feels like to be *alive.*

There beautiful thing is, we can all have this gift. What was required for us was for ego to take a back seat. We had to do the emotional, energetic work, to clean house so to speak, so that we could become the highest version of ourselves not only for ourselves and each other, but for all those we are here to serve. Ego simply gets in the way and shrouds the love we are, yet is a necessary contrast to it. Without one, we wouldn't recognize the other. There really is no secret to our successful transformation from damaged and broken to healed and whole. Simplified, the key to our success is choosing love over fear. The key to everything is that when we choose love, life absolutely flourishes on all levels.

We all arrive here with the same key, but forget we have it. We're here to remember and re-member, to put the broken parts of ourselves back together, with love as the glue, and get to be that love once again.

I know it's possible. I've experienced how it feels and continue to experience it daily. Loving more is how we can heal and create a more loving world at the same time. Just love more. Then, love even more than that. THANK YOU!

CONCLUSION

Dr Penny Sartori

I feel very privileged to have had the opportunity to work on this book with everyone who has contributed. I feel the individual chapters have served to bring up relevant points that still need addressing, despite NDEs being in the full public domain.

A crucial point this book has highlighted is the need for a greater awareness and understanding of NDEs, so that people can be provided with greater psychological support when trying to understand and integrate such a deeply profound and life-changing experience. Many people struggle for years to come to terms with their experience and some research is suggestive that the divorce rate after experiencing an NDE is quite high. It seems totally unbelievable that in 2002, despite all the information about NDEs in the media, Erica's NDE was mistaken as a psychotic episode, for which she was transferred to a psychiatric hospital where her experience was suppressed by medication. This was in 2002, not 1902! This is the epitome of how arrogant and ignorant the medical system is when considering important spiritual matters, as it only focuses on the body. Within the current healthcare system, there is currently a great disconnection between the mind, body and spirit, because science is only equipped to deal with the physical – the mind and spirit cannot be measured, so are simply not acknowledged or addressed.

Another point that was apparent is that some of these experiencers also had a sensitivity to similar experiences during their childhood. This was also noted by Ring and Rosing (1990) when they undertook a study to investigate if there was a type of personality that made people prone to NDEs. This reiterates how important it is that children are supported if they describe unusual phenomena. Reports of non-ordinary states of reality should not be dismissed; instead, children should be encouraged to express what they have experienced. Thankfully Dr Bernie

Siegel was able to embrace his childhood NDE and integrate it into his life. He did this in a way that was conducive to developing a therapeutic practice combined with the formal medical training as a paediatric surgeon, that has greatly benefited many of his patients. His ongoing work strives toward humanizing medical education and medical care as well as teaching techniques to enhance the function of the immune system, hence empowering patients.

Ironically, our science now appears to be coming full circle and studies are beginning to confirm the spiritual dimension. The fact that our scientific technology is becoming so greatly advanced and resuscitation techniques are continuously improving means that more and more people are now surviving critical illness. It seems logical to predict that many more people will report an NDE. Hospital research into NDEs began in the 1970s, and in the subsequent few decades several prospective research studies have been published which confirm that NDEs occur and have very real after-effects.

As a former nurse, I strongly feel that NDEs should be a fundamental part of the education of all healthcare workers (and also of the general public, starting as early as schoolchildren). NDEs generally occur during a period of unconsciousness, and the first people patients have contact with, after they regain consciousness, are nurses or doctors. It is therefore crucial that patients who have undergone an NDE receive the appropriate support and guidance throughout their recovery. Patients are often faced with recovering from debilitating physical illnesses but the psychological recovery is often too easily overlooked. Patient care could be greatly enhanced if each healthcare worker was trained to recognize an NDE and respond appropriately. Another welcome change to healthcare would be to ensure that each patient who survives a critical illness is specifically asked if they can recall any unusual experiences. If so, they could then be referred to the appropriate services to support them fully through the process of coming to terms with that experience.

I have always found it particularly compelling that NDEs help with the grieving process. Those who have an NDE are usually left with the certainty that something spectacular awaits them when it is their time to die. Likewise, those who haven't had an NDE, but who are able to engage deeply with NDEs, may also adopt a new understanding of death. Prior to beginning my research, over 20 years ago, I had a very different perspective on death than I do now, and I found it incredibly difficult to deal with the loss of family members or to cope with the grieving process. Now, having had the benefit of studying death and near-death phenomena, I have a very different understanding, which has subsequently given me the strength to deal with my grieving in an altogether different way. I still feel a deep sadness and sense of loss when a loved one dies – that never goes away – but my research has made it easier for me to work through this.

When I reflect back on the deaths in my own family, I recall how death-denying I was when my paternal grandfather was diagnosed with a brain tumour. He was the first of my four grandparents to die and I remember being insistent that he try any form of treatment offered to him. Since then, my other three grandparents have died, but by that time I had begun researching and studying NDEs. My attitude changed greatly from one of denial to acceptance. Whereas I was forbidden to talk about death with my grandfather, I was able to have long conversations about my research with my three other grandparents before they died, which gave them all great comfort.

As I write this conclusion, it is a month to the day that the last of my grandparents, my maternal grandmother, died. She had been admitted to hospital and two days later, as I was arriving at work, I had a phone call from my family to say that the hospital had called to let them know that my grandmother was very unwell. The university where I work is next door to the hospital where she was being treated, so I got to her bedside before the rest of the family. The doctor spoke with me about the possibility of commencing a non-invasive type of respiratory assistance. I explained that I had previously been an ITU nurse and didn't think my grandmother would tolerate the mask. I advised that palliative care would be the most appropriate course of action and told the doctor that we'd discussed this as a family.

Thankfully, the doctor agreed with me and my grandmother had a very peaceful, dignified death with her family around her. This is a stark contrast to my attitude toward death with my paternal grandfather 23 years ago. I guess the fact that my grandmother was 90 years of age, whereas my grandfather was only 68, had a lot to do with it, but I also feel that I am now able to see the long-term picture. Death will come to us all eventually, but my research has taught me to embrace death rather than fear it, and to focus on and be appreciative of life.

Many professional services that deal with the bereaved are very aware of near-death phenomena and after-death communications, and often use accounts of NDEs to help their clients. In fact, I myself have provided training in this area for grief counsellors. The fact that having this awareness of neardeath phenomena can help so much, reinforces the importance of these experiences and their therapeutic benefits. These "ripple effects" of the NDE are of particular interest to me because they can be developed further to help others. So many people struggle with grief. By hearing more about these experiences, society will begin to think about death differently and, in so doing, could develop a deeper understanding and acceptance of this aspect of being human that awaits us all.

The work of William Peters, who has created the Shared Crossing Project described in Chapter 15, transpired from his NDEs. It is of great importance because it helps those who are grieving the loss of a loved one. William's work has enabled facilitation of the shared death experience and, from the cases I have in my files of these experiences, it shows that those who have undergone them have been able to work through their grief much faster than those who have never had such an experience.

From a healthcare perspective, I am also intrigued by the remarkable healings that have been reported by some people following an NDE. In fact, I witnessed one such case during the course of my hospital research, and subsequently wrote up the case of Patient 10 (Sartori, Badham and Fenwick, 2006), who underwent a healing of a congenital contracture that he'd lived with for the 60 years prior to the NDE. Due to his cerebral palsy, his right hand had been in a permanently contracted position from birth, yet after his NDE he was able to open it out fully (all this was verified by his sister). The doctors and physiotherapists could not explain how this was possible.

Remarkable recoveries following an NDE have also been reported by others, and there are many examples in the literature such as Mellen-Thomas Benedict and Anita Moorjani. In Chapter 6, David Bennett described how, after his NDE, he was diagnosed with cancer that had metastasized to many other parts of his body, yet he overcame this. Had something about David's mindset changed as a result of his NDE that helped facilitate his recovery from this often-fatal disease?

Shelley Parker, whose NDE features in my book *The Wisdom of Near-Death Experiences,* foresaw in a premonition, in her teenage years, that she would get cancer when in her thirties, but she was also reassured that she would survive. In 2009, Shelley was diagnosed with a rare form of lymphoma and given five weeks to live. It was during her treatment for cancer that she began to have out-of-body experiences. Her health deteriorated to the point that she felt she was dying. At this point she underwent an NDE, during which she was shown that her fiancé would die. Tragically, the following day, her fiancé, a commercial helicopter pilot, was killed when the helicopter he was flying crashed.

What I find particularly inspiring about Shelley is the way she coped with the loss of her fiancé and childhood sweetheart, especially when she herself was still so poorly with cancer. Numerous studies have demonstrated that bereavement and grief can adversely affect both mental and physical health.

Shelley's case highlights just how powerful NDEs can be. The health of many people has been affected in a negative way following a bereavement, but the exact opposite seems to have happened in Shelley's case. Despite being told by her doctor that she was unlikely to make it through the night, and despite having to come to terms with the negative impact of bereavement, she recovered and remains clear of cancer over seven years later. I feel there is much we could learn and incorporate from NDEs into future treatments of this disease.

Shelley's NDE subsequently influenced the way she lives her life. As she says: "Having this experience saved my life. I now know beyond question that there is a God (I was always an agnostic who sometimes bordered on being an atheist before) and we're all here for a reason. There was a very strong feeling while I was with God that the calmness and peace I felt is something we all should be striving for on Earth."

The NDE also motivated Shelley to change her career:

I knew that, despite my postgraduate qualifications and being a published children's author, I was coasting in my life before my cancer. Suddenly, wasting time not doing something you love seemed ridiculously pointless and, a year after my chemotherapy ended, I started to retrain as a psychotherapist; something I always wanted to do, but procrastinated about for years. I qualified in 2014 and now work as a personcentred psychotherapist.

My experience has made me realize that we're here to be fulfilled in life and to do what makes us happy – also what will help other people likewise. We really are all one. There was a very strong feeling of belonging in my NDE: that we're all in this together, and how much happier and "complete" we would all be if we realized we're more similar than different and can accomplish so much if we pull together and unite.

Shelley's concluding thoughts are echoed by most NDErs, including Robert Tremblay. The fact that Robert was diagnosed with end-stage AIDS and had been admitted to hospice to die, only for an NDE to change his whole outlook on life, is again testimony to how powerful NDEs are. He continues to fundraise and spread the word for AIDS awareness over four years after he was expected to die.

I am really astonished at the lack of attention given to cases of truly remarkable recoveries. Why do so few people seem interested? When cases of remarkable healings were investigated by Carlyle Hirshberg and Marc Ian Barasch (1995), they discovered many cases that had never been discussed in the literature and even suggested that less than 10 per cent of remarkable healings are ever recorded in journals. As they say on page one of their book: "Remarkable recovery is a phenomenon so spectacular, elusive, and almost scientifically disreputable that few researchers have bothered to look for it, let alone pursue its implications. When not dismissed as a mistaken diagnosis, it is considered almost a nuisance..." It is encouraging to see so many recent positive changes toward NDEs. I am optimistic that, in the future, there will be enthusiastic healthcare professionals who are also intrigued by these cases, and undertake research to investigate these aspects further.

Anyone who survives a close brush with death is likely to have a changed attitude to life after being given a second chance at it. Is this the case only for NDErs or are *all* people who survive death changed in the same way? These were questions asked by clinical psychologists Gary Groth-Marnat and Roger Summers, who published their research in the *Journal of Humanistic Psychology* in 1998.

The study consisted of 53 NDErs and a control group of 27 people who survived a close brush with death, but did not report an NDE. There was an additional group, comprising significant others for those in the first two groups, these being used to corroborate the life changes reported. The authors investigated changes in participants' lives, such as values, beliefs and attitudes, following their brush with death.

Notable changes included reduced fear of death with a reinforced conviction of an afterlife, reduced interest in material possessions, increased transcendental experiences, increased concern for others, increased self-worth, a heightened capacity for "paranormal" phenomena, and an increased appreciation of natural phenomena.

Analysis of the results showed that the NDErs exhibited greater changes than those who had survived a brush with death, but without the NDE. These changes were corroborated by the significant others in their life. It also showed that those who reported a deeper experience had more positive changes. The overall conclusion of the study was that it was the NDE itself and not just coming close to death that instigated the life changes. Despite this research having been published nearly 20 years ago, the medical system still does not appear to embrace the implications of this. Why aren't more people curious about this finding? Just what is it about the NDE that is so powerful that it literally changes lives? This is something that both interests and inspires me, and it gives me hope that one day funding will be available to investigate it further, so that we can develop new treatments within our healthcare system that embrace our spirituality and psychological health as well as the physical.

In his book *The Varieties of Religious Experience,* published in 1902, Harvard Professor of Psychology William James wrote that "by their fruits ye shall know them." How wonderfully each contributor to this book has fulfilled that statement. The steps they have taken speak for themselves. Many have developed support systems or new interventions that have great benefits to the health and well-being of others. They are a light to those around them, but they also have a great vision for the whole of mankind. They are no longer the centre of their own little world, but see themselves as part of the great whole of mankind and the planet. Their actions and accomplishments, ranging from personal transformations to setting up healing centres and support groups, make them stand out. Each of these is a step toward a more positive and loving world.

Another reason for writing this book has been to convey the vast potential that NDEs have for the continued well-being and evolution of mankind. The most prevalent and probably biggest thing conveyed by NDEs is a feeling of pure, unconditional love. This love is experienced to a depth never known before and seems to be exuded from NDErs. Loving and being compassionate to others becomes a natural state of being for them.

To be transformed in such profound ways, as demonstrated by each contributor in this book, highlights the power of NDEs. They can no longer be dismissed as hallucinatory. Indeed, the techniques developed by Diane Goble, Krista Gorman, Barbara Ireland, Katherine Baldwin and other NDErs are all conducive to good health, which in turn will positively impact on our evolution as a species.

In Chapter 10 Diane Goble stated that "We are rising above our animal nature and developing into fully integrated spiritual-human beings" and that she now feels her mission is to raise the consciousness of mankind. Something similar was suggested by Richard Maurice Bucke in his book *Cosmic Consciousness,* published in 1901. He believed that the consciousness of mankind was evolving to the next level. When people engage with the message of the NDE, they become aware of a deeper dimension of life and they realize they are part of a great whole. They intuit that every person on the planet is interconnected and that the behaviour of each person can impact on the planet itself. Once this is understood, life is lived from a perspective of love and respect: for others, as well as for the environment. Not only is the consciousness of mankind evolving, but so too is the planet, because when we mature and become aware of the environmental damage that human behaviour is causing, we then address this problem and ensure that we care for the planet as much as we care for ourselves as individuals.

Before I end this book, I would like to mention that, without Kelly's persistence and overwhelming enthusiasm, it would never have come to fruition. I was so busy with work and family commitments that I didn't have any spare time to devote to the project, but Kelly's long-term vision, and other projects she has planned, persuaded me to be a part of it. Kelly has undertaken the majority of the work behind the scenes, including contacting each contributor and liaising with the publisher. It has been great working with Kelly. Whenever I have felt overwhelmed by my workload, she has always been there with encouragement and help.

During her experience in hospital, she told the other patients around her that "like-minded souls would collaborate to change the world." Those words were reinforced when she recently contacted Caz Simms, one of those fellow patients. Caz remarked on how Kelly was doing exactly what she had talked about while in hospital. Kelly's motivation to act on what she learned during her experience has not waned; on the contrary, it continues to gather momentum despite all of the difficulties she has had to overcome. Though she's had to deal with fully integrating her experience and the changes that come with that, her father's suicide, and subsequent ridicule and rejection from her family, she still strives to make a difference and be of service to others.

Kelly is already making a positive impact on the world through her Positivity Power Movement and the Love, Care, Share Foundation, even though the latter is in its early stages. As this grows into its full potential, Kelly's determination and hard work will be a legacy for future generations.

Once people engage with the message of the NDE, it becomes "infectious"; Professor Kenneth Ring has likened NDEs to a "benign virus". As well as undertaking fascinating sociological research into NDEs in the 1980s, Professor Ring taught a course on NDEs. He found that many of his students were changed in ways similar to those who had undergone an NDE simply through learning about them. The changes weren't as significant as those who had experienced an NDE, but there were still noticeable, positive changes.

I believe that as more and more people engage with the message of the NDE, there will be great advances in our evolution as we begin to understand that we are all interconnected and that ultimately our actions impact on ourselves. We will then begin to live from love and not fear.

This book has featured only a handful of cases and there are many more out there awaiting your discovery; I would encourage everyone to seek these people out, be inspired by them and learn from them. You, too, can play a part by engaging with the message of the NDE and spreading the word.

EPILOGUE

Kelly Walsh

This book has been a labour of love, from conception to completion, and we do hope it touches the hearts, minds and souls of every single person who reads it.

NDEs are, for most people, transformative in nature. However, they often come with their challenges and, at times, many experiencers, including myself, can feel quite lonely and isolated when not in regular contact with others who fully understand and embrace what we have been through.

The turning point for me came when I connected with Dr Penny Sartori and subsequently started to connect with other experiencers from around the world via social media. It was like being reconnected to my long-lost soul family and I found it extremely cathartic.

What struck me the most when I connected with other experiencers, is that the vast majority of people, regardless of colour, creed, gender, sexuality, religious beliefs or any other differences, came back from their experience with a similar message of oneness and unconditional love. More interestingly, many – like me – had redirected their life's purpose following their experience, and in some cases made life-changing decisions that had completely altered the direction of their life and the lives of those around them.

It was the realization that so many people had been impacted in the same way as me, following their experiences, that gave me the idea for the concept of this book. The words I shouted out following my NDE –"like-minded souls would collaborate to change the world" – had never left me and I knew that one day I would be sharing my experiences and knowledge in collaboration with others to help make a positive contribution to the collective consciousness of our planet.

I was delighted when Penny agreed to co-author this book with me. We faced a few challenges along the way, which resulted in the book being postponed for 12 months. However, I truly believe there is an ebb and flow to life and that things happen when they are supposed to do and all in perfect Divine timing. We often get little nudges and guidance from God and the universe to help us realize when the time is right. To give you an example of this, I want to tell you a little bit about my puppy Coco and how she influenced the timing and importance of this book.

Following the death of my dad to suicide, my partner suggested buying me a puppy to help with my healing process. Interestingly, I chose Coco from a collection of lots of different breeds. She is a miniature schnauzer and I was surprised to discover that her birthday falls on 9 October, which happens to be the anniversary of my NDE. A few months after getting Coco, I was feeling much stronger and texted Penny to say that I thought we should consider completing the book as I intuitively felt the time was right. Penny agreed and that very same day I turned on my laptop to start work on the project. All of a sudden Coco ran across the keyboard and a website appeared called "God's New Message to the

World", which subsequently froze on my screen. At the time, I thought, *Wow, my intuition is correct. And now it's been reaffirmed and given the thumbs up by God and the universe.* I guess some people would struggle with my viewpoint and say that these incidences were just a coincidence. To that, I would simply smile and respond that our deceased loved ones, God and the angels are communicating with us all the time, but whether we are open to accepting and receiving these messages is totally down to us and our spiritual awareness.

I sat finalizing the words for this epilogue a few short days after the first anniversary of my dad's transition to the other side. I was in a contemplative mood, thinking about what I'd been through in the previous 18 months. That period in my life was by far the most difficult so far and, at times, I struggled with feelings of isolation and kept asking "why?" It's only on reflection that I have realized that the knowledge and wisdom I gained during my NDE experience helped me enormously during that painful time, particularly in relation to remembering how much I am loved, as we all are, by our Creator and that life truly is eternal.

If anyone reading this is struggling right now, whether through the loss of a loved one or through any other circumstances, please hold onto the healing power of Divine Love and know that the dark clouds will pass and the sun will shine again very soon. At all times you are in safe, protective, loving arms.

Let me assure you that you were guided to read this book for a reason. Nothing happens by chance or fate. Perhaps it has fallen into your path to assist you with your healing journey or, quite simply, to help you open your heart, mind and soul to new ways of thinking and living. There is no right or wrong answer; only you, and you alone, will know the real reason you chose this book and the impact it has had in your life.

I believe that part of the Divine purpose of this book is to unite like-minded souls who are passionate about making a positive difference to the world. If, like me, you don't want this to be the end, but, instead, just the beginning, please join our growing global community www.positivitypowermovement.com and forge new friendships with people who are committed to creating a more loving, caring, sharing world.

On our own, we often feel we can't do enough to create the lasting change our planet needs, and we can start to feel powerless. What I try to remind people of is that when we join forces and focus on what we *can* do, even if it's just giving a smile to someone who is feeling low, we can create a culture of kindness, unity and love that creates ripples of change across the globe.

Together we can create a better world; one where children have enough food to eat, where people live in peace and harmony, where all that unites us far exceeds the things that divide us. A united human race can build a better world through the work of a compassionate and loving, caring, sharing global community.

You are helping to do this simply by purchasing this book and encouraging others to do the same. Every single penny of the royalties raised by our global sales will be used to support the children's projects that the Love, Care, Share Foundation is aligned with.

Thank you for being part of our individual and collective journeys and we do hope that you feel inspired to play a part in this transformational movement. If this book has one clear and concise message, it is that we can all make profound changes in our personal lives, and when we link with other like-minded souls, we have the potential to change the world. Many of us are starting to wake up to the deeper realization that we are all a reflection of the Divine, which can be expressed as love for self, others, other species and the world. Everyone is capable of experiencing fear, isolation and trauma, etc., but such "shadow" experiences are an integral part of our healing journeys. The lesson for all of us in these troubled times is to believe that we can transform difficulties, such as fear, guilt or hatred, into love, forgiveness and compassion. One thing I can say, with growing confidence, is that the more we love, the more we

care, the more we share. These are the foundations of Positivity Power, which can change the world.
Love conquers all!

AFTERWORD

Neale Donald Walsch

The nature of spiritually transformative experiences is varied indeed. While I have never had an NDE such as those explored in this remarkable book, I have had three out-of-body experiences in my life – and I was intrigued to find that the accounts of NDEs here vary little from my most wondrous OBE, which has been included on these pages.

The narratives of others here also match in many ways the messages about life following our Continuation Day that I have received in dialogues I have published under the title *Conversations with God.* So I am doubly motivated to encourage you to let yourself hold closely the information you have found here.

Among the many special experiences in my life, I had the honour of working on the personal staff of Dr Elisabeth Kübler-Ross, a physician and psychiatrist, who may have done more than any other single individual to alter our understanding of death and our embracing of it as a natural and joyous part of life. Elisabeth said to those of us around her a hundred times: "Death does not exist. When you are no longer afraid of dying, you are not afraid of living."

The book you are holding in your hands can do more to release humanity from its fear of dying than any book in recent memory. If you found the *Conversations with God* material helpful to you in your life, or if you are familiar with any of the writings of one of my life's most wonderful mentors, Dr Ross, I am sure you have experienced these personal chronicles to be timely and powerful confirmations, coming from many separate sources, of what you may expect in that which we have come to call the afterlife – as well as of the reality and nature of God.

In *Conversations with God – Book 4: Awaken the Species* (2017, Watkins), humans everywhere are invited to self-select to be among those who commit to moving forward their own individual evolution by sharing the stories of their journey in a way that serves to awaken the entire species to who and what all human beings really are (Individuations of Divinity). The others who agreed to place their personal testimonies in this exceptional collection have done just that, offering us first-hand details of what surely must be their most intimate and sacred life experience. In doing so, they have played their part in that mission, awakening us all to what William Shakespeare meant when he wrote: "There are more things in Heaven and Earth, Horatio, than are dreamt of in your philosophy."

I asked God in the dialogue found in *Home with God in a Life That Never Ends* to define death. In reply, She said: "Death is a process of re-identification." Before that moment I never thought of it in quite that way. Now, the contributors here have placed an exclamation point at the end of God's sentence. What they have shared on these pages can bring comfort and clarity, peace and a deep assurance of Deity's goodness, a direct witnessing of His unconditional love for us, and an affirmation of the absolute safety in our never again fearing the end of this physical life.

For those who are dying, for those who have loved ones approaching death, and for those who have died and come back to life and wonder if they are alone in what they experienced, I can't imagine a greater gift. I know that thousands who read this book will be grateful to Penny Sartori and Kelly Walsh for placing it before us. They, too, have self-selected, and we are the better for it.

CONTRIBUTORS

Most of the contributors to this book can be contacted via our community website www.positivitypowermovement.com. Additionally, a number of our contributors can be contacted directly via their own websites.

Sue Stone
www.suestone.com and www.suestonefoundation.com

Mick Collins
www.epiczoetic.co.uk

Neale Donald Walsch
www.CWGConnect.com

Dr Penny Sartori
www.drpennysartori.com

Kelly Walsh
www.kellymichellewalsh.com
www.positivitypowermovement.com and www.positivityprincess.com

Gigi Strehler
www.neardeathexperienceuk.com

Krista Gorman
www.kristagorman.net

Ainsley Threadgold
www.positivitypowermovement.com

Tibor Putnoki
www.szeretetfenye.hu

David Bennett
www.Dharmatalks.com
Podcasts: "Contemplative Living" on PodBean – http://contemplativeliving.podbean.com/

Penny Wilson
www.positivitypowermovement.com

Mike Moon
www.positivitypowermovement.com

Jeff Olsen
www.jefferycolsen.com and www.atONEnow.com

Diane Goble
www.BeyondtheVeil.net

Barbara Ireland

www.HowToStopNegativeThoughts.com

Deirdre DeWitt Maltby
www.whileiwasout.com

Erica McKenzie
www.ericamckenzie.com

Katherine Baldwin
www.angelsoulhealing.com.au

William Peters
www.sharedcrossing.com

Robert Tremblay
www.twenty-seconds.net

Paul Ammons
www.positivitypowermovement.com

Jessica Harper
www.positivitypowermovement.com

Bernie Siegel MD
www.berniesiegelmd.com

Dr Barbara Mango
www.drbarbaramango.vpweb.com

REFERENCES AND FURTHER READING

Bennett, D (2011), *Voyage of Purpose: Spiritual Wisdom on the Road Back to Life.* Scotland: Findhorn Press.

Bucke, R M (1901), *Cosmic Consciousness: A Study in the Evolution of the Human Mind.* Originally published by E.P. Dutton and Company Inc.

Collins, Mick (2014), *The Unselfish Spirit: Human Evolution in a Time of Global Crisis.* Abingdon, UK: Permanent Publications.

Futterman, A D, Kemeny, M E, Shapiro, D and Fahey, J L (1994), "Immunological and physiological changes associated with induced positive and negative mood". *Psychosomatic Medicine* 56(6) (November – December): 499–511.

Goble, D (2015), *Beyond the Veil: Our Journey Home.* Sisters, OR: Cosmic Creativity.

Gorman, K (2014), *I Died and Learned How to Live.* USA: CreateSpace Independent Publishing Platform.

Groth-Marnat, G and Summers, R (1998), "Altered Beliefs, Attitudes, and Behaviors Following Near-Death Experiences". *Journal of Humanistic Psychology* 38(3) (Summer): 110–25.

Hirshberg, C and Barasch, M I (1995), *Remarkable Recovery: What Extraordinary Healings Can Teach Us About Getting Well and Staying Well.* London: Headline Book Publishing.

Ireland, B (2016), *How to Stop Negative Thoughts: What My Near-Death Experience Taught Me About Mind Loops, Neuroscience, and Happiness.* CreateSpace Independent Publishing Platform.

James, W (1902), *The Varieties of Religious Experience: A Study in Human Nature.* New York: Longmans, Green and Co.

Maltby, D (2012), *While I Was Out...: My Near-Death Experience & Soul Altering Journey.* Bloomington, IN: Xlibris Corporation.

McKenzie, E (2015), *Dying to Fit In.* USA: CreateSpace Independent Publishing Platform.

Mellen-Thomas. B (1996), "Through the Light and Beyond", in *The Near-Death Experience: A Reader,* ed. Lee W Bailey and Jenny Yates. New York and London: Routledge.

Montgomery, R (1979), *Strangers Among Us: Enlightened Beings From a World to Come.* New York: Putnam Publishing Group.

Moorjani, A (2012), *Dying to be Me: My Journey from Cancer to Near Death to True Healing.* United Kingdom: Hay House.

Olsen, J (2012), *I Knew Their Hearts: The Amazing Story of a Journey Beyond the Veil To Learn.* USA: Plain Sight.

Olsen, J (2014), *Beyond Mile Marker 80: Choosing Joy After Tragic Loss.* USA: Plain Sight.

Prakasha, P A (2010), The *Christ Blueprint: 13 Keys to Christ Consciousness.* Scotland: Findhorn Press Ltd.

Putnoki, T (2014), *9 Minutes: My Path to the Light (9 Perc: Utam a Fenybe).* Budapest: Szeretet Fenye Kozhaszu Alapitvany.

Ring, K and Valarino, E (1998), *Lessons from the Light: What We Can Learn from the Near-Death Experience.* Needham, MA: Moment Point Press.

Ring, K and Rosing, C J (1990), "The Omega Project: An Empirical Study of the NDE-Prone Personality". *Journal of Near-Death Studies* 8(4) (Summer): 211–39.

Ross, E K (1969), *On Death and Dying.* New York: The Macmillan Company.

Sartori, P (2014), *The Wisdom of Near-Death Experiences: How Understanding NDEs Can Help Us Live More Fully.* London: Watkins Publishing.

Sartori, P, Badham, P and Fenwick, P (2006), "A Prospectively Studied Near-Death Experience with Corroborated Out-of-Body Perceptions and Unexplained Healing". *Journal of Near-Death Studies* 25(2) (Winter): 69–84.

Siegel, B (1999; new edition), *Love, Medicine and Miracles.* UK: Rider Books, Penguin Group.

Stone, S (2010), *Love Life, Live Life: How to Have Happiness and Success Beyond Your Wildest Expectations.* London: Piatkus (an imprint of Little, Brown Book Group).

Tremblay, R (2015), *Twenty Seconds: A True Account of Survival and Hope.* Bloomington, IN: Balboa Press.

Walsch, N D (1997), *Conversations with God, Book 1: An Uncommon Dialogue.* London: Hodder & Stoughton.

Walsch, N D (2017), *Conversations with God, Book 4: Awaken the Species – A New and Unexpected Dialogue.* London: Watkins Publishing.

WATKINS
Sharing Wisdom Since 1893

The story of Watkins dates back to 1893, when the scholar of esotericism John Watkins founded a bookshop, inspired by the lament of his friend and teacher Madame Blavatsky that there was nowhere in London to buy books on mysticism, occultism or metaphysics. That moment marked the birth of Watkins, soon to become the home of many of the leading lights of spiritual literature, including Carl Jung, Rudolf Steiner, Alice Bailey and Chögyam Trungpa.

Today, the passion at Watkins Publishing for vigorous questioning is still resolute. Our wide-ranging and stimulating list reflects the development of spiritual thinking and new science over the past 120 years. We remain at the cutting edge, committed to publishing books that change lives.

DISCOVER MORE...

Read our blog

Watch and listen to
our authors in action

Sign up to
our mailing list

JOIN IN THE CONVERSATION

Our books celebrate conscious, passionate, wise and happy living. Be part of the community by visiting

WWW.WATKINSPUBLISHING.COM

Index

A
acceptance, *129*
Advance Healthcare Directives, *221*
after-effects of NDEs, *55, 334*
afterlife,
  certainty about, *170, 172, 225, 316, 319*
  communication with, *263, 271*
  experiences of, *71, 76, 78, 80*
AIDS/HIV, *311, 334, 336, 337, 341*
alcohol abuse, *202, 291, 346, 355*
alternative medicine, *359*
Ammons, Paul, *343, 346, 348, 349, 352, 354, 355, 357, 359, 362*
anaesthetic complications, *381, 382*
anaphylactic shock, *136*
angel cards, *14*
Angel Soul Healing, *296, 304*
angels, *4, 27, 71, 198, 352, 390*
Angeni, Hazel, *23*
animal intuitives, *394*
animals, *53, 55, 343, 352, 392*
antidepressants, *234*
anxiety, *2, 4, 127, 234, 236*
archangels, *298*
auras xxi, *127, 289*
'Back from the Light' (TV documentary), *321*

B
Baldwin, Katherine, *285, 287, 289, 291, 293, 296, 298, 300, 302, 304, 306, 307*
Beings of Light (spirit beings), *4, 108, 120, 123, 125, 127, 164, 166,*

169, 204, 213, 215, 349, 352, 375, 376, 378, 381, 382, 409, 411, 413
Bennett, David, *114, 116, 118, 120, 123, 125, 127, 129, 131, 133, 134*
bereavement, *22, 23*
Bereavement Rescue Centre, *239*
Beyond the Veil: Our Journey Home (Goble), *218*
BeyondtheVeil.net, *218*
Bible, *4, 16, 213*
brain, *45, 83, 110, 204*
  and consciousness, *149*
  NDEs attributed to, *76, 174*
bulimia, *265, 271, 369*
bullying, *87, 263*

C

cancer, *278, 293, 399, 403, 405*
  Exceptional Cancer Patients, *395*
  recovery following NDE, *133, 134*
cardiac arrest, *38, 42, 65, 76, 78, 83, 100, 104, 110*
Catholicism, *200*
channelling xv, *298, 300, 304*
childbirth, *61, 63, 65, 68*
childhood difficulties, *2, 9, 16, 19, 25, 87, 263, 289, 291, 343, 346, 362, 366*
childhood NDEs, *87, 89, 285, 287, 289, 306, 388, 390, 394*
  recovered, *91, 93*
  to return to life, *71, 155, 182, 194, 202, 215, 232, 287, 309, 311, 321, 323*
  and tapestry of life, *248, 250, 254*
  as universal rule, *192*
Christ Blueprint, The (Padma Aon Prakasha), *16*
Christianity, *10, 13*

collective consciousness, *114, 394*

collective unconscious, *108*

Collins, Mick *xvii–xxiii*,

colony collapse disorder (CCD), *359, 362*

colours, in NDEs *xxx–xxxi, 243, 325*

Compassion & Choices, *206*

conscious dying, *218, 226*

consciousness,
    altered states *xxxv, 174*
    evolution of, *221, 225, 282*
    existence outside the body *xxviii, 65, 118, 131, 149, 243, 394, 401*
    heightened, *316*
    transformation following NDEs *xix, 76, 78, 259*

Consciousness of the Light, *120, 123, 125, 127, 129, 131*

Conversations with God (Walsch) *xxxviii, 4*
    Book 4: Awaken the Species,

cord, binding body to spirit, *149, 157*

D

Dass, Ram, *259*

death,
    as blissful experience, *42*
    continued existence after, *23, 42, 43, 149, 209, 211, 252, 258, 403, 405*
    fascination with, *37*
    losing fear of, *131, 133, 170, 223, 316, 319, 341*
    as spiritual event, *405*
    as transition, *218, 319*

see also shared death experiences,
Death with Dignity (DWD), *206, 221*
deceased loved ones,
　certainty of seeing again, *319*
　communication with and from, *289, 314*
　encountering in NDEs, *91, 145, 147, 149, 182, 188, 190, 192, 194, 321, 323, 332, 337, 341*
　feeling them near, *196*
　knowing they are well, *23, 25, 316*
depression, *2, 9, 234, 278, 311, 370, 373, 403*
Diana, Princess, *32*
disseminated intravascular coagulation (DIC), *71, 73*

divorce and separation xiii, *161, 334, 346, 355*
　following NDEs, *81, 169, 202, 293*
dreams, *55, 76, 78, 250, 259, 357*
drowning, *114, 116, 118, 200, 202, 211, 215, 217, 285, 287*
drugs,
　abuse, *202, 271, 346*
　addiction to medicinal, *265, 354*
　AIDS, *330, 336*
　not conducive to NDEs, *198*
　for 'mental health' issues, *22, 271, 273*
　to suppress NDEs, *57, 271, 283*
dyslexia, *95*

E

Earth energies, *127*
Earth school, *262, 263, 268, 273*
eating disorders, *2, 263, 265, 271, 278, 369, 370, 373*
Einstein, Albert, *362*

electrical sensitivity, *53, 89, 100, 330*
energy ball, *93*
energy fields xxxv
Eternea, *399*
evolution xviii, xxi, xxii, *221, 225, 282*
eye muscle surgery, *375*

F

Fen-Phen addiction, *265*
Fenwick, Dr Peter, *59*
forgiveness xxix, xxx, *51, 339*
Freeman, Morgan, *61, 114*

G

gender dysphoria, *370*
global crisis xviii, xxiii Goble, Diane, *200, 202, 204, 206, 209, 211, 213, 215, 217, 218, 221, 223, 225, 226*
God (Creator/Source) xxxviii, *2, 4, 16, 27, 49, 51, 198, 248, 256, 258, 359, 369, 390*
   connection with xxxix, *10, 13, 157, 254, 263, 278, 280, 298, 357, 381, 385*
   Divine unconditional love, *6, 9, 13, 23, 32, 190, 198, 245, 248, 250, 252, 263, 268, 381, 382, 385*
   doubts and ambiguity about, *10, 366, 373, 382, 386*
   experiencing in OBEs, NDEs and STEs xxix–xxxiv, *47, 123, 151, 153, 155, 190, 192, 194, 196, 241, 245, 263, 265, 268, 270, 296, 311, 382*
   faith/belief in, *276, 392*
   messages from, *29*
Gorman, Krista, *61, 63, 65, 68, 70, 71, 73, 76, 78, 80, 81, 83, 85, 97, 100*
Gossard, Stone, *228*

grief, *185, 200*
  helped by NDEs, *22, 23, 145*
  reduced by shared death experiences, *319*
  STEs following, *386*
Griffiths, Roland, *282*
guardian angels, *55, 213*

H

Hall of Knowledge, *204, 215, 225*
happy sticks, *304, 306*
Harmonic Convergence, *206*
Harper, Jessica, *364, 366, 369, 370, 373, 375, 376, 378, 381, 382, 385, 386*
healing,
  abilities following NDEs, *293, 296*
  centres for souls, *213*
  following NDEs, *9, 80, 273, 302, 307, 330, 332, 336, 354, 401*
  potential of transformative experiences, *278, 280, 282*
  remarkable, techniques developed by NDErs, *112, 395*
  with healers, *390*
healthcare,
  system humanizing, *395*
  limitations, *22, 273, 283*
  need for holistic approach, *22*
healthcare workers, *61*
  need for education in NDEs, *283*
hearing, last sense to go, *38, 42*
Heaven,
  experiencing in NDEs, *70, 71, 265, 268, 270, 352*
  in the little things, *198*

Hell xxii, *13, 47, 49, 270*
  as period of reflection, *6*
higher-consciousness thinking, *206, 215*
Hitchhiker's Guide to Cosmic Consciousness, The (Goble), *218*
honey bees, *359, 362*
hospices, *330, 332*
  care at home, *403, 405, 407, 409, 411, 413*
  volunteering in, *170, 172, 174, 175, 206, 311, 313*
How to Stop Negative Thoughts (Ireland), *237*
hydronephrosis, *61*
'I Survived...Beyond and Back' (TV series), *239*

I

idiopathic anaphylaxis, *136*
immune system, *136, 332, 336*

Indra's Net, *83*
inner guides, *392*
interconnectedness (oneness) xv, xxxii, *6, 32, 81, 83, 100, 133, 136, 155, 158, 175, 223, 234, 236, 245, 259, 289, 327, 334, 339, 415*
International Association of Near-Death Studies (IANDS) UK, *59, 61, 114*
Iraq War, *211, 213, 215, 217, 218, 221, 223, 225, 226, 228, 230, 232, 234, 236, 237, 239, 241, 243, 245, 248, 250, 252, 254, 256, 258, 259, 262, 263, 265, 268, 270, 271, 273, 276, 278, 280, 282, 283, 285, 287, 289, 291, 293, 296, 298, 300, 302, 304, 306, 307, 309, 311, 313, 314, 316, 319, 321, 323, 325, 327, 330, 332, 334, 336, 337, 339, 341, 343, 346, 348, 349, 352, 354, 355, 357, 359, 362, 364, 366, 369*
Ireland, Barbara, *228, 230, 232, 234, 236, 237*

J

Jesus, *13, 19, 215, 298, 392*
John of God, *313*
Judaism, *392, 405, 413*
Jung, Carl xxii, *394*

K

Kainth, Amit, *262*
Kinkade, Amelia, *394*
knowledge/information download xxxiii, *43, 45, 68, 108, 120, 153, 166, 190, 192, 196, 204, 215, 245, 248, 268, 283, 327, 332, 334, 349*
Kübler-Ross, Elisabeth, *405*

L

laryngospasm, *388*
learning disabilities, *343*
Life Beyond Death programme, *313*
life reviews xx, *6, 25, 47, 108, 120, 123, 133, 134, 209, 213, 232, 234, 265, 268, 309*
  regular xx–xxi
  self-generated judgements xx, *47, 49, 108, 123*
Light of Love Foundation, *102, 112*
light/lights inner, *302*
  in OBEs and NDEs xxvii–xxx, *106, 118, 120, 142, 145, 151, 153, 155, 179, 182, 188, 211, 241, 265, 287, 309, 323, 325, 348, 349, 352, 375, 381*
Limbo-land, *42, 43, 47, 51, 55*
Long, Dr Jeffery, *78*
Lorimer, David, *59*
love, *78, 80, 85, 185, 188, 198, 221, 223, 280, 283*
  Ainsley and Krista, *97*
  as the answer, *245, 263*
  and the art of living, *83*
  capacity for, in NDErs, *73, 97, 131, 184, 256, 306, 334, 339, 341*

and connection, *263*
experienced during OBEs, NDEs and STEs xiv, xx, *6, 43, 68, 70, 108, 118, 120, 125, 153, 166, 179, 182, 188, 190, 192, 211, 245, 248, 250, 252, 265, 348, 349, 401*
for NDA experiencers, *405, 413, 415*
power of xv, *198* see also God; self-love,
Love, Care Share Foundation xxiii, *14, 25, 27, 32*

M

malignant hyperthermia (MH), *169, 170*
Maltby, Deirdre DeWitt, *239, 241, 243, 245, 248, 250, 252, 254, 256, 258, 259*
Mango, Dr Barbara, *136, 397, 399, 401, 403, 405, 407, 409, 411, 413, 415*
material world, unreality, *45, 47*
McKenzie, Erica, *262, 263, 265, 268, 270, 271, 273, 276, 278, 280, 282, 283*
Meckel's diverticulum, *37, 38, 53*
meditation, *206, 289, 293, 296, 302, 306, 311*
memory loss, *76, 78*
Mental Health Act, *22*
mikvah, *411*
mind-body-spirit connection, *134, 206, 395*
Moody, Dr Raymond, *313*
Moon, Michael, *161, 162, 164, 166, 169, 170, 172, 174, 175*
motor neurone disease, *172*
multiple sclerosis, *104*

music, in NDEs, *108, 243*

N

Native Americans, *127*

nature, *170, 175, 341, 343, 354*

Near Death Experience UK, *57, 59, 89, 95*
  flashbacks, *204*
  hospital research, *100, 198*
  misdiagnosed as psychosis, *271, 283*
  'negative', *42*
  potential for mankind,
  prevalence, *409*
  reluctance to discuss, *9, 78, 127, 129, 202, 225*
  study of changes in NDErs,
  transformative aspects xix,

Nearing Death Awareness (NDA), *399, 405, 407, 409, 411, 413, 415*

negative thought patterns, *234, 237*

Nin, Anais, *405*

9 Ds of De-Looping, *234, 236*

9Minutes: My Path to the Light (Putnoki), *102*

nitrous oxide, *161, 162, 174*

O

Olsen, Jeff, *177, 179, 182, 184, 185, 188, 190, 192, 194, 196, 198*

out-of-body experiences (OBEs) xiv–xv, xxvi–xxxviii, *157, 409*

P

painkillers, *354*

paracetemol, *4*

past-life regression, *14, 16, 206*

Patrias, Lovetta, *145, 147, 149, 157*

personality change following NDE, *55, 57, 73, 76, 202, 221, 223*
Peter, The Rock, *16*
Peters, William, *309, 311, 313, 314, 316, 319*
photosensitivity, *53*
Pitocin, *63*
Planet Positavia, *25*
Pollak, Melville, *399, 403, 405, 407, 409, 411, 413*
positivity, *25, 27, 29, 337, 339, 341*
Positivity Power, *25, 27, 95*
    Facebook group, *61, 85, 95*
Positivity Power Movement, *32, 114*
Positivity Princess, *25, 27, 29, 32*
positivypowermovment.com, *27*
Post-Traumatic Stress Disorder (PTSD), *22, 57, 369*
Pot ceremony, Hungary, *112*
potential roadblocks, *278*
Powers of Ten, *204*
premonitions, *357*
psychiatric hospital xix, *271, 273, 280, 283*
psychic abilities, *293, 307*
psychosis, *19, 22, 271, 283*
pulmonary embolism, *346, 348, 355*
purpose (soul mission) xxii, *6, 10, 13, 78, 87, 89, 93, 125, 127, 134, 157, 170, 209, 217, 223, 225, 234, 256, 258, 263, 273, 282, 293, 304, 306, 307, 316, 319, 359, 362, 385*
Putnoki, Tibor, *102, 104, 106, 108, 110, 112*
'quiet ministry', *131*

R
regression hypnotherapy, *89, 91, 93*
    dangers, *100*

see also past-life regression, reincarnation, *211, 213*
Reincarnation and the Evolution of Consciousness (Goble), *221*
religion, *47, 161, 200, 209, 211, 373*
   deeds more important, *49*
road accidents, *87, 89, 91, 93, 169, 177, 179, 239, 241*
Ruane, Alistair, *27, 29*

S

sacral fracture, traumatic, *401, 403*
Sartori, Dr Penny xvi, xxv–xxvi, *14, 89, 95, 321*
sciatica, *89*
science xv, *282, 407*
   'inner scientist', *76, 83*
Seekers Open Forum, *218*
self-doubt, *230*

self-love, *6, 23, 29, 81, 196, 252, 254, 258, 259, 280, 296, 336, 337*
shadow beings xxi, *70, 81*
shamans xviii
Shared Crossing Pathway, *313, 314*
Shared Crossing Project, *313, 314, 316, 319*
shared death experiences (SDEs), *311, 313, 314, 319*
Siegel, Dr Bernie, *388, 390, 392, 394, 395*
Simms, Caz, *29*
Sitting in the Lotus Blossom (Goble), *218*
skiing accidents, *309*
sleep state, *55*
Socrates, *38*
Story of God, The (TV show), *61, 114*
soulmates, *9, 10, 293, 302, 304*
spirit,
   outside the body, *136, 149, 182, 184, 265*
   within all, *134*

spirit guides, *16, 287, 293, 296, 298, 307*
spiritual awakening xxiii, *22, 289, 359*
spiritual beings, humans as, *23, 211, 262, 263, 280*
spiritual growth, *6, 95, 209, 401*
spiritual journeys, *13, 170, 215, 405*
spiritually transformative, experiences (STEs), *4, 6, 9, 188, 190, 192, 194, 206, 248, 250, 252, 282, 382, 386, 399, 401, 409*
States of Consciousness Research Team, *262*
Strangers Among Us (Montgomery), *206*
Strehler, Gigi, *34, 37, 38, 42, 43, 45, 47, 49, 51, 53, 55, 57, 59, 85, 100*

Stress Management Centre, Florida, *206, 226*
Sue Stone Foundation, *25*
suicide, *22, 37, 355, 382*
    attempted, *2, 4, 9, 10, 370*
    raising awareness of, *23, 25*
Swanson, Dr Claude, *282*
synchronicity/ies xvii, *13, 27, 32, 61, 83, 87, 95, 100, 102, 133, 321, 334, 357, 401*

T

Threadgold, Ainsley, *85, 87, 89, 91, 93, 95, 97, 100*
Through the Tunnel (Goble), *217, 218*
timelessness, *43*
tolerance, *129, 131*
transformation xvii,
    butterfly metaphor, *202*

collective xviii, xxii, xxiii and Full Life Experience xx–xxi networks of xxi and NDEs xix,
see also individual stories,
transgender issues, *382, 385, 386*
   transition process, *373*
Tremblay, Robert, *136, 262, 321, 323, 343*
trust, *185*
truth, *131*
tularaemia, *354, 355*
tunnel experiences xxviii, *169, 265, 270*
Twelve Principles, *80, 81, 83*
Twenty-Seconds (Tremblay), *334*

U
uniqueness, value of, *276, 278*

V
Virtue, Doreen, *13*

void, *42, 55, 138, 140, 142, 145, 157*
Vortex healing modality, *298, 300, 302, 304, 306, 307*

W
Walsch, Neal xxv–xxxix, *13*
Walsh, Kelly xvii, xxv–xxvi, *2, 4, 6, 9, 10, 13, 14, 16, 19, 22, 23, 25, 27, 29, 32, 34, 61, 85, 95, 100, 114, 136, 161, 177, 200, 239, 259, 262, 285, 321, 343, 397, 401*
Walton, Rod, *239*
Williams, Helen, *102*
Wilson, Penny, *136, 138, 140, 142, 145, 147, 149, 151, 153, 155, 157, 158*
   Experiences, The (Sartori), *100*
Worrall, Olga, *390, 392*

www.ingramcontent.com/pod-product-compliance
Lightning Source LLC
Chambersburg PA
CBHW060310230426
43663CB00009B/1653